A TOUCH OF AFRICA

PART II: ONTO THE AMAZON

by
BERT D'AMICO

1663 Liberty Drive, Suite 200
Bloomington, Indiana 47403
(800) 839-8640
www.AuthorHouse.com

© 2005 Bert D'Amico. All Rights Reserved.

No part of this book may be reproduced, stored in a retrieval system, or transmitted by any means without the written permission of the author.

First published by AuthorHouse 06/10/05

ISBN: 1-4208-4043-6 (sc)

Printed in the United States of America
Bloomington, Indiana

This book is printed on acid-free paper.

*To Katharine and Christopher
who are always sources of
inspiration*

Table of Contents

ACKNOWLEDGEMENTS	xiii
PREFACE	xv
A TOUCH OF AFRICA	1
MUGOIRI SECONDARY SCHOOL	2
MURANG'A FORT HALL	7
NYERI	9
BUSH NEIGHBOURS	11
SCHOOL DAYS	12
MARY WAIRIMU	13
THE COO COO MAN	14
THE NORTHERN FRONTIER DISTRICT (N.F.D.)	16
THE SAMBURU	18
MARALAL	22
THE GREAT RIFT VALLEY	24
BARAGOI	26
TO SOUTH HORR	28
SOUTH HORR	29
LION ON THE ROAD	30
THE COKE LINE	32
FAMINE	34
LION IN THE LAGA	38
SCHOOL SAMBURU STYLE	41
MYTH OR FACT?	42
WATER WATER	45
LORRY, LORRY, HALILEUH!	46
THE LABOURER	47
EPUR	50
THE OLD RENDILLE	56
MOUNT KULAL	58
FIRST BURIAL	60
MOUNT NYIRU AND N'GAI	62
LOIYANGALLANI	70
KIBOKO KILLER	75
STRANGE ISLAND	81
COBRAS AND OTHER POISONS	83

ELEPHANT	88
CROCODILE	95
UASO NYIRO RIVER	97
THE HONEY BIRD	105
SAFARI ANTS	110
CHIGGERS AND OTHERS	113
STONED IN NYERI	115
IRELAND COMES ABOARD	120
A CHARITABLE BALL	120
WEEKEND GUESTS	122
OCEAN SAFARIS	123
A LADY FROM YORKSHIRE	127
TARZAN	129
A SINGING SHEPHERD	130
BUSH TELEGRAPH	132
THE SERENGETI	132
JACK FARREL	135
THE PEACE CORP	139
IT'S A SMALL WORLD AFTER ALL	139
WANDERING IN LAKE NAKURU	140
JOHN THE COOK	141
A PLACE TO LEAVE YOUR HEART	142
AND TODAY?	145
PART II: ONTO THE AMAZON	155
MANAUS	156
SANTA LUZIA	160
LAGO DO ALEIXO	162
BOA VISITA AND INTO THE JUNGLE	169
CATRIMANI	172
SPIRITS OF THE RAINFOREST	181
A DAY IN THE LIFE	189
A JUNGLE HUNT	196
YANA, YOU ARE YANOMAMA COME BACK	205
CONCLUSION	212

The three of us stood on the wind weathered shore of Lake Turkana, awaiting the arrival of the El Molo. Behind us, filed and chiseled, stretched a mute landscape, testimony of the epochs of ill treatment. In the midst of all this volcanic ruin was a solitary oasis, which betrayed a lone source of water, Loiyangallani. The bandy-legged El Molo pushed into the Lake and onto a rocky island by warring mainland tribes, was probably one of Africa's smallest groups. Their language, like their origin had been lost long ago. A few old men remembered the secrets of the past. How will people ever know they were here? I was accompanying Maeve and a medical Sister who were going over to their island to treat the remnants of the tribe, whose numbers were less than two hundred.

Two dom palm rafts arrived, poled by El Molo lads who greeted us with ivory white smiles. The rafts were simple affairs.... two logs lashed together with strips of palm fibers. I was to man the rubber raft with the medical sister and several boxes of supplies. Seemed like a normal request until the Padre handed me a rubber bladder. I had seen the likes of these toy boats in backyard swimming pools over the years and even then shook my head. Once blown up, it looked like a like a pillow that someone had sat on. With plastic paddles secured in the oarlocks, I loaded up the medicines along with the Sister who appeared very uncomfortable with the arrangement. Her silence was my first clue. I eased myself into the stern and set my rifle across my lap. The bladder sank to within inches of the waterline. Meanwhile, Maeve was busy adjusting herself in the middle of one of the narrow log rafts, barely able to keep her legs out of water. We shoved off and I wondered if a similar sight had once inspired Jerome K. Jerome. The raft pressed ahead and the shore fell behind. This was no quiet inland sea since prevailing easterlies ploughed its surface and threatened our craft with every wave. The lads ahead of us used short, deft strokes as they thrust their poles into the murky bottom leaving me bobbing behind. My plastic oars skimmed the surface with little evidence of our passing. It would hardly be a contest.

It wasn't long before Maeve was in a dilemma. The raft was unable to sustain her one hundred pounds and continued to sink until only her upper body was exposed. One might say the raft was shipping water at a distressing rate. She gave the impression of a floating torso. Throwing her sandals over to us, and following an impulse doubtless born on the rocky shores of western Ireland, she slipped into the water and swam effortlessly alongside of us, keeping up a conversation all the while. Crocodile infested waters? Our trust was in the El Molo who assured us that no 'mamba' lurked nearby.

Thirty El Molo, a good portion of the tribe greeted us. Bare breasted women with bottoms covered in discarded netting along with scantily clad elders led us to an area cleared of rocks. Their huts were flimsy pieces of work, lashed together with dom palm leafs carried over from the mainland, with thatched roofs weighed down with turtle shells which also served as drinking cups. This volcanic outgrowth called an island was devoid of greenery and we knew it was the fishing and relative safety from the mainland raiders which made the place attractive to the El Molo. Amidst smoldering ashes, charred remains of enormous Nile perch lay strewn about, picked so clean that even the flies felt cheated. Gaping crocodile skulls, teeth intact, stared lifelessly through hollow, charred sockets. It was a desperate place indeed, as high above us, soared winged predators pinned in an up draught.

My neck burned as rivulets ran down my back. Finally, the headman who acted as chief, called the group together and the three of us found ourselves in the middle of a semi circle next to the medicines. Squatting on their heels, the El Molo waited patiently for the 'barazza' to begin. Each person was called before us. The patient would then gesture and in rapid-fire Samburu and relate the nature of the complaint to the chief. Few present remembered or understood the practically extinct El Molo language. (I couldn't imagine another language being thrown into the proceedings.) Everyone sat hushed in concern as the drama unfolded on center stage. Only when the tale of suffering was complete, did the spectators turn to one another nodding their approval. The chief would then turn to the medical Sister and translate the nature of the complaint into KiSwahili. Shaking her head when not fully understanding, she would question the chief who would invariably return the question to the expectant patient who would in turn retell the story from the very beginning, all the while under the watchful eyes of the audience who waited their turn. After the second round of storytelling, the sister would finally turn to Maeve, and in halting English, the symptoms of the patient were retold with a smattering of KiSwahili, heavily doused with gesture and body language, finger pointing and sighs. With further dramatization on everyone's part, the story would reach an uncertain consensus, all the while under the still watchful gazes of the El Molo. The medical supplies from America were written in English and so the reason for our presence there.

Maeve with El Molo women in front of reed house.

Most ailments were related to lung and bronchial disorders while the children suffered from eye infections, and burns from open fires and windowless huts. Malaria was also rampant along with venereal diseases. The mainland tribes had left their mark. At one point Vick's Vapor Rub was used as a placebo for a chest ailment. The pungent smell in the stifling heat with the addition of the burning sensation won instant approval. Finally, this was the real stuff. Not only did it smell bad but it burned too! The fiery effect was so popular that everyone added chest problems to their list of personal ailments. The island never smelled so good.

ACKNOWLEDGEMENTS

I started this manuscript many years ago and left it to ferment in an old cardboard box. It was in bits and pieces and I must admit, somewhat pretentious in style since I was forgetting to tell the stories on paper in the same way I would often tell them to family and those friends who were ever so polite to listen. At the insistence of my daughter Katharine, Maeve my wife, and my mentor, Adrian Roscoe, I was determined to commit my experiences while in Africa, on paper and to satisfy a lingering need. Upon completing the African section, I fortuitously added, 'Onto the Amazon,' almost as an aside. Well, it grew into more pages than I had anticipated and while keeping in contact with my anthropologist friend John Saffirio, I was left no choice but to include Yano's letter, a touching account of a young girl's life upon realizing she was a child of the jungle.

I would like to express my sincere gratitude to Katharine, who upon reading my messy thoughts in the numerous revisions which I emailed to her in Barcelona, both corrected my errors and encouraged me with her delightful sense of humor. She constantly laughed at my standing in line in Nyeri with my butcher friend being dragged along, swathed in wrappings. To hear her burst out in delight over the telephone from Spain would send me scurrying back to my computer to reread the tales she so enjoyed.

Adrian Roscoe was my reason to begin this story many years ago. An accomplished author, I felt it would be difficult to refuse his constant encouraging words to, 'Get on with it.' I found his comments on my original hand written sheets dating back some twenty-five years ago, still insightful and constructive when I finally resurrected the manuscript. I thank him for his patience and unfailing encouragement.

Maeve read the rough work and was careful not to discourage me while gently prodding and coaxing.

A friend with a critical eye, Colleen Conway, read my nearly completed manuscript and penciled in her insightful comments for which I thank her. Mark Melloni Sr. kept me in hard copies during the many revisions of the manuscript. Linda Pizzacalla's creative mind designed the brilliant cover which caught the essence of the text. Thanks to Juan Kratzmaier an accomplished photographer who has traveled the world and graciously contributed his spectacular acacia tree from the Serengeti for the cover.

Christopher, my son in Ottawa, was my technical savior and stored hard copies of my manuscript while keeping my computer virus free. He, along with my daughter Katharine, downloaded the material since I was forever losing and messing up my floppy discs. Hardcopies in Ottawa and Barcelona seemed like a safe bet to me.

John Saffirio was invaluable and taught me the ways of the Yanomama from afar. His original documents were given to me to use freely in my research. John is a gracious man and a joy to call a friend.

I lost many friends in Africa and I choose to keep them alive with words. I can still hear them and catch their smiles. It would be easy to give in to grief over lost friends but then I would only remember them in sorrow. I choose to think of my pal the Padre, still traveling the treacherous roads to the N.F.D. uncomplaining and stretching his hand out in welcome. The Old Rendille, hunched and ever watchful, spitting out an ancient blessing in Samburu must surely be waiting under the spreading acacia in the South Horr compound. Longodiki, one eye misty and useless, spotting game and smiling back to me as we trudged along over hills and ravines, looking for water. Jack Farrel slouched over the wheel of his Land Rover, hat low, will be standing guard over uneasy cattle as hungry lions pierce the blackness with shiny eyes. I think of Maureen's cheeky comments, of Greg Filo speeding down the highway, and Mary Knox, wide-eyed in disbelief. Rossano will be on the concrete porch behind the elephant moat, hands tucked into his sleeves, quietly nodding a farewell.

PREFACE

Friends have often asked me why I ventured to Africa. In the early 1960's, Africa was not a common destination for most Canadians. Africa had always intrigued me because of the unknown along with the myths, which came to us in North America. It was the Roscoes, who had recently arrived at McMaster University in Hamilton, Ontario who showed me it was possible to cut the strings. Adrian and Janice from Cheshire, U.K. came to Canada from a teaching assignment in Nigeria, their first of many subsequent years in Africa. Adrian was completing an M.A. in preparation for his doctorate at Queen's University where he would become a world authority on West African literature. I had recently completed an undergraduate degree and was newly married to Maeve and completely free from any obligations. We were both qualified teachers and with the encouragement from the Roscoes, we left Canada on our first wedding anniversary, December 26, 1965 for Kenya, East Africa. We passed through the sights of London, Paris, Rome, Florence, Athens, and finally Cairo, but it was in Kenya that we felt we had finally left our home behind.

This is a story about people and animals and punctuated with personal experiences. Some of the people I met and listened to wore their memories like old scars. From the animals I learned that I had a lot to learn. My personal adventures were a mixture of foolishness, naivety, and sometimes even thoughtful planning. I am surprised at the infrequency at which I must return to my personal diaries. I read an African saying that went something like:

> 'There is a place where the Sky meets the Horizon,
> and the name of that Place is called the End.'

I have never been to that place called End, but I knew that I was at a place called, ' Beginning.'

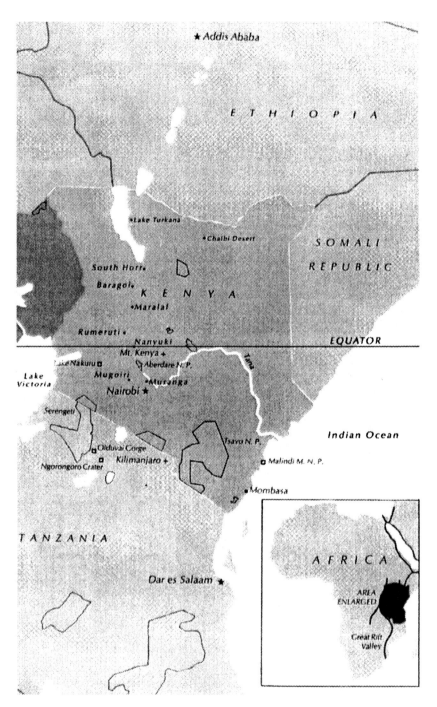

KENYA, EAST AFRICA

A TOUCH OF AFRICA

It was Kenya, East Africa that I knew best, a country of superlatives and contrasts, a staggering diversity of wildlife and people. From low lying torrid coastal regions of tropical Mombasa and the Indian Ocean, to the lofty inland capital of Nairobi, to snow covered peaks at the equator melting into the southern savannahs, Kenya with Lake Victoria, Africa's largest, was never without its surprises. The richness of the numerous African tribes was only outdone by the abundance of her wildlife. One found that the sophisticated urbanized Kikuyu were a direct opposite to the towering Nilo-Hametic nomads of the distant north. It is the Maasai who are probably the best-known nomads, who along with their cousins the Samburu, are wed to their herds. These nomads prod bone lean cattle across vast and silent plains. Some tribes fished for a living, others cultivated the land, while still others, like the WaKamba, carved Africa into flint hard ebony. In the remoteness of the forgotten Northern Frontier District, the N.F.D., was the little known El Molo, a rickety, diminutive people who had been driven off the mainland by more aggressive tribes and forced to seek refuge on a barren island in Lake Turkana. The El Molo, suffering from rickets, survive on giant Nile crocodiles and the enormous Nile perch, some weighing in at over two hundred pounds. On these same bleak shores of Lake Turkana, in later years, anthropologists would discover fossils revealing man's origin.

In contrast, market places in cities and towns and in rural villages were a riot of colorful costumes, which in turn blended into the piles of exotic fruits and vegetables all strange and unfamiliar, assaulting the newcomer. Nairobi National Game Park, only several miles from city's center is 70 square miles of wild game, which included lion. One encountered Arab traders, Asian shopkeepers, globetrotting businessmen, overlaid with international tourists, making Kenya the most visited African country south of the Sahara. Languages too, were abundant. KiSwahili, a mixture of Bantu and Arabic from the coastal regions and the lingua franca of East Africa, proved to be the savior for the novice. Christian churches could be found next to mosques and Hindu temples while in the bush, the trained eye could discover traces of animism from primordial Africa. Soon after my arrival in East Africa, an old timer told me I would contact African fever. After contacting malaria, I imagined he was prophetic. It was only years later that I realized he meant a fever of the spirit, not of the body.

MUGOIRI SECONDARY SCHOOL

My wife Maeve and I arrived in Kenya from Canada in late January 1966. We were assigned to a 'bush' school some ninety miles north of Nairobi, near the equator and some twelve miles off the main tarmac road called Mugoiri Secondary School. The school was built in the foothills of the lush Aberdare Mountain forest, where bamboo thickets hid ponderous elephant alongside previously unknown antelope, once considered just another African myth. The lower reaches where we lived were devoid of the natural forests, having been cleared away for Kikuyu shambas.

Our teacher's house was surrounded by the neatly cultivated gardens or shambas of the rural Kikuyu, the same people who had led Kenya to her recent independence from the British. Each Kikuyu shamba had several thatched mud huts, which reminded me of ripe acorns. These huts were nearly always hidden beneath waving banana trees, surrounded by rows of beans and towering corn stalks. During the chilly monsoon rains, these thatched roofs would be all smoky and steamy from the cooking fires inside. Smoldering mushrooms.

The entrance leading into the school compound deserves comment since it was obvious that a lot of loving attention was given to the grounds. Neatly pruned bougainvilleas garland the drive. Carefully tended rock gardens interrupted the hedge where delicate storm crocus were mixed with bleeding hibiscus, all surrounded by hydrangea and delicate oleander. Cactus and poinsettia grew among golden allemande. Glaring flame trees towered overhead, dripping cardinal plumes. Tall and stiff succulent euphorbia stood sentry-like, saluting the newcomer. Dagger leafed sanserveria looked menacing. A wedge wood sky seemed to hover especially low. The driveway was reminiscent of the splashes on an artist's apron. It was a vibrant entrance.

The drive continued on and around a small central pool where tilapia swam, surrounded by birds of paradise (Strelitsia) and leafy reeds. A flagpole protruded upwards and boasted the newly won Kenyan flag. At the end of this circular driveway stood the classrooms and dormitories. Constructed from the local stone, these buildings were topped with tin sheets called 'mabati.' A small chapel, cool, and heavy with lingering smells of burnt candles, completed the compound. Lilac breasted rollers, scarlet sunbirds, yellow backed weavers and finches flew among the diminutive green parrots only to be outshone by the splendid glossy starling.

A TOUCH OF AFRICA

The end of the long driveway leading to classrooms

Our teacher's house was being built on a nearby hill with an open-hearth fireplace, a small kitchen, a washroom, and a large living room with an open dining area and two bedrooms. A dry pantry for hanging meat stood in the hallway. We would have running water, which came in various colors depending upon the time of year, and at what stage the coffee factory upstream was processing their beans. (The washed beans dyed the water a burnt, rusty color and maintaining a normal appearance could be challenging. A full beard covered a lot of the problem for me.) Electricity came in short bursts from the school's generator each evening for a few hours. This always depended upon the resident fundi (handyman) and the amount of 'pombe,' (homemade brew) he had consumed that night. Smelly oil lamps were always on standby. Our first temporary house had a serious problem, which we were happy to have left behind.

Once in our new house, which was completed months behind schedule, it was comforting to finally settle in. I was itching to light a roaring fire and during the first rains with a chill in the air, I had my chance. The local wood stacked in anticipation was on the front porch and smelled great. I learned it was mango with the odd piece of ebony mixed in. It was months later that I realized that the woodpile also included very fat and hairy tarantulas, which became a favorite distraction for our Siamese cat, Elsa. Dishes put away, and with the chesterfield placed squarely in front of the fireplace, the evening for our very first fire was shaping up beautifully. Using a little kerosene to hasten the operation, the first match set the wood off to a roaring start. The monsoons pounded away and beat mightily on the panes. Inside it was warm and aglow. Glasses filled with Cinzano, with a twist of lemon from our neighbor's tree, set the mood. We were finally in our permanent house. We had a memorable experience in our temporary house on the first night several months ago and so I looked forward to peace and contentment in this our new home on the hill.

Neither Maeve nor I acknowledged the first crack. It wasn't long before the second one got our attention. I figured it was the hard ebony logs expanding with the heat. We looked at each other and continued with our drinks when a missile flew between us and landed on the opposite wall with a crunch. In rapid succession, several more volleys came menacingly close. It was obvious there was a problem as we both dove behind the chesterfield out of range and bewildered. Summoning up my courage, I ventured to peek over the chesterfield and at the roaring inferno, all the while dodging sizzling chunks as they whizzed by. It was time for action. The fiery pieces were piling up against the opposite wall and I had serious reservations that our new hand crafted table and chairs were about to become kindling. I struck upon a plan. Groping around the side of the chesterfield, I pulled at the scatter rug we had bought in Nairobi. Once I dragged it around, I was safe to use it as a shield to block the missiles which showed no signs of letting up. From behind the carpet I could feel the full wrath of the venting hearth. I eventually managed to cover the fireplace and after awhile the barrage ceased and it seemed safe to look. The source of the eruption came from the back of the fireplace's disintegrating wall as the heat became more and more intense. The contractor had failed to use firebrick to line the hearth and the back wall was blasted out leaving a large depression, which was just short of becoming another entrance to the room. I was told that at one point, as I bravely fought off the barrage, I looked like a bullfighter waving and twirling about with my rug. An *olé!* during the performance would have been encouraging.

Several months before and our first evening in Mugoiri at our temporary quarters, deserves comment. Maeve recalls it vividly. The house we were assigned to stood vacant for many months, that is to say vacant of people. We finally unpacked our bags and sunk into bed, exhausted, recounting our travels from Canada. We had been on the road for a month or so, and had sampled a half dozen countries across Europe. From ancient Rome and Florence and the smoky bistros in Paris, to the lofty Acropolis in Athens and a climb inside of the Great Pyramid near Cairo and the Nile. Our adventures ended in Nairobi and Mugoiri. The generator sputtered, the lights flickered and we were immersed in the blackness of Africa. Somewhere between sleep and awareness, I heard Maeve calling out. Fumbling for a light switch was a natural reaction. Remembering the flashlight on the floor, which the headmistress had given to me, I groped in the darkness. All the while I was conscious of a strange sensation about my arms and neck. Flicking on the flashlight, I saw the intruders dashing for cover. Spiders. Black ones and furry ones but mostly dazed ones, made off for their ceiling hideaway. They were everywhere by the hundreds and covered one wall. Their entry was easy enough to discover as they scurried between the wall and the ceiling. Sitting equally as dazed was Maeve, who began to cry. Only after reassuring her that the intruders were after insects and rearranging the bed in the middle of the room, did I shut off the flashlight but this time I hid it under my pillow. Submerging beneath the sheets, she refused to talk further. Meanwhile, I expounded upon the benefits of the hairy kingdom in great detail trying to convince the both of us. I promised that at first light, I would stuff the cracks with toilet paper thus sealing off our visitors' entranceway. This suggestion seemed to ease matters somewhat and once again we drifted off. My face and neck itched. This invasion of spiders was never repeated again during our stay in Africa. In fact, we decided later on that Mugoiri's altitude discouraged most insect life. It was only during the monsoons that flying ants (termites) by the tens of thousands and voracious safari ants were a nuisance. I find it difficult to explain the invasion on our first night and like to think of it as a most curious welcoming committee.

Early next morning, ceilings carefully stuffed, I accepted an invitation to Fort Hall later renamed, Murang'a. Maeve remained behind to unpack our luggage and to inspect our quarters in the revealing light, which included a spider-eating lizard. The school budget allowed for the purchasing of some new household utensils and the headmistress from Florence, Italy had thoughtfully invited one of us to go along to approve the purchases. Stanley, a short, mustached Kikuyu school driver, who was to become my good friend, handled the Peugeot wagon skillfully as we sped along the edge of the sun baked road, kicking up rolls of red laterite dust in our wake. I settled in the back seat and wandered over the green knolls while trying to imagine the recent turmoil called the 'Mau Mau Uprising.'

Our nearest Kikuyu neighbour.

Later that week, as I walked across the compound to the principal's office to help out with the timetables which were a priority since classes would be starting soon, a most stunning scene unfolded before me. The clouds suddenly opened and to the north and on the equator, a few miles away, majestic Mount Kenya burst into view at 17,058 feet above sea level. It was my first clear view of the mountain and it was like a splash of watercolor. Snow covered, it is Africa's second peak after Mount Kilimanjaro, (19,342 feet) which rose behind us to the south. Mt. Kenya is by far the more spectacular of the two with snowy peaks, serrated and piercing skywards while Kilimanjaro sat squatty and not unlike a plum pudding, dripping warm, white icing. Mt. Kenya caused a sensation in England when it was first reported. A mountain on the equator with snow? Impossible! A Kikuyu creation myth, tells of N'Gai their mountain dwelling deity, who embraces Gikuyu and his partner Moobi, the first people. The story goes on to tell about the nine daughters born to them and their fear of dying without heirs and how, after a sacrifice under a fig tree, nine handsome men appear. The story gets better as it goes along. Creation mythology, whether it is the Kikuyu version, Yanomama from the Amazon or the West's Genesis, allows a people to justify their actions towards one another and the world they live in. Creation mythology is an interesting study into the nature of a people and reveals who they are.

A TOUCH OF AFRICA

Mt. Kenya, snowcapped on the equator

Our former temporary house was near the center compound and close to all the activity. On our first Saturday morning, hoping for a sleep in, I was awoken by a blood-curdling squeal that had me rushing outside, shoes untied and shirt flapping. I followed the commotion down to the livestock pens, which were at the bottom of a steep incline behind the classrooms. As I inched my way down, already drenched with early dew, a pink shaped maggoty looking creature raced past me dragging a long rope around its neck. In hot pursuit, the school's cook and several helpers charged by, hooting and hollering at the top of their voices. Joining in the chase, we were led down valleys and up again, all the while following the lead man who in turn kept disappearing in the undergrowth. The hunt ended in a tangle of arms and legs, but only after several Kikuyu staff straining on the rope, heels dug in, were pulled like ploughs through a field. The school's beady-eyed boar was duly subdued, hastily bound, and unceremoniously dragged off to the kitchen to meet its fate.

MURANG'A FORT HALL

Fort Hall (Murang'a) some dozen miles north was originally a colonial outpost for the British and our nearest shopping village. Asians, who were probably the descendants of the early migrant workers brought over from India to build the Kenya-Uganda railroad from Mombasa, usually owned the shops. (This railroad ran through Tsavo Park where it was held up for many months because of two lions who ate many of the laborers. These lions can be seen today in the Field museum in Chicago.) Filo's, a Goan family, owned and operated a grocery store with an attached bar where one could meet the local people, while your list was being filled and the bags packed safely in your Land Rover. It was a pleasurable chore, especially when the local Africans found out that I was a teacher in an African school with African students, a most honorable profession and one, which placed me in high esteem. Utensils, cloth, Kikuyu beans and yams, could be found among the cigarette lighters, whiskey, hair ribbons, dresses and curried sausage rolls, brooms, shovels, canned goods and fountain pens. The sausage rolls or samosas, were a favorite of the 'white hunter' from Nairobi, who with eager clients, would stop for a cold beer and a snack before continuing upcountry on safari.

Greg and Victor Filo, the storeowners, were to become friends in the coming years. I recall my final farewell party years later. Greg and a half dozen African friends built a small fire alongside the bar one balmy night and roasted a goat in my honor. The meat was served with Tusker beer. My parting present included the dried scrotum of the goat, containing a needle and thread, a symbolic start for my new home in far off Canada.

My next stop would normally be the butcher's shop, a block building, which lacked both refrigeration and glass for the windows. This sweating, concrete cell was always busy on slaughter day when a blank eyed carcass was hauled inside on a wheelbarrow, tied by the legs and hoisted unceremoniously onto the table. One had only to point to a particular part of the carcass and that portion was efficiently dispatched for the customer. All parts of the animal were sold at the same price. One uncomfortable aspect was the ubiquitous African dog. Proceedings were nearly always carried out under the watchful gaze of these half starved, lecherous creatures. Flying pieces of bone and meat never reached the floor but were snapped up and swallowed with an expressionless leer. Flies were also present in vast numbers and I imagine the dogs had a few of them during lean times. I would order several chunks of meat, which were carved out and wrapped in a recent issue of the East African Standard newspaper. It was often a source of amusement to examine our meat at dinner for invariably one could uncover an interesting byline, well hidden between the mashed potatoes and vegetables.

NYERI

Some forty miles north of Fort Hall was the town of Nyeri, located near the equator. Nyeri was famous for its impressive Outspan Hotel and nearby Treetops. It was in Treetops, a cleverly constructed big game viewing lodge, nestled high in a clump of giant baobab trees, with bedrooms, kitchen and a dining room, that a lady ascended one evening as a princess and the following morning, descended as the future and present Queen of England.

Treetops outside of Nyeri

Nyeri was always an exciting destination for us since we could buy so many of the goods, which were unavailable in Murang'a. We could gawk at European tourists who became a novelty for us while the girls would get a first-rate look at the most recent fashions. It seemed that the safari hat with the leopard skin band was a prerequisite for most visitors viewing game or on safari. Our problem getting to Nyeri was the twelve miles of leached laterite 'road' from Mugoiri to the tarmac during the monsoons. As rookies, we spent many hours stranded in our V.W. Beetle, hopelessly mired in oxidized mud. It wasn't very long before I found myself in Nairobi, where I became the proud owner of a canvas-topped Land Rover, never to be stuck on the infamous Mugoiri road again. The highway to Nairobi deserves mention. The many times I drove south to Nairobi from Murang'a, I cannot recall the ride without passing the scene of at least one accident. Suicide Peugeot taxi cabs raced overloaded diesel belching buses as they groaned for position on blind hills or S shaped curves. It was a virtual free for all. Twisted wrecks punctuated the highway for the ninety odd miles. Without a scrap steel industry, the demolished vehicles became rusting signposts, piled on the side of the road telling of the most dangerous stretches of the highway.

Mary Knox, a teacher friend, told us of an incident on the highway outside of Nyeri. As Mary approached the bend in the road, she saw an elderly lady about to hazard the dangerous crossing. The lady, complete with sunhat, parasol and a frock fit for a tea party, seemed hesitant, if not confused. Stopping her car, Mary volunteered her services and escorted her across. Once on the other side of the tarmac, the elderly dear proceeded to the over grown cemetery but only after thanking Mary for her kindness. As she picked her way through the grave markers, she called back to Mary that she was going to visit her sweetheart. Mary recognized the imposing gravestone where the lady stopped. It was the resting place of Lord Baden-Powell, the founder of the Boy Scouts and the lady was his wife, Lady Olivia Baden-Powell. It wasn't very long afterwards, that the site held both sweethearts.

Founder of the Boy Scouts, Lord Baden-Powell

BUSH NEIGHBOURS

Dotted about the finely cultivated valleys of Kikuyu land were other bush schools like Mugoiri. It wasn't very long before we made an international group of teacher friends who like ourselves came to Africa with their own stories. K.C. Jones was our piano bashing Welshman, who, when finally leaving Kenya years later, hitchhiked around the continent. Tony Smith, a diehard Londoner at the time, had the principalship of Kaheti School thrust upon him. Al Butler, known to all as Cumberland Al, was a classically trained scholar who also taught in Kaheti. Mary Knox from Coventry saw rainbows and talked in tongues and along with Irene Mortimer from downtown London, were both originals; they taught in Nyeri at a wonderful elementary school. Gerard, an outgoing Dutchman, was a volunteer engineer at the coffee factory and lived in Murang'a with two Dutch nurses. Our spud-bashing Irish colleague, Breda Sherwin, was not only a favorite at Mugoiri but was to become as close as family. Adrian Roscoe and his wife Janice were soul mates and mentors lecturing at the University of Nairobi shortly before our departure from Kenya. We all shared Maureen Thompson for a brief while. All in all, it was an amazing collection of fascinating people who came together like the pieces of a mosaic and completed our Africa.

The house of spiders

SCHOOL DAYS

Our African students during their four years at Mugoiri Secondary School, prepared for their external exams, a throw back to former colonial times and a Russian roulette experience to say the least. They wrote a possible total of nine Cambridge Overseas exams in English, a language that was usually their third. Four years were tested during exam week, testing knowledge with little reference to their personal life experiences. I recall one site passage dealt with Scotland Yard, which had no terms of reference to their personal understanding since they never had yards in their shambas, and a Scottish yard was even a further stretch of the imagination. Trying to convince some younger students of the London underground where moving steps took you deep into a tunnel in the ground and where trains raced back and forth through holes in the wall was also an interesting lesson. Despite their lack of Western experiences, my Mugoiri students were to become my finest group of academics with the most incredible work ethics. Once written, completed Cambridge exams were bagged under strict supervision, sealed and sent off to the U.K. for grading. Parents, brothers and sisters had worked many long years to save enough money for one fortunate offspring to attend higher education. Mothers carried crippling loads of maize meal on their backs through miles of dusty roads or ankle deep mud to collect a few shilling for tuition fees. The demands upon the chosen child to succeed were intense. One unfortunate student committed suicide because she felt she would be letting her family down in the approaching final exams. Failure was not an option.

Some of my senior students in front in the school compound

MARY WAIRIMU

Letters we received from Canada thought it unusual when we hired a full time house girl for just the two of us. Help was a must. Living without the creature comforts of home, included sporadic hydro for two hours at night, water, which was undrinkable and often unusable for bathing, no telephone or electrical household appliances, and a battery powered transistor radio for world news. T. V. was unknown as was a reliable propane refrigerator. Mary Wairimu who had graduated from a domestic service program, was hired from more than twenty eager girls who lined up at our door for employment. Some of Mary's skills, besides speaking English, were ironing with a contraption that at first glance had me guessing. This ten inch high cast iron appliance was a weighty apparatus, with a removable top, which slid around on a rusty hinge. Inside the dark interior, charcoal was stacked and after a good soaking of kerosene, hastily lit and firmly clamped shut. Then the fun began. The whole appliance, which was kept outside at a distance, looked as if it would launch itself as sparks and smoke rose ominously from belching air vents. Clearly, an impressive sight for the uninitiated. When the smoldering stopped some minutes later and with the top securely hinged shut, Mary would then take the wooden handle with two hands and with dizzying twirls, spin around and around like a whirling dervish, until the thing began to glow like a cherry. Once the twirler decided upon a predetermined heat, she would rush to the ironing board and hastily begin her pressing with exaggerated thrusts. As soon as the appliance cooled down, the twirling started all over again, all the while sending out smoke signals and flying pieces of charcoal debris threatening all combustible items in the immediate vicinity. Teaching all day and marking papers at night under kerosene lamps, didn't leave much time for learning the art of ironing.

A regular source of foodstuffs was often a problem for us since the road to Murang'a was a hazard during the rains. Eggs, not always fresh, appeared on the table more than several times a week, camouflaged but eventually recognized. Through a network of neighbors, our daily milk requirements were solved. Down the driveway and through a crack in the hedge, a path led to the shamba of our nearest neighbor. Two very handsome young boys lived with their mom while dad, working in Nairobi, was an absentee father for months at a time. Mathew, the oldest boy, always led with a pearly, infectious grin. It was decided that each morning a bottle of milk would be delivered to our doorstep and a price was agreed upon. Milk finally arrived but only after we realized that we were supposed to supply the bottle. A hastily washed bottle solved the problem and each morning, without fail, our milk appeared on the doorstep, fresh from the cow, in a warm bottle, which read 'Cinzano.'

THE COO COO MAN

As milk was now a regular and much appreciated item on the menu, chicken we thought would be an indulgence and so, through 'bush telegraph,' the message circulated about that the teachers who lived in the new white house on the hill were in the chicken market. The chicken man came calling within a few days. The 'coo coo' man's first visit was memorable. I opened the door one misty morning to a very tall, toothy African gentleman who stood resplendent in his khaki shorts, barefoot, hand outstretched and grinning. Perched on his head, sat a tea cozy. Upon hearing of our requests for weekly chicken and fresh eggs and maybe, even some fruit of the season, it appeared we had a deal. As a gesture of things to come, he leapt off the front porch, ran to his bicycle and returned with a 'cock hen' for the muzungos (white man.) Thanking him for the delivery of such a fine, plump bird and after much gesturing and shaking with good will, I implied that there might be a slight problem. The coo coo man froze and appeared perplexed at my obviously not so subtle change in attitude. What could be the problem? The chicken was fresh and surely it was in fine shape, as anyone could see. After shuffling a bit, while secretly hoping Mary would materialize to translate for me, I made it clear that the chicken was in good health but it was still alive. Could he bring chickens that were dead and featherless? Realizing the simplicity of my predicament, he flashed an indulgent grin and with a mighty leap, this time chicken under one arm, he ran to his bicycle, unleashed his panga, and taking the bird with one hand, let out a victorious yell. Off came the head. 'Was there anything else we wanted?' came the toothy grin as he returned the chicken flapping in its death throes. I left the request for a featherless bird for Mary to sort out.

The 'Coo Coo' man with newly acquired business clothes

THE NORTHERN FRONTIER DISTRICT (N.F.D.)

From Kenya's Northern Frontier District (N.F.D.) came legends and myths and tales of Africa, baked in the forbidden reaches of a remote area of the continent, a place on the edge, a place seldom visited, a place unknown. Many old timers who had spent a life in Kenya had never ventured into the N.F.D. Stories abounded and held the listener spellbound and wide eyed. It was a place where one had to contend with unsuspecting hardships. It was through the goodwill of my recently made contacts that I was able to travel into this forbidden region using the isolated and scattered Italian mission stations as contacts for accommodations. Rooms for rent did not exist. Neither did motels or hotels.

Safaris into the N.F.D. varied with the season and could take days. It was during the rains that a small boat would have been more useful than my Land Rover, since many times, the way simply disappeared under water, and then for years, the entire area would suffer from devastating droughts where famine reigned and burial mounds marked the way. From Murang'a, the road passed through Nyeri, some forty miles of paved delight. Kikuyu shambas continued to dot the landscape but not for long.

The road to the N.F.D. during the very rare rainy season

More typical road conditions to the N.F.D.

Rumeruti was the last stop before entering the N.F.D. It was also the last petrol station and the end of the paved road. An elderly Asian gentleman, a dukawallaha or shopkeeper, along with his wife and daughter operated this last chance duka. The inventory was expertly displayed. One could purchase canned goods, clothing, Land Rover parts, shoes, soft drinks, glass figurines only to mention a few of the unusual items which were stocked on sagging shelves. Whiskey with mix and a groaning refrigerator for ice elevated the dukawallaha's status as a fine host and yet another reason to make the last stop. The prices were prohibitive and without apologies and so the shopper bought only seriously forgotten items and then in small quantities. Rumeruti boasted this one duka, a wooden sidewalk, and pointed to a dusty road, which led north to the N.F.D. Here, for the first time, the traveler could see tall, richly decorated warriors, brandishing shiny throwing spears while bare breasted women stood tall and elegant covered in dazzling beads gazing at the newcomers with unabashed stares. Travelers were novelty, white faces rare.

Further down the road, the border crossing into the N.F.D. blocked the way. This consisted of a flagpole gate heavily weighted down at one end opposite the sentry's box. A barefooted askari (soldier) would appear, slender and grinning ivory white. Dressed in a khaki green sweater with tan shorts and a matching hat, the traditional 'Jambo' is exchanged. Passes, stamped and documented from the District Commissioner's office are handed over, officially stamped once again and the conversation invariably turns to the condition of the road and the recent movements of the wildlife. The ever-present dangers of the Shifta bandits are never discussed, a forbidden topic. Standing nearby the sentry box are several Samburu warriors or L'Murran or morani. With long, scrupulously neat hairdos carefully braided in pigtail fashion, often flowing past the shoulders, they stand one leg tucked behind flamingo like, holding their spear, wondering who we are. Thick bangs fall over foreheads; dripping red ochre accentuate lithe, sinewy frames.

Our first crossing into the N.F.D.

Anthropologists have interesting theories about the origins of these Samburu and once connected these Nilo-Hametic people to lost Egyptian sources far up the Nile. Like the Bantu speaking peoples of Africa, linguistics offer clues to their origin and movements over the centuries. Left without the benefit of a written history, scholars delve into the subtleties of language. It is often said that oral literature has too often been overlooked in piecing together the history of a people, especially these Nilo-Hamites.

THE SAMBURU

The Samburu numbering some 30,000 are a Maasai speaking tribe who inhabit the arid N.F.D. along with several other groups of nomads. The Samburu society is based on gerontocracy, power and wealth held in the hands of the elders over the younger morani or warrior. Women have little status and do not hold any decision-making roles. Included in this elderly male power structure lies the threat of the curse, the supervision of ceremonies and rituals, and the judging of disputes. The young morani can neither marry until they are at least thirty nor exert themselves as full tribal members. Initial resentment gives way with age and as they too mature, support the system of rule they once found so offensive. An elaborate age set phenomenon is inherent among these polygynous Samburu wherein members move within it throughout their lives, forming a special bond with each other, unknown in the West. This age group association provides a buffer to the various strains in Samburu society, develops lifelong obligations among its members, and eventually furthers the gerontontic structure of the tribe.

Samburu warriors (morani) with throwing spears

Their society is composed of eight large segments called phratries, which serve as units or segments from which to exchange women. The incest taboo, like most non-technical peoples, is stringently enforced and these phratries ensure that only legitimate couples meet for marriage. So intense is the fear of incest that a married man must avoid his mother-in-law at all costs even if it means diving headlong into the brush to avoid passing her along a path. Phratries are broken into clans and from the clans, morani form their clubs. These clubs are social in nature and can be viewed as that institution which acts as a pressure valve for maturing, frustrated morani who are thwarted by their elders. No longer as useful as defenders against warring neighbors, the clubs still serve as a place where the young at heart can boast of their daring deeds, where mistresses can be met and where the incredible leaping dances are performed. Oftentimes, clubs will hold competitive dances and upon being taunted by rival clubs or even from their youthful mistresses, cattle raids are planned and sometimes killings result to show their bravery. An ever-present strain within the club is the loss of one's mistress for it is from here these young girls are taken on as additional wives by the elders.

Samburu morani with his young mistress

    The aridness of the N.F.D. precludes any hint of agriculture as a way of life. Hence, these nomadic Samburu, live in small settlements which are in a state of constant change both in location and composition. Demands upon the family necessitate these moves to and from various settlements which themselves are in a state of flux since cattle inflict a taxing drain upon the barren terrain.

Cattle for the Samburu can only be appreciated if one attempts to look into the role they play and the tremendous impact that the herds make upon virtually all aspects of Samburu life. Cattle literally sustain the family with the milk they yield and the blood they give. Puncturing the jugular after the neck has been tightly bound with a cord, the women collect blood. A small arrow pierces the vein and the blood squirts into a gourd. The animal is never over bled and the puncture is sealed with a dab of wet clay before returning the beast to the herd. Milk is either mixed with the blood or drunk straight. I was told that the gourd is washed out with cow's urine and the residue mixed in with the milk becomes a catalyst of sorts and turns the milk into a yogurt-like concoction. There is no doubt the mixture is thick. Small livestock such as goats or sheep are slaughtered periodically, but cattle are seldom killed unless ritual demands it. Roots and berries are sometimes gathered but seeds are never sown and so the Samburu looks to his cattle as the giver of life. These people are physically near perfect and look with distain upon those who till the soil and sow their crops.

A Samburu's wealth is determined by cattle, which are used in the bride price as demanded by his future father-in-law. Cattle droppings mixed with mud is used by the women to plaster their temporary huts, while hides once traditionally worn, now add to one's bartering power at the trading station. Oral literature and songs focus on the magnificence of their beasts, which carry personal names and are an integral part of Samburu life.

It is interesting to note that the Samburu do not have any way of expressing so many of our day to day familiar concepts or terms. An example would be a green lawn or an expanse of parkland. Nor is it possible to convey Niagara Falls, with its millions of gallons of water tumbling over a two hundred foot precipice each and every second. Since these phenomenons are absent in their environment, one has to wonder, if you can't say it, does it exist? The Inuit of northern Canada see many categories of snow and have names for each type. We just see snow. I once asked a Yanomama hunter in the Amazon how many animals he had strapped to his back after a day's hunting in the forest. He counted 'one, two' and then 'many' since these indigenous people of the forest can count only to two and end with many. Can they see more than two or does the concept of three and four and so on become meaningless and blurred and therefore unnecessary? Like the Pygmies of the Ituri rainforest in central Africa, the Yanomama see one dimension in distance and so a tree in the foreground is the same size as a tree on the horizon. Dr. Paul Spencer was surprised when he had several Pygmies in his Land Rover and, for the first time, these diminutive people saw a horizon outside their forest dwelling. They were amazed at how rapidly the distant Cape buffalo grew as the Land Rover approached the animals on the open savannah.

MARALAL

Rumeruti and the sentry's gate well behind, my Land Rover speeds towards Maralal, our first overnight scheduled stop. Scattered herds of Grant gazelle, graze in the distance as the dust bellows in our wake. Kongoni with narrow snouts and bent horns bounce stiff- kneed along side the road, eyes gaping white. Velvet-eyed giraffe take time from treetop meals to inspect the intruders. Enormous, tawny eland race off, dewlaps flapping fan-like, as they run unhurriedly with a pounding gait.

Reticulated giraffe on the road during the dry season.

Shy Grevy zebra startled by our approach bolt and pace alongside our vehicle only to veer recklessly in front of us before speeding away, mouths foaming, eyes saucer wide in disbelief. Africa's long distance runner, the ostrich, keeps to the middle of the road kicking furiously with two lethal toes, never thinking to veer off and away. Wild camels crunching on burnt leaves with green spittle oozing from crooked mouths barely notice our passing. Boran cattle, dust-colored and heavy chested with piercing horns, tell of our approach to Maralal. A written request for our first night's accommodation was necessary before going any further into the Great Rift Valley and the next phase of the safari.

Elephant have the right of way outside Maralal

Camping out is never an option for the traveler in the N.F.D. and to abandon a broken-down vehicle could be fatal. Two American girls became stranded not far from Maralal. Instead of sitting tight for the evening and waiting for a passing Samburu or Turkana to relay their plight to the mission station, one of the girls decided to walk for help. The girl left behind in the vehicle was hysterical when she was found the next morning by a passing morani. Lion and hyena had tormented her throughout the night. Her friend who had walked for help was missing. Several Samburu morani were engaged for the search. The next day one morani returned. He showed the authorities what he had found. The only remains left of the young girl was her one hand.

Maralal mission station is unusual because of the elephant moat, and to enter, one must drive over a shaky wooden drawbridge. This is elephant country and the moat is needed to keep the giant browsers away from the besieged garden. Nightly visits by the elephants created havoc in the compound and bearded Fr. Rosano would be up at all hours shooing away the beasts before they devoured all of his meager greens. Maralal is high and cold at night, especially during the rains. After a simple dinner, the long awaited conversation with the Padre was always a treat for he was an old timer and could recall tales now long forgotten by most. One bone chilling evening, fortified with strong coffee and my treat of whiskey, we sat around glowing hurricane lamps that bulged at the middle like fat old Santas. The Padre who lived alone was glad for our company and I feel he enjoyed our short overnight stays throughout the years.

Padre Rosano had been in Maralal for many years dispensing medicines and helping out during the famine periods. He knew most of the nomads who passed by and the few who took up permanent residence nearby. He also had intimate knowledge of the wildlife, especially one old wrinkled elephant. This ancient beast, like most old elephants, had trouble chewing the tough vegetation and the bark and thorns from the acacia trees. His molars were worn from years of grinding grit, which was part of his dusty diet. Without the hundreds of pounds of food each day, the beast was literally starving to death. The animal naturally looked for a softer, tenderer diet and found it in the gardens of the few locals, mostly transplanted Kikuyu, who had come to Maralal as government administrators. As is often the case, the animal in its attempt to survive, and after many complaints to the Game Department, was put on the 'most wanted' list to be shot. Lives were being threatened with each foraging evening. The game wardens, which were few and overworked protecting game, asked Rosano to shoot the animal. As he told the story, you knew he was talking about an old friend he had watched for forty years and one whose habits he knew as well as his own. Not wanting a stranger to do the deed, he took up his rifle and in the mid day sun, drove to the elephant's favorite back scratching tree. There he found his friend, leaning against a worn acacia; he walked twenty paces towards him, and put him down. Everyone in the area used the meat since it had to be eaten quickly without the benefit of refrigeration. During the butchering, the front foot was given to the Padre as a memento of an old friend. The ivory was sent to Mombasa. During the story telling I thought I could see a glistening in the old man's eyes.

The next morning, after a night of curdling hyena calls, as I bade farewell, I was presented with an enormous dried elephant foot, all wrinkled and hard. Months later, I took it to a friend in Nairobi where it was cleaned and cured and lined with red mango wood. Today, it sits in my living room, ghastly for some, but reminiscent of an old bearded friend, now long gone.

THE GREAT RIFT VALLEY

A chilly, dewy start, and Maralal is left behind as are the hyena whose whooping wails keep the most exhausted traveler wondering. Our route takes us through noticeably drier country, dotted with the odd Samburu manyatta, while still more wild camels, green bile dripping from their crooked mouths, nibble on parched brush. We are heading towards the Great Rift Valley. Our route leads us to a treacherous craggy track that is terrifyingly carved on the ledge of the Rift. Sharp boulders must be negotiated as the vehicle twists and groans. Looking into the yawning chasm below is truly a heart-thumping experience.

This is no river-eroded Grand Canyon, a mere waterway in comparison. This is a massive tear in the earth's crust. Blue-gray peaks line the opposite wall off in the cloudy distance.

The view from the ledge is memorable and not soon forgotten. Towards the north stretches the cavernous split leading to Ethiopia and the Red Sea, the Rift Valley's northern beginning, an enormous gash in earth's crust. Mountains stud the floor and are lost in the immensity of the scene. Clouds cast dull shadows over the yawning landscape while a scorching sun mirrors back, rare waterholes. On the floor far below us, herds of Grevy zebra make their presence known like gray maggots inching their way along the hazy bottom. Dust clouds tell of a nervous herd stampeding in the face of some unknown predator. Nomads in their trek towards some remote manyatta can be detected as spears glimmer and blink at us. Mount Nyiro on the northern horizon is a blend of purples and gold as it shelters South Horr Station our base camp in the days to come. Beyond Nyiro lies the fabled Jade Sea or Lake Turkana where beds of fossils contain the remains of man's origin, a most unlikely place for mankind's entrance.

Looking into the Great Rift Valley towards the north and Lake Turkana

A sweating canvas water bag is passed around and our descent into the valley is painstakingly slow since a recent landslide crowds the Land Rover dangerously close to the edge. Off in the distance on the Valley floor, the tin roof of Baragoi station waves mirage-like and unreal. Our descent complete, Baragoi seems only minutes away since the track becomes a smooth, sandy path with only an occasional rock. Donkey-eared zebra take time from their foraging and question our intrusion. Saber horned oryx grunt in annoyance and race alongside only to halt abruptly to become swallowed up in our dust. Northern Grant gazelle are a faded tan and lack the richer coats of their southern cousins. This piece of road is a treat and will never be experienced again while in the Great Rift Valley.

BARAGOI

Baragoi is less than a village. The settlement is an administrative one and consists of the local police, a vacant veterinarian office and one Somali duka featuring an oversupply of Kimbo lard. Rusty tins have long since lost their labels. Several African open 'pubs' are found under the modest shade that wispy pepper trees offer. Samburu warriors lean easily against these pepper trees, heavily laden with the nests of the yellow weaverbird, intent upon watching a game of bao, a chess -like game. The Turkana, who are likewise nomads, keep to their own in small groups. These two tribes have been known to have their differences. It seems a brittle friendship now exists between them since the advent of British colonial rule. Sporadic cattle raids and minor conflicts still flare up, however. A lone gas or petrol station with its rusting sign has long stopped pumping fuel of any sort, a token reminder of former colonial days.

Downtown Baragoi and pepper trees

Turkana are the more rugged of the two tribes and appear so in their dress. Even the greetings of the two people tell of their differences. In Turkana, the greeting for hello is spat out almost angrily while the Samburu's welcome is soft and lilting. The Turkana can survive the worst of famines and are never restricted by taboos and hence they eat the flesh of any animal, a distinct advantage during tough times. The warriors don the traditional beehive hairdo and build it up over the years by applying mud mixed with cow dung. A bluish dye is added to this hard crusted growth of hair and protruding from this elaborate masterpiece is an ostrich feather pom pom. Ostrich feathers are taken from the more colorful male bird, which have distinct black and white plumes with glowing red legs during the mating season. Warriors use porcupine quills to scratch and soothe their itchy scalps. Since, like the Samburu, resting one's head at night would destroy weeks of labour spent on the elegant coiffures, both tribes use a wooden bench-like pillow to support the nape of the neck, thus keeping the hairdo off the ground and intact. I found it really uncomfortable but then again I don't look as attractive as the morani. I was given a Turkana wrist knife. This circular weapon fits around the wrist and is wrapped in a leather sheath. Once the sheath is removed, a dangerous round blade is exposed and used for slashing enemies at close quarters. It is considered a collector's item because of its rarity.

Turkana women shave their hair except for a tangled patch, which is left down the middle to the back of the head. Samburu women shave completely. Both women don elaborate necklaces of multicolored beads, weighing them down and stretching the neck in time, while also restricting head movement. With the years, these beads are continuously added to, and eventually, even the bosoms are covered. So we see the males of both tribes spending hours upon hours grooming and fussing about each other while the females in comparison, appear plain and somewhat common. One can hardly miss the similarity to nature where the male is often so much more showy and grander than the faded female who sits quietly camouflaged among her young.

Baragoi station, our second overnight stop, like Maralal, would also require an invitation from our host. Unlike most of the local dwellings, which are covered in mud and dung, the buildings at the station are from cut stone and cement blocks, which thwarted all attempts of the hungry termite colonies. Having been expected, we are shown to our plain but comfortable, clean rooms and soon shed our clothing, heavy with perspiration and dust. Having washed off the miles, a glass of Vermouth settles the traveler and soon the jostling and grinding of the Land Rover is pushed beneath tender limbs. Gazelle steaks and a green salad taken from our supplies are complimented with a glass of red wine. News of the north is exchanged for news from our Kikuyu land and with a lull in the conversation, someone suggests bed and an early start as the last twenty odd miles to South Horr Station has been known to get one's attention.

TO SOUTH HORR

From Baragoi to South Horr is twenty-six miles, lonely and untravelled. Breakdowns are a constant worry and since help is some walking distance away for the bravest of hearts, I always allowed for the maximum of daylight hours. Also, during the cooler, early hours, game sighting was at its best because the herds would be returning from shrinking waterholes after an anxious night of guarding against predators. Stiff legged secretary birds, feathers protruding from behind the head like pencils, bustards and the towering crested crane with its fabulous mating ritual strut through the dried frankincense bushes. These hours were a photographer's delight even though trying to stay on the track, which often disappeared, was a chore and a constant concern. Keeping familiar landmarks in sight was a must. Scenery was nothing short of wild; unscaled peaks of the Ndoto Mountains to the east beckoned to brave hearts. Stretches of unchartered territory gave way only to the nomad. The land kept its secrets well hidden and only yielded to the watchful and the patient. This is the land of the wanderer, those who choose to wander, but were not lost.

An early start in Africa is important since there is an unwritten law, which states that the night belongs to the animals. This I can attest to. Without the use of a Land Rover, our friends were seldom able to travel off the tarmac roads and were therefore very restricted. And so it was, that I would often take one of our friends to the N.F.D., being always conscious of taxing the lonely outposts' meager supplies. On one such safari, Breda Sherwin our Irish teaching companion from Mugoiri and an excellent traveler under any condition was with Maeve and I. We were on the last leg of the safari from Baragoi to South Horr. It was understood that one brought enough food and meat to these outposts and even to leave a little behind, especially greens and pineapples and potatoes. You had to be self sufficient with petrol, as well. Several miles outside South Horr a small herd of Grant gazelle grazed quite near to the 'road.' Shooting an old male, I swung the Land Rover alongside the carcass and thought I could pull it aboard by myself. Unable to pull the heavy hindquarters over the side, Breda and Maeve gamely volunteered their help. The two girls, down on their knees, heaved and pushed the bulky still warm carcass while I tugged at the horns from the back of the Land Rover. We were unable to swing the hindquarters over the side, despite the groans and grunts from below, the girls staggering under their load, finally collapsing. In gales of laughter they reeled, prostrate on the ground while I was left straining with the animal, precariously balanced over the edge. Teetering, the carcass began to slip. Over it went. The two, unable to move in their spasms of laughter watched it come plummeting down. I followed shortly behind, still holding on to the horns. There we all lay in a heap, unable to sort ourselves out, gazelle legs tangled in and about us, holding on to our sides in hysterics, and once again sharing the unexpected.

SOUTH HORR

Nearing Mount Nyiru, South Horr was a comforting sight both for its oasis-like greenery and the suddenness of its appearance just behind a rise in the road. South Horr was at the base of Nyiru from which an intermittent icy mountain stream flowed for half a kilometer before it disappeared into the sandy bed, never to be tasted again. Why South Horr appeared on a map of Kenya always intrigued me. It consisted of one sun baked mud Somali duka, and my host's nearly completed outpost station. The duka looked like a skeleton with its wooden ribs sticking out twisted and askew. On the other hand, the station had two permanent cement blockhouses, a nearly completed two-room school, a garage-sized dispensary with an even smaller storehouse attached, and an artistically built chapel, the windows glazed with the local pink quartz. Building materials from the area were used and applied in a most effective manner. Rose quartz was used instead of glass and produced a dramatic effect when the sun poured through. Steel pipes ran around the perimeter of the roof of the house filled with gravity fed water from Mount Nyiru and by noon hour each day these pipes contained very hot water and a pleasant shower was available to the first two or three who managed to get in before the ice cold mountain water poured out. Rain water, used for drinking, the most precious of commodities, ran into a large aluminum tank strategically placed beneath eaves, with taps under lock and key.

Father Joe Polet was a remarkable man and a most gracious host. Tall and lean, thoughtful and farseeing, he was both Samburu and Turkana, a mix of the old and the new. Ice blue eyes and sallow cheeks, a whiskered chin and slender long fingers marked his aesthetic character. Known for his restlessness in his youth, this young man from the Piedmont of Italy came to Africa and became synonymous with the N.F.D. His meager station welcomed anthropologists and government dignitaries alike. The Padre as he was known amongst the Africans, sheltered the sick, fed the hungry ones, settled disputes when he could and buried the dead. He also brought awareness to a forgotten people who were living on the edge and would become pawns in the face of 'progress.' His graciousness towards Maeve and I was the beginning of a lifetime friendship.

Enjoying a laugh with the Padre on the right.

Contact while at South Horr with the outside world was made with the aid of a two-way battery powered radio. Oftentimes, I would tune in and while awaiting our call signal, listen to the first hand reports of the N.F.D. These reports would invariably be concerned with the previous evening's cattle raids and the ensuing battles of revenge, which were bound to follow. Marauding leopards or lion initiated urgent requests to the Game Department for assistance. (A Samburu women was charged by an irate rhino and died of her injuries. Her husband, in desperation, hunted down the animal and with his spear killed it in revenge. He was duly charged for killing a protected species and jailed. Such are the conflicts between man and animals.) Medical needs of some distant outpost would be relayed to the Flying Doctor services in Nairobi, while most emergencies went unanswered. It was disappointing on subsequent visits to find the batteries dead or corroded and so we were unable to hear the news of the north or to make contact with the outside world from South Horr.

LION ON THE ROAD

The Padre believed in the dignity of work and felt that free handouts was a loss of self-respect. When food from America became available during the frequent bouts of famine, he would have the recipients give up their labor so that the foodstuffs were not handouts but earned through their own efforts.

Self-respect was left intact. Such was the road-building project from South Horr to Baragoi, a most progressive and outlandish idea at the time. He convinced the Samburu and Turkana elders that a road would greatly improve their chances of survival, especially during famines and raids. With hammers and picks, thirty nomadic tribesmen were put to work carving out a road to Baragoi starting at the South Horr Valley, a tremendous undertaking. The work was as slow as the soaring thermometer. The road would pass through gullies and flint hard rocky knolls and each day the workers earned food for themselves and their families, another idea as foreign as the tools they used.

After several miles and many months of intense labor, construction came to an abrupt halt. The men who slept on the side of the road each evening, were kept supplied with food and water by the Padre. One night, a lion leapt over their thorn bush boma, enclosing them for the night, and carried off a young morani, leaping with the hapless victim in its jaws over the five-foot thorn hedge. It was only the chasing and yelling by the aroused warriors that saved the young man from being eaten. He was unceremoniously dropped, as the animal made its escape, spears flying at the fleeing would be man-eater. This did not stop the pride from returning nightly and prowling around the perimeter of the boma. Finally, the worker warriors had enough and wanted the Padre to take action. I was in South Horr when the lion problem came to a head and one late afternoon, the Padre asked me to accompany him to the scene. Maeve decided to come along to watch.

We arrived at the roadside boma in my Land Rover, guns in hand, looking very confident out in the open. As it turned out the plan was that I was to take three or four of the warriors and the Padre would do the same. We would enter the undergrowth separately and apart from where the lions were last seen. After that, I wasn't sure what was supposed to happen. We were both followed by towering, spear toting warriors, completely forgetting Maeve, who was left sitting on the hood my Land Rover. As we entered the thick bush, I knew it was a poor plan since whatever was inside the undergrowth would have all the advantages of surprise. We hadn't got very far before we were stopped by the blast of several shots to our left. Well, loud pops would better describe the sound. Almost immediately, there was a rush from behind us. The bushes parted and there stood the warriors from the Padre's party. I decided it was wise to return to the Land Rover and find out what happened. Apparently the Padre thought he heard a movement and fired his small bore .22 caliber hoping to scare the would be man-eaters off. Well, there was no doubt upon hearing that the pitiful pop, the Padre and his gun was no match for a charging lion and so his warriors had serious misgivings about their leader and decided to follow the bwana with the big gun since my rifle was a 9.3 m.m. and the boom could be heard a long way off. I was grateful not to have been challenged by a charging lion but it wouldn't be the last time I was confronted by these determined beasts.

Like their Maasai cousins, the Samburu hunt lion with only a spear in hand, but in the open savanna and never in thick bush. It was a custom, not so long ago, for a future son-in-law to present the scrotum of a lion he killed to his father-in-law to be as a sign of his worthiness and ability to protect a wife. After hearing the pathetic shot from the Padre they must have had second thoughts and maybe guessed why he never had a wife for himself. Well, after several years of scorching drought, a deluge swept through the area. The torrential rain erased any semblance of a road and the project came to an end. Ironically, there was no more rain for years to come.

As previously mentioned, it was in 1898 during the building of the Kenya-Uganda railroad when construction was brought to a halt. Two man eating lion feasted on nearly one hundred Indian laborers until one Colonel Patterson shot them. In a nearby cave, human remains were found and the lower jaw of one of the man-eaters was malformed and rendered useless. The railroad was passing through the lions' territory. These man-eaters from Tsavo became the subject of a popular movie that falsely shows the Masai running away while the hero from Hollywood braves the wild beasts. Today, lion still threaten human populations in Africa. In 1991, six people were eaten in Mufe, Zambia. With hearing three times that of humans and the need for only one fifth the light we require, the animal is a fearsome night stalker weighing in at 425 lbs. with a roar, which can be heard five miles away. Roaming the grasslands of Africa, the lion is surely king of the savannah.

THE COKE LINE

On one of my many return trips to Africa, I found myself with the Padre leaving Nairobi on safari to his beloved N.F.D. and to the South Horr Valley. As we neared the Valley, we crossed the ubiquitous dry riverbeds called lagas. It was a blistering afternoon and we had been pushing it hard with two of us as drivers in his new Land Rover. When we came to the famous laga called the Morani, because so many young warriors died there in battle, we decided to turn into the riverbed for a rest and after several hundred yards found a shady spot alongside the bank and under a welcoming overhang. We took out our soggy sandwiches and several warm cokes, our treats for the day. Sitting in the sand and next to the Land Rover with the hood raised to cool off the engine, we anticipated our lunch no matter how badly it looked.

It was just about then when we heard the tinkling of a wooden bell used on a lead animal. Around the bend in the laga, came a small herd of goats being coaxed on by an even smaller Samburu young girl. Barefooted and apron clad, smeared with red ochre, she showed the beginnings of womanhood.

A typical Samburu young girl returning with gourd of milk

Brandishing a hefty stick she hastened along, looking anxiously behind her all the while. Wide-eyed, she seemed both stunned and relieved to see two white men, muzungos. When the Padre spoke to her in Samburu, relief filled her face and she returned his greetings, still looking behind her all the while. When asked how the day was going she replied that a lion was stalking both her and the small herd of goats and she was determined not to loose one single animal for fear of the consequences back at the manyatta. Our presence seemed to have a calming effect upon her and she chattered away with the Padre. Maybe she knew that the strange smells of an overheated Land Rover, a mixture of gasoline and oil with rubber tire odors thrown in, would temporarily discourage even the most nervy lion. This was not to forget muzungos' body odors, which were found to be extremely offensive to most wild animals. I offered her a warm soda. Holding the can at arm's length, she followed our example and put the open can to her mouth and took a deep gulp. Well, the effect was disastrous. She never suspected the sudden rush of carbonated bubbles and gas as she gasped, gagged and retched, soda pouring from her nose and down her chest and apron. Down went the can, its contents disappearing in the sand. We had played a nasty trick on her. With her trusty stick in hand, she glared at us menacingly and off she went, shooing the goats in front of her. Better to take her chances with a hungry lion. Her simple taste buds had been ruthlessly assaulted. I sat in amazement until I realized that she had never tasted pop in her life. It was not often that one ventured past the 'coke line,' a rare experience indeed. It was many years later that I had a similar experience in the Amazon jungle, with Yanomama Indians and a stick of chewing gum

FAMINE

During our many safaris to South Horr, we assumed various jobs that in turn helped me gain a better understanding of Nilo-Hametic nomads. I was primarily interested in creation mythology, a fascinating study of man's place in the world as dictated by the stories, which allow us to justify our actions to each other and the way we treat the world around us. Each morning lines of women carrying infants, some holding on to small children, waited patiently in the dusty compound. Sacks of American cracked wheat and powdered milk were distributed from under a large fever tree. The dignity of these hungry people made a lasting impact on me. There was never any pushing or shoving and there was always room in line for the orphaned or the old and very weak. It was unfortunate when we had to halt the distribution of these extremely limited supplies especially when I knew there were tons of donated foodstuffs stored in warehouses in distant Mombasa on the Indian Ocean. The problem was transporting the food to the N.F.D. since a lorry or truck was necessary and the 'roads' would test the toughest of ordinary vehicles.

Medical supplies, despite the expiry dates, donated by Europeans and Americans, had to be sorted out into useable categories. Knowledge of English was a necessity and so huge cartons of smelly bottles were put into some kind of order for the medical nurse who knew little English. At other times, the day would include a Land Rover full of hungry children and driving off to a nearby laga, spot a herd of gazelle and return with food for several days. Several times a year, I would exercise my resident's zebra license and then there would be meat enough for many manyattas. All the while I observed the ways of the nomad.

I recall one lazy afternoon, returning from a hunting trip with a dozen children hanging on to the Land Rover like barnacles, and being barely able to steer over the bumpy track. Over the constant chattering and laughing which usually came before an anticipated meal, I could hear a strange sucking sound from the back where a Grant gazelle lay stiff and lifeless. Curiosity got the best of me and I stopped the Land Rover and looked behind and there I saw a lasting sight. Sitting on top of the gazelle, a Samburu girl of about five, barefooted and wrapped in her scanty shoulder cloth, was holding the exposed leg bone of the animal and was sucking out the raw marrow. She was unable to contain her hunger. Having now drawn attention to herself, she froze in fear, brown eyes fixed unblinkingly on me. Had she done something wrong and was the Bwana upset?

When the children gathered a particularly hard-shelled seed, it was a sign that there was little food left in the family's scant reserve. I noticed that elephant ate these same brown seeds, the size of a small nut. I tried to chew one, and finally gave up in frustration. They were tasteless and not unlike a small peach pit and had to be swallowed whole to fill the stomach. Powdered milk from the U.S.A. was available periodically when, on rare occasions, several bags would be delivered from Mombasa via Baragoi. The children would do a curious thing with their powder. Using the much sought after discarded Kimbo lard cans to collect their rations, they would top up these rusty containers with water from the stream, place a twig inside and with tiny hands, twirl the contents until the white foam rose to the top. An illusion of more milk? Another common sight in the long lines, was an infant sucking on the withered breast of a glassy-eyed mother, who after awhile would pass the child to a neighbor, where the baby would once again, try its luck. When the young ones with distended tummies and faded hair appeared, the end was often predictable. It was then you noticed that the mother had been to a witch doctor to thwart the inevitable. She wore a green leaf in her headband.

Maeve distributing powdered milk in South Horr

Late one afternoon, a Turkana mother, wrapped in crusty skins covering one shoulder, holding a shriveled infant at her sagging breast and clutching a naked youngster with her free hand, appeared in front of the dispensary. She had arrived from the north, which meant she, along with her two children, had walked over the lava-strewn land during the day, in the tremendous heat, a most remarkable feat. There was something different about her as I stared. It was her face. The salt from perspiration had eaten away her eyebrows and eyelashes, leaving her face raw and unfinished. She had heard that powdered milk had arrived at the station…another example of bush telegraph at its best. What she didn't realize was that the few bags of powdered milk were already distributed several days before. 'All tears are equally salty,' and for this mother born on rations, the taste was bitter. An excerpt from the Padre sent to me in Canada:

Oct. 6/1968

Dear Bert

I would like to buy a good stock of blankets for our old men and women as well as for the poorest students in order to give them a place and cloth for spending the night here at the station. In fact many of them have to walk for many miles every day in order to come to school and go back. The fear of Elephants is not un-reasonable .Our school children from far away have been charged by angry elephants many times.
Fr. Polet

One cloudless afternoon in South Horr, when even the insects knew to be quiet, a pounding at the front door awakened the Padre from his siesta. To his surprise, there stood an elderly Samburu, his broken spear in one hand, the other hand grasping his shoulder, which was gashed and torn. Holding out the broken spear, his modest request was for a replacement. The Padre kept a supply of spears in the front hallway, which he traded for goods in far off Nairobi. First things first, however. Without the benefit of any anesthetic, he sewed up the old man's shoulder and put a crude sling wrap around it. With his new spear in hand, the elder told his story.

Earlier, he had been walking to South Horr through the maze of lagas. He heard the trumpeting of an elephant and the shrieking of children. Rushing to the scene, he saw an elephant, trunk curled, blaring angrily, ready to charge two helpless young girls pinned to the side of the laga. Without hesitation and with spear poised menacingly, he jumped between the animal and the terrified children. As the elephant rushed at this new intruder, the old man threw his spear deep above the curled trunk. When the animal bent down to crush him, the spear was driven deeper and deeper into the trumpeting animal, finally snapping off at the wooden insert which held the spear together, leaving the hardened metal end firmly embedded in the elephant's face. Backing off the bleeding elder, the animal stood over him, swaying back and forth, trumpeting mightily and looking like the fabled unicorn. The elder had pantomimed this scene for me, and it was truly living theatre as he swung about, one finger pointing away from his forehead, mimicking the broken spear and the swaying animal. The elephant in a terrible rage, trying to rid herself of the embedded spear, swung around, crashed through the underbrush and disappeared, blaring a terrible wrath.

Looking down into a laga with several elephant foraging on the opposite side

The two young girls who were walking through the laga on their way to school had unwittingly cut off a female from her calf. The frightened mother went for the intruders. Some weeks later it was mistakenly reported that poachers had killed a female elephant that was found dead with a broken spear protruding from her head. This was sixty desert miles away. I look at the remnant of the broken spear here in my living room, and can only imagine the fright, which took place on that afternoon, and the agony of the dying mother who was only following her instincts in protecting her young calf.

LION IN THE LAGA

It was the dry riverbeds, which I found most fascinating. Sand-filled arteries, these lagas were named and familiar to the nomads, since battles had raged in many of them, and cattle, stolen during raids, were kept hidden and secure in the maze of countless dry beds. Only the foolish adventurer would venture alone into the lagas, which spread out like the veins in a body builder's arm. Loose, sandy bottoms challenged even the most steadfast Land Rover. Often, these dry riverbeds would be reduced to narrow gaps with overhanging vegetation, only to open up into a sunlit clearing, a wide expanse filled with evidence of passing wildlife. The uninitiated was soon confused and hopelessly lost. The simplest solution was to have a Samburu onboard, since even the children had an uncanny knack in finding the main artery and the route back to South Horr. Leaving the lagas and going overland was a lesson I learned never to repeat. As I plowed through the bushes, sharp thorns broke off in my tires, and worked their way through resulting in many slow leaks for days to come. I learned to stay in the lagas. Overland routes were for the elephants.

Crossing the Morani laga named after the warriors who were killed there

It was during one of our dinner hunting forays into a laga, that we came upon the unexpected. The Padre was driving his Land Rover, Maeve was in the passenger's seat and I sat behind with a young Samburu lad in the open, gun resting on my lap. Driving into one of the many entrances in the maze, it wasn't very long before we came face to face with a herd of Grant gazelle. The Padre remarked how strangely they were behaving, since the animals would run a short distance, only to stop and look around at our approach. As the herd stared at us suspiciously, I jumped out of the Land Rover, clamored up a hill and once on top, looked down upon the scene. Spotting an old male, I took it down. Half sliding down the slope, I stood over the still warm animal. After removing the stomach, I used the sand to clean my hands and knife, all the while under the watchful gaze of several patient vultures perched in nearby trees. These scavengers had the knack of appearing within minutes of a kill. The odor of rotting carrion can be detected forty miles away while stomach enzymes and acids allow them to consume enough botulism in one ghoulish meal to kill an entire village. With the help of the Padre and young boy, the gazelle was lifted into the Land Rover and off we chugged through the sandy laga, now heating up like a kiln. Both the boy and I sat on the gazelle since it was much more comfortable than the steel wheel-wells. Land Rovers were known for their reliability, not their comfort.

Having to turn around, the Padre shifting the vehicle into low gear, climbed up the bank, with the idea of backing down to make his turn. We were still climbing the steep bank when I heard the first shout, 'Lion!' The nasty desert type that was not especially particular about their diet had surrounded us. I was uncertain whether it was the vigilant vultures, the reeking stomach remains, or the dead gazelle, which we were sitting on that got the lions' attention. These same lions had terrorized the road builders and stopped the road construction. The only clear memory I have is of a very large scruffy male, chin pointed skyward, sniffing the air trying to locate the fresh meat, which was thankfully mixed in with the smell of gasoline and fumes from the vehicle. I was told that there were half dozen females scattered around and peering at us through the bushes. Gears grinding, the Land Rover lurched backwards and spun around in the loose sand, but not before the Padre pitched a gun to me. He had both our guns in the front with him and in his haste, I ended up with his gun with a telescopic scope. I fumbled the scope to my eye, nearly poking it out, and located the sky, several clouds and a nesting bird. I hated those telescopes. Could never find a target in the best of times. I looked up as we ground away, realizing the cats could cover the short distance between us in mere seconds. The open back of the Land Rover was not a reassuring place to be, and sitting on a dead gazelle was definitely not the greatest seat in the house. It was a quiet ride back to South Horr as I rubbed my sore eye, silently cursing telescopic gun sights.

Years later, I found myself with an African driver Masawa, in Mikumi, Tanzania, on a fact finding mission of sorts. We were on a deserted road when our shiny tire blew apart. The Land Rover was without a spare, and this was not surprising since everything including soap was rationed and most items were simply not available. (I remember stopping at a lodge and pointing to a bottle at the back of the bar for a sundowner. The barman shook his head. I was using my best KiSwahili, peppered with some obvious impatient gestures. Finally, I realized his refusal was nothing personal. The bottles were filled with cold tea for display purposes only.) Masawa left our stranded vehicle and walked back the several miles to town with the hopes of locating a second hand tire. He knew the language and the means to scrounge for a replacement. It was unbearably hot as I sat in the Land Rover, swatting sleeping sickness carrying tsetse flies, with their scissor like wings. Even a direct swat never seemed to bother these flying menaces. It didn't take me long to figure out that the roof of the Land Rover was the place to wait. As I sat on my perch, I was high enough off the ground to avoid the pests, since these carriers hover around six feet. Sometimes you get the feeling you're being watched. I got that feeling as I sat there. Looking around, some twenty feet away in an acacia tree, belly sagging and eyelids droopy, stared a fully-grown lioness. She too was avoiding the annoying flies in the heat of the day. She too found relief like myself, higher up. We never much bothered with each other after that. It was only much later that I questioned my nonchalant attitude.

Lion in a tree avoiding the dreaded tsetse fly

Later that same evening, tire replaced and on the way to our sleeping quarters and avoiding cavernous potholes in the road, Masawa turned sharply around an especially deep cavity. A lion could be seen in our headlights, squatting in the hole and probably relieving himself, massive head quite visible in our lights, and completely fearless as we swerved around the animal.

It was on this same safari, on our return to Dar es Salaam, that Masawa and I stopped at Kaole on the Indian Ocean, where 13th century mosques and eroding gravestones told a story of Arab society long ago. The local doors were awesome, all carved and studded with brass and geometric designs. One Mr. Samahani M. Kejeri, the self appointed caretaker of the ruins who had been there for years, gave us a lecture in faltering English. It was his custom to have each and every visitor sign his book and in return you were given his name and address and a number. I was visitor number 2297 and would now be considered one of his friends. When I asked him about his archeological background, he invited me into his wattle hut and produced a document with a flourish of great pride. It told of his reading books about the early ruins and was signed under the stamp: 'Prison Warden.'

SCHOOL SAMBURU STYLE

The nearly completed elementary school in South Horr, with two unfinished classrooms and windowless gaping holes where one day glass would be installed and sporting a shiny new corrugated roof, was the pride of the station. It was insufferably hot inside. When good times were at hand, due to fresh grass and nearby waterholes, the enrollment would soar to nearly thirty students. Lessons in basic hygiene and writing, with simple calculations, were conducted in KiSwahili, the lingua franca of East Africa. The Samburu and Turkana children were assigned to their seats by size. Some boys wore khaki shorts while others were draped in the traditional sheet, tied at the shoulder. The girls, in an attempt at modesty, were issued bloomers. These roughly tailored panties once contained wheat and powdered milk from America. You could still see the faded picture of a white hand shaking a black one in a gesture of friendship from the States.

Samburu school girls

The teacher told us the following story. One of the Samburu students, a girl of about six or seven, was having a difficult time concentrating in the confinements of the concrete block building. She was constantly being scolded for her inattentiveness. She was disturbing her neighbors. Discipline problems were rare indeed. One blistering afternoon, sun peaking in a cloudless sky, she decided she could tolerate her confinement not one lesson longer. Getting up from her wooden bench, she made a dash to freedom and with a mighty slam of the door, was last seen heading towards the nearest laga. Our teacher, interrupted from her painted plywood chalkboard, made for the door, wrenched it open, only to hesitate. In a crumpled heap on the floor, lay a pair of bloomers, a final gesture of revulsion and indignation!

MYTH OR FACT?

The Padre, who was told the story first hand from two unrelated sources, related the following to me. The first tale was from a Samburu morani who had recently returned with a small herd of goats from the Koroli Desert, a truly forsaken region of the north. A camel herding Rendille tribesman who was passing through the South Horr Valley told his story. Both accounts are as unusual as they are similar.

In search of pasture, the Samburu morani had walked four or five days from the Valley. The terrain is as lonely and desolate as any moonscape, the thorn scrub offering dry, burnt leaves to desperate animals in need. As is the custom, herd animals are sheltered each evening in a makeshift boma. This circular thorn bush enclosure offers some protection for the herdsman and his animals. Once inside, the morani can relax since his herd is relatively safe from desert lion or errant leopards. Lions have been known to leap over these enclosures, while the slouching spotted hyena is a formidable predator as well. (The myth of the cowardly hyena would be put to rest, when years later, research in N'Goro N'Goro crater in Tanzania would document hyena not only killing on their own, but driving off prides of lion. African oral literature told of the hyenas' prowess for generations but these stories were always downgraded to the category of myth. In addition, it was learned that hyena pups practice fratricide to establish dominance in the group. This practice remains a rarity in the animal world.) And so, the warrior proceeded to drive his animals into the enclosure as the late afternoon shadows hung long and heavy. Using the butt of his spear, he coaxed the stragglers through the small opening, to be sealed with the 'enclosure' bush or key. Suddenly and without any warning, there appeared from behind the thorn bushes and his animals, a peculiar looking 'muzungo' or white man. Startled and unsure, the herder was unable to stop the visitor who flanked the herd and followed them into the boma. Unwilling to have his animals wander outside of the boma with the approaching darkness, he was left with no choice but to pull in the key bush, thus sealing off any escape route.

The warrior's constant terms of reference when describing the 'muzungo' was behavioral traits as opposed to physical description. Standing as high as a white man, the Padre is slightly over six feet and short for a Samburu, the herdsman told how the creature was covered with body hair, which Africans lack. Long finger nails constantly brushed the 'muzungo's' overgrown hair from his eyes, another characteristic, which the African lacks, long hair. This continuous brushing away of hair was a constant throughout the story. During these first moments inside the boma and throughout the night, there was no attempt at oral communication. Our herder, using caution, sat himself down on the opposite side of the boma and struck a low fire, all the while under the watchful gaze of the intruder and the shuffling herd. The herdsman unwrapped a piece of goat meat from his skin bag, and proceeded to roast it. The solitary meal began, spear close at hand. The 'muzungo' obviously stirred by the smell of food, continued brushing his hair to one side with curved fingernails, all the while staring at the herdsman intently, while motioning towards his mouth in an attempt to share some of the meat. This performance continued throughout the meal and at no time was there any conversation or attempt at language. Neither did the morani share his meat. The continuous separating of the hair from the forehead and eyes was constantly related during the herdsman's narration. Throughout the sleepless night, with knobkerry between his knees and throwing spear at hand, he returned the steadfast stare of the intruder. With dawn the entrance bush was removed, the goats passed noisily out into the open acacia scrub followed by the 'muzungo.' Without looking behind, the silent visitor disappeared into the wasteland without the least sound or even a backward glance.

Months after the Samburu tale was told, a Rendille tribesman, known for their camel herding expertise, related the following tale. His story is not as complete in detail but the description of the 'muzungo' is identical. The chance encounter took place east of Lake Turkana and once again in very inhospitable surroundings, the Chalbi Desert. The camel tending Rendille warrior, came upon a 'muzungo' covered with hair, all the while separating long strands from his eyes. Both accounts tell of the creature's fair skin, most of which was covered with long hair. Long fingernails were emphasized in both stories. Again, both nomads agree that the 'muzungo' was not aggressive.

I only encountered Rendille once in my travels. Maeve and I were following the Padre to Loiyangallani when we came across a Rendille encampment. As we neared the gathering of temporary huts, the children and women came running to see the travelers, a rare sight indeed. The crowd surrounded the Land Rovers and stared at us in amazement. They had seen the Padre before but Maeve and I were an additional attraction with my black beard and a woman next to me. The Rendille women were spell bound by Maeve's appearance while the children begged for 'sedimenti' or sweets. They had never seen a 'white' woman and stared in disbelief. The tall and silent warriors stood quietly behind the gathering, looking on, leaning easily on shiny throwing spears. I threw out a handful of candies and the scrambling children were lost in a cloud of dust amidst thrashing arms and legs. From the rear of the group, a handsome warrior approached us and in faltering KiSwahili, asked who was the owner of the 'muzungo' woman. I took ownership. He wanted to make a deal. He offered me several fresh ostrich eggs if I would barter her hair. No doubt he would have woven the strands into his own hair. Maeve's hair was blonde and must have appeared unimaginable. She was an apparition. We drove off after I carefully wrapped the two ostrich eggs in a towel. Maeve's hair was left intact.

Imagination? Over taxed mythology? A forgotten feral population? It is difficult to determine the authenticity of the stories. These two men from different tribes are certainly not influenced by the outside world. There are no radios, televisions, newspapers, or magazines available. Neither can they read. Visitors to the north are rare indeed and would, by necessity, travel by

Land Rover. There was no apparent reason to fabricate such a tale since no one gained. The N.F.D. is a virtual wasteland to the north and east while European settlements are non-existent. Both reports absolutely concluded that they had encountered a 'muzungo' and not a fellow African. The Rendille and the Samburu are two distinct peoples with different languages, customs, and mythologies. They are also unfriendly with each other. Their separate lifestyles preclude any possibility of collusion for gain by relating to their mutual friend, a most unusual tale.

It must be mentioned that, in the past, Africans already knew about various 'discoveries.' Unfortunately, in most cases, some explorers and contemporary Westerners, relegated these tales to more fanciful African myths and discarded them into the realm of fantasy. Several examples would include the okapi. The animal was described by natives as part zebra and part giraffe. Just another African myth until its recent 'discovery' in the Abedare Mountains. The same story can be told about the mountain gorilla, which was 'discovered' by the military from German East Africa in the Verunga Mountains of central Africa. In the formidable swamps of the Congo, Africans tell about Mokeli Mbembe, a dinosaur like creature of enormous dimensions. The Mokeli Mbembe story has been around a long time and some anthropologists agree that if a remnant of the Cretaceous period has survived, this inhospitable and isolated region of central Africa would be an excellent location.

I have never studied the arguments of the cryptozoologists nor am I inclined to do so. The Yetis and Big Foots, if they indeed do exist, need hard evidence as proof. I have no idea what the Rendille and Samburu saw in the forsaken wastes of the N. F.D. but the existence of a 'muzungo' needs the same hard proof, as do all 'discoveries.'

WATER WATER

One afternoon, as I was brooding over the thorns in my tires, the sound of an approaching Land Rover could be heard as it ground laboriously over the last few miles of road. Visitors to South Horr rarely dropped in and were usually invited and expected, and when they failed to arrive, it would be necessary to send out a search party towards the south. No one ever arrived from the north and Lake Turkana. We waited. The Padre finally recognized the Land Rover as the game warden's, one Mr. Rodney Elliot. The game warden and his passenger were welcomed and I returned to work on my sagging tires. I could hear the Padre offer them refreshments as they disappeared inside. After a short while, Mr. Elliot's passenger appeared with an empty canvas water bag and kindly asked if I would fill it for him since I had the key to the water tank.

I just as kindly refused, telling him water was scarce and they had just left Baragoi where water was plentiful and maybe they should have filled their bags there. Somewhat embarrassed, he returned to the house. Refreshments over, the game warden and his passenger walked over to their Land Rover, and the Padre came over to me with the empty water bag and said it was o.k. to fill it up. I did so begrudgingly since water was at a premium and poor planning was costly to all. Having filled the canvas bag, I walked over to visitor's vehicle and tied it on to the front rack. They thanked me sheepishly and drove off towards north and to the Lake. North? No one traveled north and furthermore, where would they stay and what was their purpose? You had to wonder.

I found out the purpose for their safari north that night, as the Padre and I ate our dinner and recalled the incident. He asked if I recognized Mr. Elliot's passenger, an American actor. I said I hadn't and the Padre went on to say that he was the American who owned the Safari Club in Nanyuki, one Mr. William Holden. He along with the game warden, were laying out the plans for a documentary on Lake Turkana to be called, 'A Journey to the Jade Sea.' The Padre was asked to play a part in the film. I guessed then and there, it would have been absolutely pointless for me to appear at a casting call.

LORRY, LORRY, HALILEUH!

A brand new ten-ton Bedford lorry was purchased in Nairobi for South Horr. Students from Denis Morris High School back in Canada were responsible. Door to door fundraising, car washes and personal donations made the purchase a reality. We were pretty excited. The lorry would be used to haul free powdered milk, peanut oil, and cracked grain all generously donated by the Americans and warehoused in Mombasa on the Indian Ocean. (It was explained to me that notwithstanding these generous gifts from the U.S.A., all seeds were put through a dry machine to crack the kernels, thus eliminating any chance of planting for a sustainable future crop.) The foodstuffs were a lifesaver except for the problem of transportation. A ten-ton Bedford lorry was the solution.

Many months later, and bushels of red tape overcome, the deal was signed, sealed, and settled. We arrived at South Horr Valley weeks later, and saw this handsome shiny lorry, glistening in front of the nearly completed elementary school, awaiting the arrival of the 'muzungos.' The entire school population was marched outside and onto the back of the lorry. Once assembled and under the watchful gaze of their teacher, and a glowing equatorial sun, we were treated to a memorized Samburu version of, 'Lorry, Lorry, Halileuh.' After pictures and as an added bonus, we loaded on some supplies, which included an empty 45-gallon steel drum and with the entire school population, drove in the new vehicle to a nearby laga. Once settled, a large, male Grant gazelle was shot along with several guinea fowl, the steel drum serving as a make shift butchering table. As always, I couldn't help but notice how no one displayed the least signs of greediness or pushing to get at the food. These were very hungry children.

THE LABOURER

Throughout my many trips to Kenya, I always considered myself a visitor and as such forced myself to avoid making judgments. This was not an easy task because I came from Canada and we do it like this and so you too, should do it our way. Well so I thought. Such were my feelings about the elementary school in South Horr and M'Bacazi. Officialdom was creeping into the North. Signs of government bureaucracy were in the air. Anxious veterinarians began to show up, checking cattle. Forms began to appear and even census data became an issue. Demarcations setting up boundaries were being drawn up and discussed. The Kikuyu government in Nairobi was extending her long arm of control. Strangers appeared and used KiSwahili, the common language of East Africa but foreign to most of the nomads of the N.F.D. The Padre felt that the Samburu had to face the new wave of progress or become swallowed up in its wake. Perhaps a Samburu from South Horr might one day voice the needs of the tribe through parliament in far off Nairobi. An elementary school was to be the first step towards this goal. The thought of this intrusion disturbed me. Should these nomads fight a battle for cultural survival against a burgeoning bureaucracy without the slightest chance of succeeding or must their way of life be torn away in order to prepare for their future against forces that were foreign and overpowering?

M'Bacazi, literally the 'laborer,' was named when his father first saw and heard of men working and being paid for their services. Kiberetti or 'matches' was another popular name. M'Bacazi, a Samburu boy of about eleven when I first met him, was quick, bright eyed, and could charm the shine off Sunday shoes. His laugh was contagious. His wide-eyed pleading would earn him a ride in the Land Rover or send me digging through luggage for sedimenti or sweets. He attended the elementary school and helped out around the house of the Padre. He would help us set table and was a whiz at controlling the finicky oil lamps. We followed his progress keenly. Was he the future of the Samburu? Some people thought so.

M'Bacazi the houseboy and student

For every Samburu lad, circumcision became the event in his life that marked him both as a man and full-fledged member of the group. The ceremony and operation would begin his journey with his age mates through life. He would become a morani, dance in front of the various clubs, live with his equals in the bush, brag of bravery yet to come, and dress like a Samburu warrior, all the while brandishing a shiny, throwing spear. One day with the help of family and age mates, he would gather enough cattle to purchase a first wife. This lifestyle was the antithesis of a potential Nairobi-bound Samburu member of parliament. This was the conflict that existed between the traditional and the contemporary in Africa.

M'Bacazi faced the upcoming circumcision ritual with trepidation, since not only would the ordeal be a major test of his manhood, but how could he conform to the ceremonies and demands leading up to it and still maintain his status in school? He should return to his father's manyatta, and with his peers, begin the transformation process towards adulthood, which included living in the bush. Pressure from peers who were beginning to disappear over the mountains escalated and M'Bacazi would have to make a decision as to continue the new ways or revert to the ways of his father. A great deal of discussion took place and a very innovative solution by those concerned was hit upon. M'Bacazi and several of his remaining peers would go to the small clinic in Maralal and undergo the operation, thus satisfying the cultural demands of manhood while having the procedure done under hygienic conditions. Approval for this format was obtained from the elders and the boys were transported to the clinic. Six days later, they returned all smiling and beaming with pride. They were no longer totos; they had taken the first step towards manhood. Female Samburu also underwent the operation but for different reasons.

It wasn't very long before M'Bacazi became restless. The transformation of the boys upon their return from the clinic was amazing. I could no longer jostle with them or joke about everyday events. They had accepted their new role with deadly seriousness. M'Bacazi's peers startled us with their new appearance. Khaki shorts were abandoned along with the loose t-shirts. Colt-like thin legs, once clumsy and stork-like were partially covered with the reddish toga tied around the waist, while rows of beads adorned the bare neck. Red ocher highlighted their hair, while intricate chest and facial designs further marked their new positions. Lethal throwing spears, hand-rubbed and gleaming completed the transformation. They were nearly morani. No longer did they race alongside of the Land Rover and beg for rides. Profuse greetings became solemn nods. They shuffled uneasily at the sight of bare breasted maidens who taunted them with long and private conversations. M'Bacazi, in his khaki shorts and stretched T-shirt looked pathetic next to his former playmates.

It was suggested that M'Bacazi needed a change and so upon our return to Mugoiri and Kikuyu land, he took his first safari away from South Horr and the N.F.D. The change was less than satisfactory. He longed for the freedom of the North. We arranged for his return. He was a stranger in Kikuyu-land despite a genuine affection for the D'Amicos.

Piecemeal reports informed us that M'Bacazi was spending more and more time away from school and the Valley. When we returned to South Horr, M'Bacazi had been gone for several months. The station seemed empty. M'Bacazi was sorely missed. No longer did we walk the quiet paths with our young friend darting in and out about us, sometimes throwing stones at scolding monkeys, sometimes admonishing the younger children for misbehaving. Obviously, M'Bacazi, the 'laborer,' had made a decision to quit South Horr and return to his father's ways. Several days before our departure, a young lad casually summoned me behind my Land Rover. Thinking I had another flat tire from the ever-present thorns, I inspected my tires. Like a shadow, M'Bacazi stepped out from behind. His new appearance took me by surprise. More than his dress caught my attention as he walked towards me. His eyes spoke of an inner assurance. We greeted each other European style as his grin filled the face of the young boy I once knew. He asked about all the friends we had known together. Hurrying off, I returned with Maeve, his favorite and whom he welcomed with his boyish eagerness. He told us of life in the mountains and a girl he had met. He was a morani. He pointed to the route he would take and disappeared. We never saw M'Bacazi again.

M'Bacazi the newly transformed morani.

M'Bacazi made a choice. There was disappointment from those who had pinned the Samburus' hopes on him. For M'Bacazi, it was the right choice at the time and despite my own concerns, I could only agree with M'Bacazi's decision. I often wondered about the life he choose to live and trusted that he remained true to his age mates, his new, extended family. M'Bacazi was a Samburu and he had responded.

EPUR

One evening the three of us sat on the front porch of the Padre's house, a most incongruous situation, even as I sat there talking. There was nothing really to look at. The porch faced a wire mesh-enclosed garden, and beyond that, low scrub and then even more low scrub, which faded away to the north. There were the scattered acacias or fever trees about but the view was nothing to warrant anyone going out and sitting on the front porch. Ethiopia, a country away, was a neighbor if you considered many horizons away a neighbor. Porch sitting is for when you have sidewalks, and next-door neighbors, and people walking by and cars honking and all the other reasons there are to sit outside. It wasn't the way you spent your evenings in South Horr, sort of wondering what to look at. Besides sitting on the porch under a hissing hurricane lamp attracted lots of flying insects who like moths always managed to get just that one wing too close with the obvious consequences. The light also attracted orange-colored scorpions whose sting was not fatal but left you with a very sore groin.

I noticed a movement near the garden and shushed everyone, thinking a leopard or serval cat was on the prowl. We all strained into the darkness when finally the Padre said that it was Epur. Epur? Poking along in the African night, completely naked and smudged with the day's dust, a little boy shuffled along perhaps attracted by our voices. He was blind. I could not fathom the situation. In the blackness of the African night, one that could be filled with every sort of nightmare you may well imagine, a little Turkana blind boy was making his way to nowhere.

The Padre told us the little he knew of the boy called Epur. His parents were dead and thought to have been killed in a raid or battle of sorts as rumor had it. There was an older brother, now a warrior who lived the nomadic life out in the plains. Epur was shuffled from one manyatta to another, and when food and resources were low, and when the strain he put on one family was too much, he was pushed to the next boma. We made sure he was safely installed in a nearby manyatta that night and the next morning we addressed Epur's immediate problem, clothes from a huge bundle sent from the Catholic Relief Service in the U.S.A.

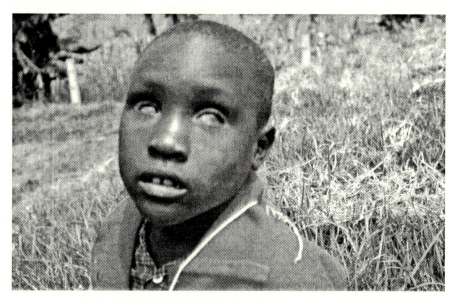

Epur the next morning with first clothing

I remember digging through the compressed pile of clothing for a hat. To save shipping costs and space, all articles were firmly compacted by a machine to get the most into one bundle. This meant that you peeled the articles away like the pages of a book. I found a white sailor hat for the Old Rendille, a favorite of mine. He had lost his hat the night before in the cooking fire as he slept. After he bestowed a blessing upon me, which included lightly spitting and pounding on my chest while he chanted 'N'gai N'gai,' (God, God), he proudly set off with his newly acquired cap. The huge letters on the front of the hat read, 'Come on baby, let's Rock'.

Maeve, Adrian Roscoe and I were busily preparing for the long safari to Mugoiri and Kikuyu country and then to Canada. I packed skins, throwing and lion spears, and beadwork of all kinds for the tourist shops on Bazaar Street in Nairobi. (A Samburu lion spear was all blade with a short piece of wood in the middle as an insert to attach the two ends. Unlike a throwing spear, the warrior would wedge the lion spear in the ground and as the animal charged and leapt, it would impale itself on the blade.) With the money from the artifacts, I would purchase goods from a prepared list I had recorded. I was glad to lend a hand since their needs told me a lot about the nomad. It was during our preparation for Kikuyu country that the Padre offered Epur. I had never been offered a person before and was unsure of the implications. Epur would not survive given the way he had to struggle. The Padre had his plate full and seldom asked for help. So Maeve and I said yes, and away we went with a little orphaned, blind Turkana boy who knew no English or KiSwahili, a boy who had no one to even say goodbye. Adrian recalls the ride back many years later, even though it was uneventful enough as safaris went. Not wanting to sound quixotic, it was extremely unusual to see the number of animals on the side of the road as we passed. It was a sad farewell safari for all of us and one particularly large rouge elephant approached the Land Rover in full view before he side stepped and disappeared into the scrub as they are known to do. One could imagine we were being given a final send off.

The author and Maeve in background with Epur in plaid shorts.

It is a custom of the Samburu and the Turkana to put a sheet over their heads when they sleep or when they are sick. I don't know the reason for this but I know of one incident when a lion leapt over a thorn bush boma and made off with a sleeping Samburu warrior. It was the man's knee in the lion's mouth, not his head like the animal thought. Sleeping under the sheet, knees bent, the lion thought it had its meal secured. The man survived. Well, Epur was packed between the cases and wrapped in blankets for security. He immediately covered himself including his head and lay there for the whole safari. At one point, Maeve asked us if we could hear music. Well, not really since the open window, the banging of the Land Rover over treacherous road, and all the dust pouring in, had my attention. Adrian however heard a faint but unmistakable tune coming from beneath the mound of sheets in the back, eerie and fairylike. Epur must have brought a whistle or flute with him and why we hadn't seen it or where it came from was a mystery. He was singing, 'Lazy, Lazy life in South America,' the only English words he knew and repeated them over and over again. Where he would have learned the tune was also a big mystery.

There are the obvious practical problems when oral communication and body language are absent. Communication becomes tenuous at best. We hoped Epur would sense our intentions and feel comfortable and safe. His stay with us was not a real big success. We were in class during the day and Mary, our Kikuyu house girl whose help was our salvation, was not too keen to get involved with a non-Kikuyu, blind boy. Even food and going to the bathroom became mini adventures for all of us. Imagine, sitting on a toilet seat and having someone flush the apparatus and then the noise of rushing water filling the room? Rushing water! Never heard such a noise before, coming from the bone-dry N.F.D. What could have been going through Epur's mind and keen senses? So many new sounds and smells and strange objects in the way. A solution was found and it was Nairobi.

The Roscoes, Adrian and Janice and three young children, were only recently settled in Nairobi. We were confident that our idea for moving Epur to the city would be for the best. Janice a qualified nurse and with the experience of three demanding children would surely help us out of our dilemma. We were already making preparations for our departure to Canada Sure enough and with their usual graciousness, the Roscoes added another plate to the table and off went Epur. Not only did Epur find a new home but also the Roscoes located a school in Thika, a school for the blind. Off went Epur, to a professional institution, one where he would settle in and grow and thrive throughout the years. I never knew the school existed and to my surprise, the Salvation Army who ran the school had personnel from Canada. The Roscoes had worked their magic once again.

Maeve and I left for Canada with the intent of returning to Kenya as soon as we had settled our affairs. I returned to Africa many times throughout the years but only after two children and a long delay. It was fourteen years later and with the Roscoes long since gone, that I knocked at the door of the Salvation Army School for the Blind in Thika. The door opened and I inquired about Epur. I was told that Epur's teacher and mentor, a Canadian gentleman was in Nairobi and leaving for Canada the next day. He would have information on Epur who was also in Nairobi and attending school. The gentleman told me that Epur was now called David Epur and besides being a very successful student was also an excellent trumpet player since his musical talents knew no bounds. So the whistle in the back of the Land Rover many years ago was indicative of things to come. I was staying in Nairobi and leaving on safari with the Padre who had come from the N.F.D. to pick me up. I would be a guest of another friend on a rice plantation in Mwea, and so I had a few days before all this would happen. The Salvation Army fellow would try to contact David Epur through his roommate in Nairobi but was doubtful. They had my temporary address and I was hopeful for a long overdue meeting with David Epur.

It was my last day in Nairobi when the house girl knocked on my door to tell me I had a visitor. African telegraph once again, just like the old days. I took the steps two at a time and pulled open the front door. There before me tall and handsome, stood a man in a gray suit, with an open white shirt, and obviously blind. Could this really be the same little boy, covered in dust, prodding about with a stick in the blackness of the N.F.D.? Epur sensing my presence, stuck out his hand, with a 'Mr. D'Amico, Sir!' His English was perfect. We sat in the living room for a long time and he told me of his successes under the most trying conditions. His closest friend and roommate had been recently shot in Nairobi during a political skirmish, a great loss for Epur who found himself alone. He was at present attending the University of Nairobi and had ambitions. With the years covered, it was Epur who now had questions for me. He wanted to know if he had any family in the far off north. He dug for answers. I could only offer to put him in contact with the Padre who still lived with the nomads and knew Epur's story first hand. I guessed however, that there was little information on his family. What did he recall of his childhood? The safari from the north, playing his whistle under the sheet and a very kind and loving lady who made him feel wanted for the first time in his short life.

The following is a recent extract from Dr. Adrian Roscoe, and his recollection of Epur.

'You and Maeve took me up to South Horr during my first six weeks in Kenya- one of the most extraordinary safaris of my life and, shamefully, into a landscape I never revisited. It was on that trip that you brought back Epur. I recall him in the back of the LR. And I recall him singing (amazingly) 'Lazy, lazy life in South America' perhaps the only English words he knew. When he (Epur) came down to join us in Nairobi, he stayed for perhaps two weeks. I especially recall his voracious appetite. You know how our Western kids are so fussy about food and not cleaning up their plates. Our kids would watch in astonishment, as Epur, having finished off his own meal, would swiftly finish off every last crumb they had left. He was a sort of eating machine you couldn't stop. I recall, yes, his habit of always sleeping with the blanket pulled up over his head. Also, his prize possession of a pair of shoes you and Maeve had given him. These he kept by his head when asleep, as a Samburu moran might keep his spear. Waking up one morning and finding them not there led to a pitiful tearful outburst and it was a while before we realized what it was all about. We took him to Kenya's top eye surgeon, a Brit, who took one look at him, declared loftily something like 'total corneal opacity' and said there was absolutely nothing he could do. It was then that we decided to try the Salvation Army School (in Thika) and drove up there one Sunday afternoon. I recall it clearly. Sunny. Very quiet grounds. One of those timid knocks on the door and a long story prepared to make the case persuasively, and all manner of hoops, hurdles, difficulties and hesitations anticipated. There was a long pause. Nobody in, alas? Then the door suddenly opened. A man in Sally Army uniform stood smiling before us. We exchanged

greetings, and before we'd got into our third or fourth sentence, he said something like "Of course he's welcome here" and took Epur in there and then. It was all done and dusted within three minutes! Absolutely amazing. The sort of incident you'd never forget and which, by the by, has earned the Sally Army a bob or two every time I've encountered them since. We visited Epur during the rest of our stay and soon heard that he was taking to music like a bee to honey. I even recall seeing him try to play a bit of soccer with his friends. He certainly seemed happy. That was reassuring. In later years, not often enough, we contacted Epur, and heard of his move to Kenyatta University to read for a B.Ed.'

Adrian Roscoe

THE OLD RENDILLE

The 'Old Rendille' was in fact Samburu on his mother's side, with Rendille blood from his father. Stretched and lean, the old man poked about with his worn stick supported on his stork-like legs, carrying his years. His bony head was splashed with patches of gray; a sunken mouth gathered beneath regal cheekbones. Ear lobes cut and pierced long ago as a morani and inserted with the traditional ivory earplugs, now dangled lifelessly down to his shoulders. With one hand he clutched his army issue blanket from the Padre's stores, which was used as a bedroll at night and a covering by day. Scarred feet no longer left traces of arches in the dust. He did not know his age and neither was that important. None of his circumcision age group survived and everyone agreed he had witnessed tribal wars, famine years, and the advent of the 'muzungo.' The 'Old Rendille's' body was used up but his watery eyes, an ashen gray, were alert. We became friends over the years despite the lack of a common language. He had two wives left, one blind son who was married and led about by holding on to a stick guided by his five year old, and one single daughter who bare-chested revealed her buxom accomplishments with obvious pride while flashing her father's eyes.

A TOUCH OF AFRICA

The Old Rendille trying a cigarette

Arriving in South Horr with a Land Rover filled with supplies, it was the 'Old Rendille' who would be the first to greet us with a blessing, by spitting on our chests and uttering 'N'gai, N'gai' many times over. Sometimes he would render upon us the shortened version if he caught sight of a particularly interesting package or if the crowds of people were threatening his first choice of a gift. When we had washed off the miles of dust and greeted our host, I would distribute the parcels, many which had been requested months before having bartered with their artifacts in Nairobi, a place foreign to the tribes of the Valley. Kikuyu snuffing tobacco wrapped in dried banana leaves was the most popular treat and a string of packets was always reserved for the 'Old Rendille.' After inspecting the packets very carefully and fondling them for their veiled contents of snuff, the old man would settle himself under a nearby acacia tree, conceal his dangling garland of tobacco beneath his blanket and with deliberate satisfaction, undo one of the wrappers. Coaxing the cocoa colored dust onto his palm, he would hold it to his nose and with a mighty snort, inhale the powder until his palm was wet and shiny. Content with the results, he would oversee the Land Rover proceedings from a distance, careful all the while to conceal his gift from would be borrowers. His all-knowing wives would take a heavy toll when he returned to his manyatta, so he could ill afford more losses. The 'Old Rendille' wonders where we have gone.

Maeve and I with the Old Rendille in front of his manyatta

MOUNT KULAL

Sometimes, you see something completely out of context and so unusual that it takes a moment or two to sink in, and only then your jaw drops in disbelief with, 'Did I really see that?' It's like the black leopard I swear I saw, one misty morning, coming through the bamboo forests of the Abedare Mountains. Crouched on the side of the road, eyes yellow hard and as cold as morning air, it watched me pass and I watched it vanish before me without ever moving my gaze. And so it was, one afternoon in South Horr Valley, as I tinkered around my Land Rover, probably removing more thorns from my exhausted tires, when I not only heard but watched a Land Rover pass by the compound with what looked like an American family, father driving, mom sitting next to him and several kids in the back, staring at me through the dusty window. All very normal and commonplace as a carmine bee-eater, with green head feathers and a scarlet chest, darted about after a tasty meal. I think I even waved and continued on with my work, as the Land Rover disappeared in the dust. I couldn't have been more surprised if an ice-cream cart had peddled by. Shaking my head, I sauntered, nonchalantly, over to the Padre and told him what I thought I had just seen. Yes, it was an American family, heading to

Mount Kulal where they would set up living quarters and work the nomads. We were to have neighbors, one misty mountain range away.

At first hearing about the family and their intentions it might seem normal, notwithstanding the philosophical implications of their presence. (It seemed to me that the nomads already knew about life.) Now this family, kids and all were off to a mountaintop, 7,812 feet high, to set up shop. One must understand that there was nothing there, despite the meager building supplies they had already delivered to their lofty quarters. Having previously stopped a month or so ago when they introduced themselves to the Padre, the entire family had now arrived to take up their new mountain top quarters.

On one particular safari to Loiyangallani on Lake Turkana, we felt we should drive up Mount Kulal for a visit since the folks there had not been seen for many weeks. It was somewhat on our way to the Lake. Up and up we drove, four-wheel drive spinning and kicking rocks behind us as we negotiated a pass fit for goats. We arrived at a very humble abode, a misty perch, damp and unappealing. Conditions were disturbing. There stood the family, obviously hearing our Land Rover, waiting for us in the chilly mountain air, anxious and thankful at the same time. Several youngsters stared at us in disbelief. Their situation had deteriorated. Household goods and foodstuffs lay scattered about their 'house' in disarray. It was dark, damp, and uninviting. It was the most miserable of places to call home. There was really no reason for it to be there. Also, after our initial greetings, it was apparent that there were more serious problems than their tenuous living conditions. The night before, outside their quarters, a full-fledged battle had raged. They were not sure if the murderous Boran were involved but the night was spent in fear of their lives. We could only wonder at their situation all the more. With words of encouragement, we left the mountain roost, feeling helpless and wondering at their fate. South Horr Valley was considered remote. The top of Kulal was bleak.

Wild game kept many villages supplied with meat in famine stricken areas.

FIRST BURIAL

Oftentimes, we would take a short siesta during the heat of the afternoon, awake refreshed and continue on with the chores of the day. Thorns always worked their way into my tires and slow leaks were a sweaty irritation. Sometimes, medical supplies were sorted out or I would be with my morani friends discussing local folklore or often, with a Land Rover filled with children, off to a nearby laga for gazelle. Sometimes I chased Kudu, without any hopes of photographing them.

In the early morning before anyone stirred up the dusty compound, I always found it fascinating to examine the tracks of the night before, tracks made while we were all asleep, a few yards away. I could identify the small cats, porcupine, hyena, leopard but it was the rifts in the sand that confused me. These waves invariably led to the water tank and its condensation. It was only when a young Samburu boy showed me in pantomime, that I realized it was the snakes, cobras and the likes, which had made the waves in their search for moisture. Not my idea of a good place for a nightly walk.

This particular day, mail had arrived from our school in Mugoiri via Baragoi on the rare chance that it would reach us. I have no recollection how the mail got to the Valley from Baragoi but it was a pleasant treat to get outside news. The note was from my brother Bob in Canada who had been to Expo '67 on Montreal and he wrote of the international prestige Canada had gained with the exhibition. He mentioned the East African pavilion in which he took great interest.

K.C. Jones and Maeve outside a Samburu manyata

Arising from a brief siesta and testing a steaming cup of black Kenyan coffee, the sudden pounding on the door had us rushing to the dispensary across the compound. Opening the door, it was a moment or so before my eyes became accustomed to the dark interior. On the floor, curled in a fetal position, lay a waxen-faced Samburu girl, perhaps sixteen years old. Large almond eyes held us in their disbelief. For the moment no one spoke. I returned her fixed gaze. She was dead. Wrapped tightly around her tiny limbs were strings of traditional Samburu beads. Under her stiff skin apron, her fragile legs looked unnaturally twisted. The nursing sister told us how she was called to the dispensary a few minutes before, to find the young girl weak and bleeding. She was carried inside where she collapsed on the floor. An injection was no help. Her manyatta was over the mountains, in a place called the Ol Doinya Mara. Apparently she had suffered from a miscarriage and in a desperate attempt for help, she began her last walk days before, over the mountains and to the station in the Valley. Several Samburu women who had assisted her in the final approach had scant details and knew nothing of her clan or family. Wrapping the child in sacks once filled with life giving wheat from America, the Padre and I carried her to a hastily dug grave behind the dispensary. Once buried, I was told to hack away a pile of thorn branches and heap them over the shallow grave. Thorns would thwart the hungry hyena that night. Years later, an old tracker friend of mine would also lie next to her, bitten by a red cobra while he hunted on the forbidden slopes of Mount Niyru. Dinner that night was unusually quiet and everyone went to bed extra early.

A Samburu wife adorned with gifts of beads

MOUNT NYIRU AND N'GAI

The following account belongs to Samburu mythology and is only one facet of their supernatural belief system. We must remember the so-called myth of the now famous island kingdom on Crete and the lost empire of the Minoans, complete with its maze and the fabled Minatour. The Samburu believed that one of their gods, N'gai, resided on the peak of lofty, 9,201 foot Mount Nyiru, which sheltered the South Horr Valley. Blanketed by a thick covering of thorn and unfamiliar forests, the mountain was the home to the harried elephant and Cape Water buffalo both of which took refuge each night in the higher, protected reaches. Every evening, these herbivores would leave the security of the highland forests and walk slowly down the slopes to lowland pasture, only to return before dawn the following morning. Leopards and smaller cats lived undisturbed in the pockets of dark undergrowth and were seldom seen or disturbed by poachers.

The regal Greater Kudu also called the mountain home. This splendid animal deserves mention. Tawny with six to eight white stripes across its back with large donkey-like ears, well proportioned to the head and body, a male might weigh in at more than 300 pounds and stand five feet plus at the shoulder. Mounted on an angular head, the Kudu male wears a pair of spiral horns with two and a half twists on a mature adult. Tips are complete with ivory points. When running, the male must toss these weapons back over his haunches to avoid entanglement in the overhang. Racing with high stepped paces, head tossed arrogantly back, horns stretched over broad hindquarters, eyes flashing saucer- wide with nostrils flared, the male Kudu is a sight to remember. I always pestered the Samburu to lead me to a Kudu so I could photograph one. My sightings were rare indeed. I became known as, 'Where's the kudu?' or in KiSwahili, ' Wapi Malo?' Kudu were plentiful I was told and this seemed a contradiction to me. Being ever so polite, it was only by chance and years later that I was told why the nomadic herders could virtually walk among the Kudu whereas with a brief snort, the animal was long gone before me. I was told that the muzungo or white man smelled very badly and not unlike that of a cadaver, quite unlike the natural, smoky odor of the African. One can hardly blame the Kudu for disappearing at first scent. In a paper by Dr. L.S.B. Leakey, the world-renowned paleontologist, it was postulated that early man, the Australopithecines and their hominid relatives, were aided in their survival against hungry predators precisely because they smelled so badly and were therefore avoided.

Mount Nyiru was also home to many venomous snakes, which included the cobra family and the slow moving Gabon Viper, thick bodied and deadly. This is the same mountain where my Samburu friend and tracker with whom I had spent many adventurous times, was bitten by a red cobra and died. Numerous monkey troupes lived in the lower levels. The steel blue Whydah, floated dreamlike amidst the shadows, with two-foot tails undulating wave-like and leaving one rubbing incredulous eyes. This mountain was also home of N'Gai, the Samburu God, and the ruler of the mountain, a God we were told, to best leave alone and undisturbed.

During my many safaris to the N.F.D. my good friend the Padre and I would discuss a climb to the peak to see for ourselves, the source of this popular legend. Years back, several reckless Samburu morani in an attempt to further their reputation made a climb to the summit. Their various descriptions of the peak were consistent with the popular legend. We were told that the very top of this mountain was flat, spongy, and in the center of this lofty carpet of moss, was a hole, a deep and dark cavernous entrance leading to the home of N'Gai. Pointing the way to the entrance hole, were several unmistakable paths lined with bones, bleached white and strangely split. The bones leading to the hole were always included among the various storytellers. These tales gave us many hours of discussion as we stared at Mount Nyiru's easterly face bathed orange each evening and dotted with black pockets of forest where mist rose from some mysterious brew. These Samburu morani, as the tale was told, were unable to approach the hole for no sooner had they clamored to the top of the flat summit, when clouds of mist rolled over them, leaving them in confusion. The unearthly screams, which came from the black entrance, ended in a long howl driving them backwards in fear and over the edge in a hasty retreat. We surmised that erosion had created a wind tunnel and the unearthly sounds would be the wind passing through this natural echo chamber. The bone lined path however, left us puzzling. We knew that Samburu did not know how to lie.

Our first attempt to scale the peak ended in failure. Our trackers took the southern and safer route to avoid the returning elephants. This led us to a yawning chasm and defeat. On my last safari before returning to Canada, it was then or never. My close friend newly arrived from graduate work in Canada, Adrian Roscoe, accompanied Maeve and I to South Horr. It was unfair to leave Adrian back at the station and it was equally unfair to ask him to come along on a most strenuous trek, which would test the fittest amongst us. He had been behind a desk for two years completing his doctorate on West African literature. I questioned my own hardiness to make the effort to the summit. Without the slightest hesitation, Adrian let it be known he was on board for the climb and looked forward to the adventure. Another reason why I considered him a pal and great to be around.

July 31, 1968, 5 a.m., lanterns lit, we set off for the summit of Mount Nyiru. Adrian and I, still shaking sleep from our eyes, dutifully followed the Padre and Muggi Muggi, our Samburu guide. Also along, was a boy. He was a Rendille lad of about twelve, orphaned for years and suffering from terrible nightmares. He always wore a huge, friendly grin showing large white, perfect teeth. It was black and ominously still and now unfamiliar as we walked the paths without words. My gun felt heavy. The young lad offered to carry it. We knew we had to hurry ahead of the returning elephant before dawn since it was their route we would follow up this time. Suddenly and without comment, a long and silent Samburu warrior materialized out of the shadows, and fell into line, spear in hand grasping his toga about him to keep out the cold, his sandaled feet stretching out lengthy paces. His spear seemed to point to Mt. Nyiru's shrouded peak and the home of N'Gai.

Our lanterns glowed like fireflies as we meditated over our private reservations and expectations, long shadows cast eerily ahead of us. We must have looked a strange sight indeed, a procession of silent shadows. The rolling foothills presented no special problems and we were soon swallowed up in towering elephant grass. These tunnels through the grass were well used as we avoided stepping on the numerous elephant droppings. I was always uneasy in these maze-like pathways, since secondary routes to somewhere else, constantly intersected them. I always expected to collide into a silent mammoth at one of these intersections and wondered just what would I do? Muggi Muggi who led the way seemed fully aware and so, whether it was the jungles of the Amazon in Brazil or in the foothills of Mount Nyiru in Kenya, you just had to trust the head tracker and carry on. At this point, I still trusted Muggi Muggi. Silently we marched, rising and falling with the land. With daylight and the sun streaking the path ahead of us, we stored the lanterns to one side for pick up on our return. We began our gradual ascent to the summit.

We maneuvered around giant boulders and strained on rocky inclines, only to find relief on the occasional grassy steppe. As we twisted and turned skyward in our journey, the shiny rooftop of South Horr gleamed lonely and distant. It wasn't long before we had an unexpected turn of events, which scattered our orderly column. As we were led around an outcrop, a crashing came from behind and someone shouted, 'N'dovfu.' Dropping our gear we scrambled for height and protection. Adrian, who did not understand, was left momentarily helpless as we headed for higher ground. Several elephant with young ones, led by the matriarch, charged past us. Gathering our supplies, we followed in their wake of trampled grasses, subdued, but nevertheless still determined.

Hours later, at about eight thousand feet, after pulling and slipping, grunting and sliding, it was decided that the Padre and the silent warrior would carry on to the summit. We were too cumbersome a group to maintain the speed necessary to reach the top and return before nightfall since it was imperative to arrive back before darkness. We could not spend the night on Mt. Nyiru. Our legs ached, breathing was reduced to short gasps, and our meager supplies seemed much heavier as the climb went on. It was only common sense to have the Padre and the warrior complete the final assault, since the two could maintain a faster pace without our hindering them. The two literally melted into the undergrowth but not before we had struck upon a plan. At a designated time the four of us who were left behind would begin our descent despite the whereabouts of the advance party. We were to wait for our companions until 3 p.m.

The following hour or so spent waiting will never leave me. Off the main 'path' we found an open ended covered grotto of tangled vegetation, the exposed end show casing a view of the concealed westerly side of Mount Nyiru, a side seldom ever seen. Through this break we peered down and into a vast chasm of shadowy growth, a drop into the abyss, a sight truly breathtaking. Barking baboons echoed across to us. We doubted if anyone had ever penetrated the lush entanglement of bleeding green below us. Adrian and I lay on our backs, exhausted, while Muggi Muggi and the orphaned Rendille lad, made a low fire, the smoke being drawn out and into the chasm below.

Adrian and I have since discussed the solitude of that sheltered cove where we lay prostrate, soaking in the earthy smells and distant sounds. Staring over the edge, one was transported high above the wildness. The height was awesome. Fear when looking into the abyss intensified the moment. It was like peering down through a crack in the sky. One could almost imagine flight. A commanding view. Rolls of mist hung tightly around the steep walls and seemed to flow slowly downwards like thick syrup into an uncertain bottom. Smoke stung our eyes. At 3 o'clock, the appointed time, we reluctantly gathered up our few supplies. Muggi Muggi, forever grinning a toothy smile, led us back to the open track used by the Cape Water buffalo. We were too high for elephant. He would lead us down by a new route he said and so we fell in line, feeling incomplete without our two companions.

I praised Muggi Muggi profusely since this new path sloped ever so gently and there were fewer 'leave-me-not' thorn bushes to tear at our hair and skin and shred our shirts. We walked for a while before the ascent became steeper. It wasn't long before I gasped silently at the first sight of hoof marks, deeply imbedded in the soft mud, many still filling with brackish water. The undergrowth grew closer and daylight became heavy with shadow. We were forced to help one another over rotting stumps, which were covered in a slimy moss and left us greasy and smelling like old mushrooms. Sliding and slipping, it became easier to crawl through the tangle of thorns which now seemed everywhere around us. The way seemed almost impenetrable. A quiet desperation flooded over us. Muggi Muggi kept well ahead of me knowing full well that he hadn't a clue where he was going. We were thus groping in our miserable descent when I heard the first buffalo snort. In case there was any doubt, the warm droppings confirmed the presence of Africa's most wary and dangerous animal. This was sheer madness. A professional hunter once told me never to approach buffalo in their lie-ups since they had every advantage of smell and hearing not to mention 20/20 vision in a camouflaged thicket. Always approach them coming or going to water and in full frontal view he said. The Cape buffalo was the only animal he feared after thirty years in the bush. A charging bull had nearly killed him.

Muggi Muggi, subdued and wide-eyed, exchanged a few words with the young Rendille lad. It seemed I could detect massive shadows. Was it my overworked imagination? Were we crawling through a resting herd? I kept hoping for the wind to remain constant since a swirling breeze could confuse the animals and cause them to stampede and in an attempt to move off, crush us in the process. This nearly happened to me once before and it was an experience I was glad to have behind. I was proud of Adrian who knew enough to follow and to follow silently. We hesitated and once again heard the welcomed silence. Minutes stretched into even longer silences. Every noise was carefully noted. We moved quietly and with determination. I thought of 4 o'clock tea at South Horr.

African Cape Water buffalo to be avoided at any cost.

We were thankful when we burst into the sunlit, grassy meadow having survived the treacherous buffalo lie up. It was through this open meadow that the Padre and the warrior would have to pass and from here we could make it down to safety during the remaining light. Adrian took a picture of the Rendille lad and myself and when I saw the photo, I can still feel the relief of the moment. We had survived a Muggi Muggi folly, who remained sheepish and subdued while we waited. The young lad pointed and said the Padre and the warrior would soon be here. We looked towards the summit of Mt. Nyiru and saw nothing. Only after some time, did I notice the glint off the Padre's rifle barrel. We waited feeling relieved for soon we would be a complete party again.

Muggi Muggi, the orphaned Rendille boy and Adrian Roscoe

We had a longer hike down than I thought and it was dusk when we trooped through the compound of South Horr. The fires were our beacons and we arrived feeling somewhat triumphant at our feat. On the way down and near the place where the lanterns were stored, the Padre who was in front of me, turned suddenly and fired a shot not one foot away from my boot. Needless to say I was stunned. I hoped it was nothing I had said. I never did see the Gabon viper trying to move sluggishly across the path and into the undergrowth since this non-aggressive snake is stepped upon with disastrous results. The poisonous serpent is super slow and when trod upon, turns upon the intruder and bites, usually on the ankle, leaving the victim with a slim chance of survival. The Padre simply said, 'Nyoka' and carried on. Nyoka indeed!

A TOUCH OF AFRICA

Adrian and I after our descent from Mt. Nyiru

We washed with the remaining hot water in the cooling pipes and gathered for dinner amidst a swarm of flying ants. During our lantern lit meal, the Padre recounted the events after he had left us for the final push to the summit. The path became very steep as they struggled along. Climbing over and onto the flat summit, the spongy lichen and mosses lay before them like a carpet. Numerous bones lay about along a crude path of sorts, showing the way to the center of the summit. They had only gone a few feet when the rolling mist enveloped them completely. Visibility was reduced to an arm's length. The floor sank beneath their feet, the wind swirled and rushed around them and howled like a distraught banshee from somewhere ahead. Disoriented, they could go no further. Slowly they retraced their sinking steps to the point of their approach on this bizarre summit. The sun was sinking and the clamor ahead was deafening. There was a mutual agreement to leave the place but not before the Padre picked up one of the bones for me. Several photos were luckily taken before the mist covered the summit. The pictures show the mossy covering and the scattered bones but not the path leading to the middle hole. The Samburu nod in complete agreement with the story. There is no way N'Gai would allow anyone near the entrance to his home. 'It is the way of N'Gai.'

The Padre, not one taken to hasty conclusions and in fact a very collected and thoughtful man, was nevertheless at a loss to explain the suddenness of the misty clouds and the howling rising from the hole. The bones, split lengthways were unusual too. Hyena, whose legendary jaws are the most fearsome in the animal kingdom, split bones but not lengthways. Vultures have been known to drop stones on eggs to break them, a primitive tool no doubt. However, the birds would be at a loss trying to smash bones of a mossy, summit surface. The bones remain an unsolved mystery.

The Akikuyu tell of a strange ground dwelling people who were the original inhabitants on their land. President Jomo Kenyatta in his account, 'Facing Mount Kenya,' discusses these long forgotten ground dwellers. He asserts that over time, the Kikuyu gained dominance over these aborigines. Had a vanguard of these ground dwellers migrated many miles north in the face of the encroaching Kikuyu? Similar tales of ground dwellers come from West Africa. The meal was cold when we finished and the conversation under the shadows of Mount Nyiru left us in thought. I fingered the bone the Padre had collected for me and wondered.

The Padre's photo of the bones taken on the summit

LOIYANGALLANI

From South Horr to Lake Turkana, formerly Lake Rudolph is some sixty miles of unfriendly landscape. The safari to the lake takes many hours, barring mechanical breakdowns. Any loose connections, especially front end ones, had a way of leaving the traveler straddled uncomfortably on one of the many boulders, which made up the 'road.' Miles from shade and even further from any outside assistance, the 'road' was a challenge. In fact, there was no outside assistance to call upon and I never saw another vehicle in all my safaris to the lake. Radio communication along with any other trappings of civilization was left far behind.

The terrain was volcanic in origin with the route, handpicked through miles of spewed rock. Miocene eruptions scattered hundreds of square miles with pockmarked missiles. Teleki's last eruption was in 1895. The heat was always intense, the wind an open-hearth blast. It was a land baked, burnt, dead and forgotten, a land of the Judas tree. Vipers and scorpions made this their home. To my amazement Grant gazelle and the mighty chested oryx survived in this formidable landscape. These northern species found enough moisture in their withered and thorny diet to satisfy their needs. Kori bustards, long-legged and sporting a powerful beak, high step among the rocks looking for scorpions and snakes. This is also the haunt of the ruthless Boran raiders and the murderous Somali Shifta bandits. The Samburu and Turkana tribesmen march across this land sucking a small stone placed under their tongue. Apparently this helps to assuage their thirst. When I passed either Samburu or Turkana on the 'road' they would cup their long slender fingers to their mouths in a gesture for water. These warriors without the advantages of special diets and professional trainers were probably the toughest individuals one would ever encounter. We always shared what little water we could afford from the canvas water bag tied securely to the front of the Land Rover. I would be able to refill them from the fresh springs at Loiyangallani. This scorched land remained untouched and scarred with hideous sores dating back to when this sub Saharan landscape was once lush and filled with the greenery of life. This was a strange and forgotten part of the world. It was difficult not to feel overlooked as you made your way through the past.

As I neared the lake on my first safari, several final volcanic outgrowths had to be negotiated. Vehicle and passengers twisting and grinding, it was a tortuous last mile or so. The water stretched before us, azure and hazy, a welcomed sight after the miserable lunar landscape we had endured. (Count Teleki and Von Hohnel were the first Europeans to discover the Lake. I often wondered how the Lake was lost to the Africans and needed discovering.) Long and narrow, this desert Lake, once thought a source of water for the mighty Nile, appeared mirage-like as it shimmered northwards towards Ethiopia and the Sahara Desert. This was the fabled 'Jade Sea' a tropical aquarium of nearly three thousand square miles where everything grew to outlandish sizes and where few sources of water refreshed the shrinking alkaline shores. This was the domain of the Tiger fish (hydrocyon lineatus) a superb fighter that swam alongside twenty-pound succulent Tilapia. Mighty Nile perch weighed in at a record of nearly three hundred pounds. (The large vertebrae from this fish proved useful as natural candlestick holders.)

Waiting beneath the indigo surface lurked Africa's notorious Nile crocodile and the ponderous river horse as the Greeks called the hippopotamus.

The infamous Nile crocodile

Awesome fish eagles and kingfishers, Egyptian geese, and lappet-faced vultures found a home here. Getting out of the Land Rover, I splashed around in the soapy water filled with accomplishment. My good humor disappeared ever so quickly when I saw my new and expensive tires. They were shredded minced meat. The protruding lugs dangled like pieces of burnt liver.

The Kenya-Somali governments were unofficially involved in a terrorist war over the control of these northern reaches. Somali Shifta had become more aggressive. Roads were said to be land-mined, attacks on unescorted convoys were not uncommon, while cattle raids and poaching of wild game was routine. Non-Africans like ourselves were supposedly outside the sphere of conflict or so we thought.

Before the Shifta had become brazen murderers, an Anglo-American consortium seized upon the idea of developing a luxury, world class fishing lodge on this oasis called Loiyangallani. Since driving would be out of the question, a small landing strip was built to make the safari from Nairobi a pleasant one. The plan was an ambitious one, complete with luxury eating quarters in the spacious dining room and comfortable sleeping cottages or cabanas. Next to the dining lodge and the half dozen African style cabanas, was the kidney shaped swimming pool, lined with ceramics, imported from the Czech Republic. No expense was spared. Nilo-Hametic nomads passing with their herds stared at the wonderment

A TOUCH OF AFRICA

of it all, a sight never before imagined. This lavish fishing lodge, complete to the very last silver setting, never opened its doors to one single tourist.

One Father Stallone, was in the last stages of completing his one room school near the main lodge for the dwindling El Molo when he got caught. The Seychelles manager of the lodge became the second captive along with several Samburu warriors. It all happened suddenly. The Shifta burst into Loiyangallani, raping and looting, firing guns and beating anyone in their way. After tying up Stallone and securing the manager, they packed their loot, destroying whatever else they touched. They had one fear. The generator was the sole source of power for communication with the outside world and unless it was destroyed, their captives could radio Nairobi and the military from the coast could cut off their escape as they headed east. Despite their efforts even after shooting at the generator, they finally gave up. No person who could use the generator-radio would be left alive. They shot Stallone, leaving him tied to the center pole in blood spattered cabana number six.

Cabana number six

The Seychellese manager along with several Samburu was taken at gunpoint as hostages to carry the heavy loot over the baked scrub to Somalia, another distant horizon away. Loaded down, the bloody column left, booty laden and drunk with power.

Months later the story was completed. A Samburu warrior survived to tell the tale. The Seychellese manager, unable to carry on with his heavy load sank to the ground. He was bound and skinned alive. The Shifta left him in the wasteland to perish in agony. Lake Turkana's luxury lodge at Loiyangallani was immediately shut down and a small police contingent arrived from Nairobi to guard the abandoned lodge from further attacks. The Kenyan government was forced to make a statement of force. The property and buildings were left to the Padre to use as he wished. The El Molo also became the responsibility of the Padre. It was fascinating to know that years later Richard Leakey, son of the famous Louis Leakey and his wife Maeve, anthropologists in their own rights, were to discover fossils dating back to man's beginning on these very shores of Lake Turkana just a few fossil rich miles north of Loiyangallani, and the abandoned luxury lodge.

It was always interesting to journey northwards along the shore of the Lake. This was untraveled territory and seldom if ever seen by westerners, and certainly no study had been done at this time. I was with the Padre, one afternoon, as we drove to a large, conspicuous rocky outcrop. Faded but still very recognizable, were the rock drawings of Neo Lithic man, paintings unknown to the scientific world and until this day, still unidentified to my knowledge. I wonder at the impact, if any, these rock paintings would have on contemporary evolutionary thought? I did take a picture of the site. It was near this place years later, that Richard Leakey made his startling discovery about man's origin.

Rock paintings on the shore of Lake Turkana

KIBOKO KILLER

It wasn't long before I felt particularly useless during the distribution of the medicines to the El Molo on their forsaken island that hot afternoon. The medical sister and Maeve were doing fine interpreting the pantomimes. I decided to walk the island with the hopes of gathering more data for my research. Kites and soiled pelicans never seemed to use their wings as the thermos lifted them higher and higher in the cloudless sky. A young boy of about twelve or fourteen followed me. He donned very unusual body decorations and was pleased when I inspected them using my faltering KiSwahili. I was to learn later, the reason for his appearance. He was covered with blotches of guano, which were dubbed with a feathery down. He looked odd with these white puffs of feathers sprouting out from all over his body, and glued down with bird droppings. His tale was told to me as follows

This young boy was poling on his dom palm raft one afternoon, probably getting ready to fish when he spotted a female hippo with her calf. Male hippos can measure nearly six feet high while the females are slightly shorter. Fourteen feet in length, the bulls are an awesome sight with the cows not far behind. These animals can weigh in between four and five tons while one hippo sported a record forty-one and a half inch pair of ivory canines.

The awesome hippo feeding at dusk

Without hesitation, the lad knew what would be expected from him. He slipped noiselessly into the water and once submerged took up a position behind the unsuspecting mother. His knife and cunning would be his only companions. He must have considered the possibility of a nearby bull. Patrolling Nile crocodiles didn't seem to be an issue. He was counting on the hippo to continue feeding away from him. When he was within striking range and diving even deeper, knife in hand, he slashed at her hind leg tendons. The commotion would have been deafening, the bloody water a whirlpool of angry, jaw-snapping hippo ivory. Leaving the crippled beast floundering in her torment, he hurried to the island for help. The El Molo adults returned in force. The hippo was duly dispatched and dragged into shallow water where it was butchered for not only the meat but especially for its fat, much prized amongst Africans The entire population feasted for days on the carcass. Lacking refrigeration, meat in the desert sun does not have a very long shore life. There was also the matter of hungry crocodiles.

The young boy was honored for his bravery and would be forever known as 'Killer of the Kiboko.' Hippo skin, if properly treated is highly valued for its durability and incredible strength. Long strips taken from the back of the animal are cured and shaped into whips which are called kibokos and used by the urban police for crowd control during marches and parades. I was given one such crudely fashioned whip, which seemed an effective weapon. Maasi warriors always favor the impenetrable hippo skin for their shields and only substitute this with the chest skin from the Cape Water buffalo when it is unavailable. Alongside a pile of burnt bones, I picked up a piece of hard, dry hippo skin at least one inch thick. An attempt by someone had been made to fashion a pair of shoes. It had ended in failure. The skin was just too tough for the crude tools of the El Molo. The El Molo's chief natural resource was their will power.

An El Molo family from Lake Turkana

A TOUCH OF AFRICA

NEWS OF THE NORTH

Loiyangallani

April 3/1971

Dear Bert and Maeve

I am ashamed to write you only today. I left your letter on my table with the hope to have a break on my work to answer. I hope you are well. Here things are not very good; people are near starvation because it has not rained since 14 months! I do not say it is as dry as ever, but there is not a single patch of grass, green or dry. Cattle are dying at South Horr, Maralal, Baragoi: even zebra are already dying as Mr.Elliot (game warden) told me. People are gathering near the station in order to get something to survive. I can now say that the healthiest ones are the El Molo! Almost all cattle are grazing in the lake like hippos.

Now we have four nursing sisters, one also for the school. She is doing well. I hope to hear from you soon. My best wishes for you Maeve and baby Katharine.

Gods blessing
Fr. Polet

P.S. The main lodge (at Loiyangallani) had been burned down by mistake

Lake Turkana,
Loiyangallani,

The Padre with Africa's smallest tribe, the El Molo

A TOUCH OF AFRICA

March 20th 1972

Sometime ago I have spotted a dozen lion strolling after my car (Land Rover) at half way to So. Horr; that country is always empty of people because everybody fears the Boran raiders. After the last raid (did I tell you?) of Christmas /71 where 25 turkana children and old R have been killed, we have had no more trouble...but we fear some soon, during the next rain. Sorry to send you only these poor pictures but I have none. Best wishes to you, Maeve and children.

HAPPY EASTER

P. Polet

El Molo youngsters in the Lake

When we were in Loiyangallani, the Padre would sleep in a small concrete dispensary on a mat about a half-kilometer away. Maeve and I would sleep in cabana six, despite its recent history, since it was nearest to the lodge where we had our food and close to an El Molo camp near the shore. Some El Molo would venture from their island sanctuary to the mainland and feel safe from their more aggressive neighbors when the Padre was around. Peering inside one of these flimsy reed El Molo huts one afternoon, I looked down onto an old man, naked and failing, protruding bones telling their last story. He was left on his own to die and next to his head, a Kimbo lard can filled with lake water would be his last worldly comfort. His hut would be burned upon his death.

The author with El Molo friends

Around our cabana number six, some half dozen other cabanas in various stages of disrepair stood abandoned. These units were skillfully constructed for the anticipated fishing tourist but were never used because of the raid and the killings. The woven matting and concrete floor gave a semblance of durability, especially when you compared them to the flimsy El Molo dwellings. However, there were no doors on any of the units and a bamboo screen was used for privacy and to block the prevailing gales coming off the Lake. This screen was a nuisance since it was forever falling over during the night and sometimes even becoming airborne before it crashed down. Immediately behind our cabana, in a make shift military camp, were a half dozen soldiers stationed at Loiyangallani. These were token troops.

These soldiers were from different tribal backgrounds, with families and friends far away. They felt they were being punished with this forsaken assignment and were constantly fighting amongst themselves. Usually filled with booze and having nightly wild parties with several of the local Turkana women, the revelry would continue late into the night. All in all, their presence did not inspire much confidence against the possibility of marauding Shifta bandits.

One late evening as we lay in our cots, both hands anchoring down the bellowing bed sheets, we heard the deafening crack of a rifle, smelled gun powder as someone from behind us shouted, 'Kufa, Kufu' or 'Dead, Dead.' I dove for my rifle. Yelling to Maeve to get down and under the bed, I fumbled for my shorts all the while the commotion from behind our flimsy cabana was getting much louder. If it was a Shifta attack, I fully expected the reed walls to come crashing down around us. I peeked outside warily, gun barrel leading the way. Flashlights and lanterns lit the rear of our cabana. I edged my way around the corner to see a party of bare-chested soldiers staring down behind our quarters. I fully expected to see a dead Shifta raider, as I pushed my way through the stench of bad whiskey for a better view. Lying mouth agape was a six-foot crocodile, gasping its last breath. The soldier who had done the shooting was being slapped on the back. Apparently a ten-foot female croc and a young one were nightly visitors to the camp with the hopes of snagging one of the army dogs for a snack. Our marksman, whose name I discovered was David, heard the shuffling in the dry reeds and ventured a shot. The larger female escaped to the safety of the lake. Our marksman had to hold the flashlight with one hand, the rifle with the other, take aim and fire. However, looking back at where he had stood, I could see it was a direct line to the back of our cabana and our cots and heads. I questioned what was more disconcerting, the thought of two crocs prowling inches behind our heads or David, shooting a rifle with one hand, flashlight in the other, all the while reeling from the night's libations.

STRANGE ISLAND

Several miles off the eastern shore and Loiyangallani is the 'Island of No Return.' Sounds intimidating. Oral mythology recounts how the present Lake was once a valley. One sun filled morning, a woman who was tending to her goats came upon a bubbling spring. Seizing a nearby rock she pounded idly away at the edges of the frothing spring only to create an even faster flow of water, which began to fill the valley. Hurrying with her animals, she took refuge on higher ground and soon found herself stranded on an island. Over the years she gave birth to many of her own kind and the island was soon populated.

Unfortunately her offspring inherited her idle pastime for they too sat around pounding the ground with rocks. It wasn't long before the underground demons had had enough. Burrowing below the idle rock pounders, these boisterous offspring fell into these subterranean holes and disappeared forever. Today, one finds numerous craters on the island, fragments of fired pottery, and more than two hundred hybrid goats. Bats, birds, and snakes are also numerous. The resident Nile crocodile also grows to enormous lengths.

Von Hohnel or South Island as it is also called, looms invitingly and has attracted several adventurers to its shores with disastrous consequences. Dyson and Martin, two Englishmen disappeared in 1934. Since then, few explorers have made the crossing. George Adamson, game warden and the man behind the well-known story, 'Born Free,' made the crossing in 1955. (Hence, the name of our Siamese cat Elsa, which I admit, was not very original.) It seemed the unpredictable elements on the water made the journey a hazardous one in anything but a real boat designed for heavy seas. No such vessel existed on the entire Lake. Surrounded by mysterious tales of would be adventurers, South Island, filled with craters and wild goats carries the ignomous title of 'Island of No Return.'

The comparative isolation from outside intruders resulted in a Nile crocodile sanctuary. Adamson reported that twenty-one foot crocs were not unusual. These giants are confirmed by the present day El Molo, who on a regular basis, hunt down and eat crocs measuring sixteen feet and more. These I have seen on more than one occasion. I have in my possession, the head of sixteen-footer. Back home in Mugoiri, I boiled it in a large pot of water to clean it thoroughly and to get rid of the offensive odor before I attempted to bring it into the house. I ran across one problem. All seventy odd teeth fell out in the boiling process, which I reluctantly fished out of the reeking water. To add to the mess, I discovered the teeth were telescopic to boot, and before they could be inserted into the jaws, I had to match them, stack them, one on top of the other, all the while looking for the right fits. Apparently, when one tooth breaks in the animal's mouth, a second one is waiting to take its place. Over the years, I look at my orthodontia work with great suspicion since I had several teeth left over. I later learned value of safari ants, which would attack the bone and burrow into the minutest orifice, eating all organic residues, leaving a clean, odorless skull.

COBRAS AND OTHER POISONS

I was walking along with the Padre, examining the location for a permanent house he was planning to build. Loiyangallani, an oasis in the desert with both hot and cold gurgling pools was forever green and grew some decent size acacia trees along with several towering dom palms. These same pools also attracted unwanted guests in the form of very large Nile crocodiles with nasty dispositions and a dislike for anything like an intruder. An acacia tree had fallen over and as I walked along side of the Padre, the fallen tree in my path was a natural to climb and I walked up it and he walked alongside. I was about six feet in the air when the Padre turned quickly and with a mighty shove sent me tumbling off my perch and onto the ground. I wondered yet again if it was something I had said. He quickly apologized. He had seen the infamous green mamba poised in the branches just feet away from me. A bite could have been disastrous. This was the second time he had saved me from being bitten by venomous snakes. Not a pleasant thought especially being in such an isolated area.

The Padre told me when he was building at South Horr, he started with the small dispensary first and used it as his sleeping quarters. Well, one dark and tiring night, after a long day of mixing concrete and forming homemade blocks and without dinner and exhausted, he headed straight for the dispensary for a night's sleep. Flashlight showing the way, he opened the door and with that a snake slithered across the concrete floor and disappeared. What to do? Carefully holding the light in one hand, he proceeded to remove his meager contents from the small dispensary. Having investigated under his bed and removing a few chairs and a table, he was finally left with his steamer trunk against the wall. Moving it slowly, being careful not to get too close, he felt the spray on his hand holding the flashlight. With that, he saw the culprit make for the open door and disappear into the dark. It was a spitting cobra. The snake thinking the light was an eye, targeted it. This was fortunate since venom in the eyes could have had very serious consequences. Rushing outside, he tore away several succulent branches from a common hedge-like plant, which grew wild and oozed a white milky substance when broken. This he applied to his hand and arm and off he went to bed, worn out and alone, many rocky miles from anywhere.

I often wondered how it was that the Africans knew what type of remedy to apply when in need. The common answer I received was, in the case of snakebites, observe the reaction when two snakes were embattled with each other or when an animal was bitten. The one bitten would go to a certain plant and eat it or behave in such a way as to combat the poison. It all seemed too simple to me.

It seemed there existed an array of designer poisons. There was the poison applied to arrow tips. One variety of poison would have the stricken animal seize up with rigor mortis and drop dead. This was especially useful on gazelle, which would otherwise run for miles and die in some far off hidden bush never to be found by the hunter and his hungry family. It seemed that there existed an assortment of poisons for varied uses as the situation demanded. A particular beetle was the source of Samburu poison, used to impose rigor mortis, so I was told. At a particular stage in the metamorphosis, the insect is taken, crushed and heated over a low fire until the mix became black and tar-like. The arrow tip was then dipped into this mixture and left to dry, leaving a hard, glassy look. Added to this was a fixer, a substance to keep the poison waterproofed in case of rain. As if this wasn't amazing enough, was the exacting selection from the millions of insects available and to use it during one particular stage in the insect's life. I never saw this process since it was a taboo of sorts. The old man who fashioned arrows and coated them was an outcast for his lethal work. This didn't stop the demand for the arrows however, which the warriors paid for using the barter system.

In the Amazon, the Yanomama Indians hunt quarry that live in towering trees. When a monkey is struck with a poisoned arrow, the last thing the hunter wants is for rigor mortis to set in leaving the animal stranded high above the ground, and stuck in the branches. The hunter uses a poison, which acts as a relaxant. The stricken animal releases its hold and falls into the waiting arms of the Indian hunter below, just the opposite effect to poison used by the Samburu.

I often carried Samburu and Turkana artifacts to Nairobi for an Asian dealer on Bazaar Street who owned a curio shop. Arrows, spears and shields were in great demand by the tourists. One of the shopkeeper's constant requests was for poison arrows. On one particular safari to Nairobi, I delivered several. They fetched a good price and I was able to exchange them for the goods, which had been requested by my nomadic friends in the north. It was many months later when the shop owner in Nairobi told me about a letter he had received from a customer. Apparently a gentleman had purchased several of these dangerous arrows and once back home felt he had been tricked into buying fake artifacts, and gave his very young boy these same arrows to play with. As the youngster waved the poison tipped arrows around, the family dog was scratched. The pet walked across the room and dropped dead. The American gentleman was quite upset at having been sold such dangerous artifacts and was demanding an explanation. I never bartered poison arrows again but I often wondered what happened to the remainder of the shipment.

It was in Dar es Salaam (Haven of Peace) Tanzania, where I met the snake man. His incredible stories confirmed his even more incredible reputation. His name was Luis, an Italian and he lived inland on a station among the Africans of the area. The area was plagued with all sorts of snakes. One morning as he shaved while looking into a broken mirror nailed to the wall, a movement caught his attention. Without a moment's hesitation, he reached for his stick with one free hand and gave the intruder a mighty whack. Between himself and the sink, a cobra, hooded and bobbing back and forth had interrupted his shave. With the snake stick always ready, he dispatched the serpent and he went back to his morning ablutions. He mentioned that he had nearly nicked himself shaving in the process.

Another time upon hearing a commotion from the river, which was located behind his house, he ran to investigate. There he saw a distraught mother, wailing in horror. On the ground, was a very large python wrapped around protruding arms and legs. With his panga (machete), the snake man began to chop away with mighty blows. Luis related to me, how he 'hit and hit' the snake until his powerful arms ached. Only after some time and in small pieces was the python finally removed from the boy, who was covered in blood. Taking the youngster in hand, after splashing water on him, the mother and boy disappeared down river, thanking the snake man as she dragged her terrified charge to safety.

On my very first visit to Nyeri, north of us by some forty miles, I had to pass part of the road, which had a steep embankment on one side with a sheer drop on the other, leading down to an experimental fish hatchery. I ran over a log, which was lying across the road with a mighty thump. Felt good in my new Land Rover, to be able to drive over such inconveniences. On my way back that afternoon, I slowed down as I approached the place where I had driven over the log. To my amazement it was not a log at all. A dead python lay stretched from one side of the road to the other, somewhat worse for wear, but nevertheless very recognizable as one very large snake. It must have already been dead earlier that morning when I first ran over it since I didn't see any movement. It was huge and sported a mighty girth.

I was given this 18-foot python which terrorized the neighbourhood

Adrian, who was at the University of Nairobi, would write to me after my return to Canada. He sent several articles of dogs being torn off their chains as a hungry python dragged them off to the river. This river ran through Nairobi, a sprawling urban city.

I recall the morning in South Horr when my Samburu friend, Longodiki and I went for a 'walk' in the mountains, the Ol Doinya Mara. We met in the compound near the dispensary for our outing to photograph Kudu. Off we marched, approached the foothills, walked up and over the first ridge, and continued on for hours, up and down slopes. The vegetation was open and the walk easy so we chugged along, my guide pointing out features in Samburu, which I never understood in the least but nevertheless nodded with smiles and enthusiasm. Far below, lay the rooftops of the several buildings called South Horr. It was a hot day and I realized just how hot it was as my thirst began to grow and I blamed myself for not bringing along a water bag. It got much hotter as we trudged headlong into crevasses and up the opposite sides. I was getting very thirsty.

In my very best KiSwahili, I informed Longodiki of my concern. He acknowledged it and said 'maggi' or water was very close, 'Karibo Sana.' Now for a nomad, very close is not what we think of as very close. Very close is very far. And so we continued our walk, my need becoming somewhat desperate as I hoped that very close was near at hand. My tongue began to swell and I could feel my throat starting to close. Again, I slurred the need for maggi and once

A TOUCH OF AFRICA

again I was assured that water was 'Karibo Sana.' On and on we went, while the thought of clear, fresh water fueled me as I struggled to keep up. This was no fun and the cloudless sky offered little respite from the African sun. Stopping my companion, I thought I should perhaps reemphasize my needs once again and I slowly asked how much further to maggi. Looking at me with his one good eye he slowly said, 'Karibo, Sana.' On we went for another hour, with visions of waterfalls dancing in my head.

The author, Longodiki, and Muggi Muggi

When he finally pointed that we had arrived, I was somewhat dismayed, since I could neither see nor hear the fresh, cool, mountain waterfalls, gushing headlong over rocky ledges, waiting to be tasted and then to be drenched in its coolest of mists. He pointed to a large rock. Surely there was a mistake but being in no position to argue, I raced for the rock and as I rounded the boulder, realized it was hollow on the opposite side and held a deep, dark entrance. There in the middle of the opening, stood a green pool of water, still and fostering abundant plant growth of various hues and color. What upset me were the nasty habits of the passing baboons that also used the pool for their drinking needs. They had gloriously fouled the water with large feces, half submerged and bobbing about. This behavior was meant to discourage would be interlopers, like me.

I knew if I drank the water I would be sick for months with at least amoebic dysentery and a host of other ills as the wee beasties floated about inside me. However, I foolishly reasoned out of desperation, if I gently pushed aside the most obvious pieces, maybe the water below would be more inviting. Down on my knees I sank. With my face close to the pool, I inched myself forward looking for a likely spot to clear away. It was dark and the water cool to the touch and I was desperate and so I decided to chance it. Brushing aside a flotilla of debris, I detected movement. Now I was several feet into the cave, wet and on my knees, and it was dark inside. I focused and to my horror, I made out the shape of a very large snake that was lying around the sides of the pool and was beginning to stir. It was wrapped around me on both sides. The head began to rise, hood expanding, eyes like shiny marbles, tongue tasting the air, flicking. It was an awfully large cobra. Needless to say, I must have reacted out of pure instinct because with one mighty shove, I flipped myself backwards reminiscent of the finest of Russian Olympian gymnasts, executing a somersault and coming to rest at the feet of wide-eyed Longodiki, who must have thought that was some potent water in there.

What I learned was that our physical needs are secondary to our emotions. Fear held priority over bodily desires. We marched back to South Horr, never stopping for a rest and without the slightest complaint on my part for water. Fear was a powerful drive and not to be denied. History tells of how fear ushered millions into mass graves, often without a whimper. If fear were an animal, I'm sure it would be an elephant.

During the early months of my arrival in Africa, I was given the 'black stone' from the Congo. This piece of porous volcanic rock, flat and shiny, was to be used as a poultice if bitten by a venomous snake or scorpion or insect. You simply put it on the puncture and the stone stuck like glue. After awhile, when it was saturated with poison, it would fall off. I was told to boil it in milk, and rinse it in clear water, allow it to dry, and it would be ready for the next bite. It worked well on mosquito bites.

ELEPHANT

Despite being fairly common in the animal world, several stories may help to illustrate another aspect of the world's largest land animal. A professional hunter, and former game warden, studied elephant in Meru country for nearly twenty years and gained his intimacy with the animal through years of observation. While out on patrol one evening with two African askaris (soldiers), they were drawn towards the trumpeting of an elephant in distress. What they discovered was an unfortunate young bull floundering in a pit dug by poachers who would return in the morning for the kill and the ivory. Camping nearby, they decided to wait until morning to try and rescue the animal and maybe even catch some poachers. Throughout the night these would be liberators, were kept awake with the piercing trumpeting from a large herd. The disturbance continued until dawn. When they approached the pit, to their astonishment it was empty. Under the cover of darkness, the herd had returned in search of their missing member. A joint effort was executed to free the young animal and the ingenious plan worked. The herd proceeded to cave in one wall of the pit until enough loosened material formed a crude ramp allowing the trapped animal to struggle free from its intended grave. The caved in pit was the only evidence left the next morning.

This one charged

A Turkana elder related the following story, which took place near his village. Community meant everyone had to contribute to the welfare of the village, even the very young and very old, including the blind. One morning, an elderly blind Turkana woman made her usual foray to the nearby forested area to gather firewood. She had often poked about in the dry underbrush in search of kindling. On this particular morning, the sun was more exhausting than usual and so she decided to take a nap in the heat of the day under a tree, her trusty walking stick near at hand. She tells how she was awoken by a strange sensation delicately prodding her body. Wise enough to remain completely still, the prodding continued for some time. She knew she was surrounded by elephant and stiffened with fright. The herd milled about her as she listened to the familiar stomach rumblings, elephant communication. The rumblings gave way to the tearing and ripping of branches and paralyzed with fear, she continued to lay motionless as the branches fell on her in heaps. She was being covered. Her elephant sentries stood guard around her throughout the day and night and it was the next morning before a search party of Turkana warriors found her. The young men knew the ways of the elephant and realized they had covered something. The bewildered cries of the old lady gave way to shouts of rejoicing as she was led back to the village. The elephants mistook the old woman for dead and had ceremoniously buried her.

A couple that researched elephants in Lake Manyara observed the animals' interesting traits when dealing with their own dead. When a foraging herd passed the bleached remains of a former member, not only did the herd appear to recognize the remains, but picked up the bones and mouthed them gently, passing them around to one another. The bones were then ceremoniously placed in a heap before the herd moved on. It would appear that a tribute of sorts was part of their instinctual behavior. An elephant's sense of smell is ten times that of a bloodhound. Smell becomes another set of eyes.

President Kenyatta had a team of askaris from the Game Department, protect a colossal against poachers and declared this giant elephant a living monument to be safeguarded until it died. Amhed, the living giant, lived on the slopes of Mount Meru and was said to have tusks so long, he walked up hills backwards! The ivory was of enormous length and when the animal died of natural causes, it was taken to Nairobi, and today the skeleton with its ten-foot tusks stands mounted for everyone to see. Each tusk weighed in at a hundred and fifty pounds or so, not heavy when records are examined but their length was awesome. Amhed was the nearest thing to a living mammoth.

Amhed the living monument who roamed the hills in Marsabet

Elephant graveyards? Such tales were common and still persist in some quarters. Plausible explanations for the fields of skeletons and ivory are as follows. One primitive hunting method was to set fire upwind and have the flames engulf a cornered herd. Meat was the primary motive and so the remains of bones and ivory were left to be discovered, as some sort of communal burial ground. Also, older animals suffer from starvation when their teeth fail them and they can no longer grind the hundreds of pounds of gritty vegetation. Seeking softer sources of food often led the animals to low, swampy areas where they would become mired, exhausted and die. The remains would surely look like a place where elephants went to die.

Parallels between the life cycle of man and the elephant have often been made. Age similarities, young males in the herd forced out on their own, incredible maternal instincts, babysitting and stroking of birthing mothers by her female relatives and so on, have led to the comparisons. Most importantly, it is the female who determines the path the herd will follow, and leads them for a lifetime. This alone should convince the skeptic in regards to the parallels with man. The elephant has been likened to Africa, deceivingly simple at first meeting. Both were ancient before man was.

A most memorable time with the Roscoes took place upon our return to Kenya with nearly grown children. We traveled to Malawi to meet up with our friends who were gracious as usual and had made plans for both families to go on safari to Zambia and Chinzambo Game Lodge on the Luangwa River. My two children, Katharine and Christopher were excited as we stuffed nine people into Adrian's station wagon. Despite the strains that usually accompany the traveler on the African road, we all arrived tired and filled with good will found only among old friends. Our cabana was traditional and clean. The Roscoe and the D'Amico children ran around for a quick inspection. Chris found the bleached carcass of a dehydrated hippo covered with bird droppings, probably vultures. Situated on the Luangwa River, the site was completely isolated and superb. Numerous crocs and hippo lined the nearby opposite shore. Meals were taken outside in a dining room, open sided and covered with traditional thatch and dripping flowers.

During our first evening meal, having been introduced to an English guest who was doing rhino research, we sat down hungry and ready to sample the meal being prepared for us in the open kitchen. It smelled like fine dining as we waited for the first course to appear. As plates of food were being set down, the researcher jumped up from his bench, waved authoritative arms about and barked out a sharp command that all women and children should immediately get to the back. In front of us loomed a silhouette, enormous and dream-like as it glided past, as noiseless as a whisper. It was a shadow, which vanished as suddenly as it appeared. The old bull elephant was a long time resident of the area, long before anyone had decided to build a lodge. We were on his turf. All the local Africans knew the ancient resident as Chinzambo, the lodge having taken his name. Nice to know in hindsight that we were camped on the private turf of a wild African elephant.

A TOUCH OF AFRICA

An old male set in his ways

As part of the 'program' at the lodge, besides traveling into the bush in an open Land Rover to view big game, was the nightly presentation of the flora and fauna of the Luangwa Valley. This slide show took place in the open sided all-purpose structure next to the riverbank. I think it was Adrian who was sitting next to me during the presentation. We all sat looking at the wildlife, colorfully displayed on the white portable movie screen when from behind the picture, a shadow, once again, loomed large and silent as it moved noiselessly past. Not only were we watching hippo on celluloid, one of the same was passing in front of us in the dark, unnoticed as it melted into the gloom. I tapped Adrian on the knee and pointed as inconspicuously as I could. Angry hippos, disturbed, are dangerous and have been known to chomp boats in half.

On one of my return trips to Africa and the Uaso Nyiro River, I came across a twelve foot Nile croc that lay on its back, covered with flies and bloated. My African driver told me that elephant trample crocs without hesitation when their young were threatened as they crossed the river. The Africans say. *'When two elephants fight, it is the grass that suffers.'*

After dust bath with red laterite soil

Elephants are notorious for raiding crops late at night, whether it is in Africa or India. Farmers suffer the consequences when they encroach on the elephants' territory and natural foraging becomes scarce. Also, fresh crops once tasted become a nightly treat and the clever animal will overcome nearly any obstacle to dine on the succulent fare. Electrical fences, wooden walls, nightly fires and so on are all useless against the marauder. One particular deterrent has recently been applied to the nightly raiders with excellent success. Researchers have long known how receptive the elephants' sense of smell has evolved. Apparently, this discerning organ, finds the odor of rotting eggs so disgusting it will avoid the stench at all costs, even if it means giving up a tasty treat in the farmers' fields. Yet another similarity between elephant and man?

The author with Adrian Roscoe (on the right) and giant Baobab tree in Malawi

CROCODILE

It is important to distinguish between the crocodile, the alligator and the caiman. The crocodile is the bad tempered one, larger, meaner and the one to avoid at all costs. Besides the obvious physical differences, the Nile crocodile has left horror stories in its wake, stories found only in the worst of nightmares.

On the Shire River in Malawi, a newly commissioned ferry built in England, went on its maiden voyage or at least one of its very early crossings. The posted warnings indicated that the boat would hold so many people. This was in English and translated into the local language, Chichewa. The translation of the word 'people' became 'men' and so the numbers were doubled with the addition of an equal amount of women and children who were, of course, not men. The ferry capsized and lost hundreds of people in the river, some to drowning but a great many lost to the ever-present Nile crocodile. The disaster is documented as a record for the most people eaten by crocodile in one accident. In the stomachs of the Shire River crocs, brass bracelets and neck ornaments are found as a regular occurrence. Women wear these items.

On the Uaso Nyiro River, a river, which winds its way across Kenya, passes through what is now called the Samburu Game Reserve. A mother with her young son and his playmate were at the river's edge busy with the weekly wash. While hanging several items on a nearby tree, she heard a commotion. A large croc had been scrutinizing the scene, steely eyes barely visible above the waterline, waiting for his chance to drag off a meal. The croc rushed at her youngster, who had been playing on the shore, and was dragging him backwards into the river as the terrified woman rushed in to save her son. Both the mother and playmate managed to pull the helpless boy from certain death. They dragged the torn youngster further up the embankment, bleeding heavily and nearly unconscious. Running for help, the frightened women quickly returned with friends. To her horror, the young lad was gone. The playmate told how the ravenous crocodile had returned for the wailing youngster and dragged him off and into the river for a second and final time. 'All mothers' tears are equally salty.'

I still have articles from the 'East African Standard,' which reported the incredible determination of the Nile crocodile. Contrary to belief, the croc will leave water far behind in its search for easy prey. Apparently, in one area of Kenya, the animals would roam as far as two miles on their nightly forays to find sleeping victims in their huts. Dragging the helpless person back to water, the croc would then in characteristic fashion, shake apart its anticipated meal or oftentimes drown and lodge the victim under a sunken branch. In due time, the meal would rot, be torn apart and swallowed. This was not an isolated incident and the articles appeared at least twice, recounting the latest horror story. The Game Department would arrive and wait for the cunning beasts to make their move. They shot many a croc but the article went on to say the askaris routinely shot the young animals for their valuable skins. The older scarred crocs had hides of little value. It was however, the older animals, which were responsible for the tragedies.

Chimzambo, the lodge we visited with the Roscoes, home to our nightly elephant visitor, was situated on the banks of the Luangwa River in Zambia, a river studiously documented by all the wildlife research programs and a favorite today on wildlife T.V. programs. You could sit on the riverbank and count numerous basking Nile croc on the opposite bank. In the river, every mile or sometimes even less, pods of anxious hippo yawned nervously in their respective territories. In one particular pod, we spotted an albino baby hippo.

A young researcher from the U.K. was studying the river's wildlife in Chimzambo several years after our visit. His daily habit was to go to the river's edge, towel and soap in hand, and perform his morning ablutions. As is often the case, the local Africans warned him but to no avail. Nile crocs do not discriminate in their choice of meals. As expected, he failed to return one morning and his African assistants found his towel and soap near the water's edge. The authorities were called. The conclusion was clear. The crocs had him. Evidence was needed and reports had to be completed and questions were asked. This was a muzungo and there would be consequences. The askaris, guns in hands approached the site and asked the locals for assistance. An enormous croc with an even bigger reputation was labeled as the one responsible. The not so easily satisfied askaris had one of the locals, go into the water waist deep with a stick to prod about for remains of the Englishman. As the African volunteer poked about, he swiftly disappeared beneath a sudden surge of frothing water. Two men were now gone.

With the askaris finally convinced, the large croc was shot, emptied of its stomach contents only to find the remains of the young researcher's upper torso. This was sent back to the U.K. for his family to bury. The croc that ate the African was never identified. Once again, the African had paid the ultimate price for a muzungo's folly. Adrian read this story as it was reported in the local news and forwarded the article to me.

UASO NYIRO RIVER

It was camping on the Uaso Nyiro River that will remain with me as one of the highlights in my life and certainly in Africa and only to be equaled with a time in the Amazon jungle and the Yanomama Indians, many years later. Freddie Seed was a professional hunter and in earlier times was referred to as a 'white hunter.' This term of reference always made me smile since the Africans were far superior hunters in every way and their skills were indispensable on all big game safaris. Besides Freddie Seed was pink from too much sun.

The Game Department in Nairobi using aerial photography and on the ground counts controlled the culling of all game and issued very expensive licenses to non-resident hunters who wished to shoot a particular animal for the Department. The money from the licenses went into the coffers to further protect wildlife. There were legitimate reasons to kill animals, which I finally admitted to but only after seeing first hand, starving, disease ridden animals due to their excessive numbers or raging elephants terrorizing the countryside or lean and miserable herds being ravaged with anthrax or other infections often due to overcrowding. Herds of gazelle numbered in the many hundreds since many of the predators were gone because of the ever sprawling, urban population. Kenya has one of the highest birth rates in the world, and land is being cultivated at an insatiable rate.

Freddie Seed was approached by the Department to cull Cape Water buffalo and a marauding leopard from the Uaso Nyiro River area. The buffalo were too numerous for the amount of vegetation in the area and aerial photography correctly predicted the problem months ago. Also, on the Uaso Nyiro, were several scattered villages whose livestock had paid a heavy toll because of a leopard, one, which was out of control. Each evening or when the leopard felt so inclined, into the goat pens it would leap and in leopard fashion, kill off all of the milling animals and take away only one which it would eat for its dinner. Leopards were hated for this wanton destruction. Lions would have killed only what they needed at the time and leave the remaining animals untouched. This left the villagers in a sorry state of affairs. Oftentimes lion or leopard will turn into man eaters when they are too old to keep up to wary prey or they might even have thorns in their paws or become injured during a kill and realize how much easier it is to kill a human, especially children. Killing goats in a compound was much too close for comfort and so off I went with Freddie Seed from Nanyuki. This was my first real big game safari with a pro and I would be living under real canvas on the banks of the Uaso Nyiro River. I thought to myself, 'Move over Mr. Hemmingway.' Expectations ran high. We were to have experienced African trackers, a cook, and help around the camp. I had only been in Africa several months and this was a totally unexpected adventure, my first of many in the years ahead.

As a novice I had to learn fast. First of all, the guns had to be sighted in. I didn't have a clue. This was done using a target and a lot of adjusting to telescopic scopes, which I was to learn, could be very touchy and thrown askew in a heartbeat. I passed the first step despite the fact I was a raw beginner. I had never shot a gun in my life but I never told Freddie Seed. (Nor have I fired one since my return to Canada.) Packed with all the creature comforts I never expected, Freddie sent the lorry ahead with the African personnel and we followed behind in my Land Rover, allowing them time to set up camp at a prearranged area, deep in the bush and on the river. It was enroute that I first met Jack and his Masaai wife and their children. I was to return to the area in the coming years, invited by Jack Farrel, a friend of Freddie Seed. Having married an African woman he was ostracized and lived outside the small white community of Nanyuki, alone with his family on the cattle ranch.

The setting on the river still jars my memory. The site was under several large, spreading acacia trees on flat ground and fifteen feet from the water. Now at this time of the year, the water was a series of separate gurgling streams, passing over a flat shale river bottom, all the while tumbling over mini waterfalls no higher than one or two feet. There would be no bilharzias, a schistosomiasis organism, living on the backs of snails to infest the bloodstream and bladder and cause a slow and painful death because the water here ran swiftly. A most brilliant emerald green bordered the entire scene, which in my photos appear unreal. The bush was open to a distance of twenty feet before it closed, dark but not threatening. We had a mess tent under which meals were taken in the event of foul weather, an open dining tent, and our own sleeping tents with sewn in floors, a great relief. The routine was simple. Get up at 4a.m. shake your boots for scorpions, a habit I still perform unconsciously, and with a coffee still burning its way down, follow the lead tracker, carrying your gun and anything else you might need until our return later in the morning or early afternoon, depending on what happened during the hunt for Cape Water buffalo. It was always cold despite the proximity to zero degrees latitude and the dew seemed to take forever to dry. No one talked much as we followed the lead tracker through the shadows of thorn.

Our camp site on the Uaso Nyiro River

The idea was to hunt buffalo in the morning and in the late afternoon, retreat to the blind for the marauding leopard. The leopard site was baited each day. Since it was only safe to hunt the Cape Water buffalo coming or going to water and therefore in the open, we therefore took up our positions and waited for them on their return to thicker bush where they would lie up in the heat of the day. Well, this tactic never worked and Freddie Seed was getting more anxious and more daring with each day throwing caution to the wind, we followed the buffalo to their lie ups, a serious error. In hindsight, I imagine it was a matter of pride for Freddie since he was insistent on showing me the real thing. Pride in this instance, was a dangerous luxury.

Late one morning, deep in the thorn undergrowth, and having left a good deal of skin on the trail with the leave-me-not thorns, we were in hot pursuit of a very large buffalo being guarded by two younger bulls. According to our African tracker, the younger animals will chaperone and protect the older buffalo. The mood was tense, visibility nil, and the animals were directly ahead of us in thick undergrowth. It had been repeatedly pounded into my head by Freddie that Africa's most dangerous animal with its superb hearing, vision, and smell must never be wounded since it meant the hunter had to follow the wounded beast and this was the most dangerous of tasks, especially for the lead tracker who went ahead unarmed. It was drilled into me that one must aim either above the shoulder or at the base of the tail if it were running away. A headshot was too iffy since the large horns protected the head. With this firmly embedded in my mind, I was certain to let an animal escape before taking an unsure shot and leaving a potential catastrophe for someone else to clean up. Also, it was the humane thing to do. I was thinking these thoughts as I followed the tracker with Freddie behind me, the buffalo only feet ahead of us when all of a sudden a deafening shot rang out, leaving my ears throbbing. I couldn't make out the shouts around me, the stinging and aching was so intense. When I did get some hearing back, Freddie was yelling, 'Finish him off.' Finish what off? I hadn't seen a thing. Several feet ahead of me, lying in the tall grass and on its side was the black mass of a Cape Water buffalo, legs kicking in a futile attempt to escape as it lay there bleeding from a tear in its side. I was devastated at the mess Freddie had made, especially after all instructions and warnings. I felt sick. There was no clean shot to be had and despite this he had broken all of his own rules and fired blindly into the bush without a clear target. I put the wounded animal out of its misery. I was very upset. Without the slightest acknowledgement, Freddie instructed the tracker to begin butchering the animal, which must have weighed nearly a ton. It seemed only minutes passed before the vultures were circling overhead and the women and children from a nearby village, baskets at the ready, surrounded us. The animal disappeared before us, leaving the grass bent and stained. The tail was taken for our own dinner and I must admit, reluctantly, that I have never eaten ox tail soup so tasty as that evening out in the open and under the African sky. Our tracker, who had second choice of the meat, selected the fat from the stomach lining, further confirming the rumor that fat is good and makes you strong and healthy just like the muzungos. The gun Freddie fired was a two shot Jeffery's 500, one barrel over the other and hand fashioned in the U.K. It was a small cannon, and very loud.

The Cape Water buffalo with a nasty disposition

On another occasion, once again following buffalo to their lie ups, we were very close to a large herd which were nervously snorting just feet away in the thickest of brush. There would be no way we could cull the half dozen animals required by the Game Department. It's amazing the messes one can get into, if not unwittingly at least unknowingly. As Freddie and the tracker pointed and talked in hushed gestures, the herd ahead of us caught our scent and like all wild animals, they didn't relish it. They stampeded. This would have suited me just fine except they stampeded in the wrong direction and came straight at us because the swirling wind had confused them. And so they charged, heads low, with swooping black horns spreading four feet wide and awesome, as trees and bushes flew apart before them. This was all unreal. Freddie shouted something at me and the tracker who was already hanging from a nearby acacia, feet and legs gathered beneath him, was the safest. I stood next to Freddie and without apology, knees shaking or better still quaking, down I went. On one knee, gun poised, I probably looked in control. The animals crashed between, around and about us, kicking up a dust storm. The noise added to the confusion. These creatures were massive and barrel chested. The herd finally pounded passed, leaving a path of flattened scrub in their wake. Then an amazing thing happened. The herd stopped, turned and stared. Not again, I thought! After a good look they charged off again, leaving me grateful at seeing their backsides. It was suddenly very quiet. Freddie Seed handed his gun to our tracker who had swung down from his perch, and grasped me with both arms congratulating me on my incredible bush sense and astuteness. I had presented a small target to the charging herd he said and was all the more steady to take a shot as I rested on one knee. I never had the heart to tell Freddie that filled with terror, my knees had buckled and with that I sank to the ground, gun at the ready and eyes squeezed firmly shut. Much later, a friend told me that Freddie Seed had a terrible experience as a young man. He had been thrown by a Cape Water buffalo and was shaken at the thought of facing another. I realized then why he had panicked in the thorn thicket, and broke all the rules of fair play.

I found the nights filled me with anticipation because after dinner and over a scotch and water, Freddie would tell me tales of Africa, unwritten and soon to be forgotten with the likes of the old timers. I had yet to venture into the N.F.D. and to many of the places he talked about. Because of the early morning wake up calls, someone would yawn, the hint taken, and off we would go to our beds in the chill of the evening. Our sleeping tents were five feet apart and we often talked to each other once inside. I was about to doze off when Freddie called out for me to listen. From across the nearby river came the unmistakable heavy panting of a lion as it pushed forward, one powerful leg ahead of the other, expelling an unforgettable rumble of air as it moved along. The rumblings, deep throated and steady came closer and closer until the lion was not only in front of us, but made his way between the two tents, knocking the guide ropes and shaking the tents as he passed. I shall never forget that feeling. The ground shook as the animal passed. Freddie was proud of himself as if he had orchestrated the whole affair for my benefit. He was anxious to have me experience the 'real' Africa. I think I did.

The afternoons were spent in preparation for the leopard hunt later in the day. First, we had to determine the home base of the animal. Our tracker who found the remains of a baboon, the leopard's second favorite food, established the site. (I still have the head of this baboon with the dentition still firmly set in the skull: I later used the skull in class to show the differences between man and his primate cousins referring to the molars and forum magnum.) Next, was to find a spot, which was on higher ground with a tree to hang the bait. This was an easy task since there was a nearby rock, under several overhanging branches. With our pangas, we cleared the brush away, leaving a sturdy branch on which to hang the bait. Stringing the bait high meant that leopard would have to stretch to reach its meal, thus presenting a perfect target. We also needed an unobstructed view. The blind, a hundred yards back, was a simple affair. Branches, loosely woven together in the shape of a large letter U allowed us to enter from the open back. We had a clear view from a tiny peephole. Our guns rested on forked sticks. Nothing left to do except stare quietly at the hanging bait over the rock. Bait was usually a gazelle or wild pig. The longer it sat in the sun, the riper it got until the maggots could be heard writhing from a distance. Leopards relish this tenderized meat.

So each day, after an early morning trek in the bush, lunch, and a rest, Freddie and I would follow the head tracker to the blind, crawling the last bit so as to be as inconspicuous as possible. Once inside the blind, it was absolutely paramount not to move, not even a finger since the leopard would detect the slightest motion or noise and take off, never to return. So we waited patiently, day after day, mosquitoes feasting on us since we had no choice but to watch them dine on exposed skin unwilling to swat them away. Mosquitoes could be deadly. At dusk and unable to see the bait clearly, we would crawl away through the open back of the blind to the Land Rover and drive to camp for drinks and dinner, tired and scratching all the way. A report the next day would come back to us telling how the bait had been eaten after our departure and so another animal had to be dragged to the sight, hung and left in the tropical sun to ripen. Dragging the bait behind the Land Rover encouraged the leopard to follow the scent to the overhanging branch. Later on, I realized this was totally unnecessary.

Baiting the leopard with view from the blind

Perhaps it is important to mention here that being attacked by one of the big cats in Africa would be horrendous since few survive. However, it is the septic wounds inflicted by the bacteria-laden claws which will kill you, should you be so lucky as to survive the initial attack. After seeing the rotting meals on which our leopard fed, it is not surprising.

One drowsy afternoon, after having yet another unsuccessful morning tracking buffalo, a small group of lanky, ashen-faced Africans walked through our camp. Freddie told me they were Wandorobo, an ancient people who shadow-like, live in the furthest recesses of the murky forests. They were renowned honey gathers. They were following a Honey Guide bird and were sure to find a hive in the trees. In my faltering KiSwahili and with some assistance from Freddie, I asked to join them in their quest for honey. With a fatalistic shrug of his shoulders, an elder motioned me to follow along knowing full well I would be a clumsy addition to their troupe. Off we marched into the forest, a young boy who cradled a baby olive baboon accompanied me. I thought this unusual since I knew the strong bonds between the female baboon and her young. The mother must be dead I thought.

We hadn't walked that far in the forest when the group stopped, threw down their gear and looked skyward. Bees hummed about, high in the branches. I found myself a comfortable spot to sit and watch the proceedings. A fire was started using two sticks like those used by the Samburu, while two young Wandorobo, tying their loin clothes about them, seemed to be discussing a plan of attack. (Years later, in the Amazon jungle, I was to witness a similar scene but the object then was a special seasonal fruit growing at the top of a forty foot thorn covered palm tree.) The tall, dusky Wanderobo looked on intently, appearing to be so much a part of the forest, standing on one leg with one long thin arm wrapped around their throwing spear, all the while leaning against a gnarled tree. It seemed surreal, like they too were rooted to the ground like some ancient growth. White smoke drifted lazily upwards through shafts of sunlight. The low fire crackled and the bees buzzed.

The scenario soon began in earnest. Finally the two younger men, having decided on a plan, shimmied up the tree, using wrap around cords, while holding firebrands and a dangling basket tied to their waists. The audience below came to life. The hooting and waving to the climbers became more animated as they rose higher and higher in the lofty bough and the bees grew thicker and thicker as they approached the hive. The smoking torches were placed beneath a dark shaped hive, which reminded me of a loaf of black bread. These African 'killer' bees were very upset. As they poked at the hive with branches, pieces of the comb tumbled to the ground while some even managed to land in the homemade basket they had carried up. Arms flaying, heads shaking, feet kicking, the two men had the group below in hysterics. Clouds of bees rocked to and fro, drunk with smoke of the intruders.

Once on the ground the two received wet-eyed praises as the audience mimicked the scene, holding on to their sides with bursts of laughter. High in the tree, honey oozed down, snake like, as a small bird eagerly darted about, scooping up bees and nectar alike. Indicator-Indicator had earned its reward. The contents of the baskets were dumped into a blacken pot on the fire. Honey comb, dead bees, pieces of leaves and twigs, with a healthy smattering of larvae boiled and bubbled. The charcoal laden pot had assumed the importance of a center stage prop, as everyone squatted around, occasionally stirring it with a stick. I was invited to share their spoils, which meant poking my fingers into the bubbly liquid to taste the sweet mixture. As the watery honey cooled, pieces of debris including the larvae, stuck to my fingers and gratefully eaten under the approving eyes of my hosts. Now and then someone in a language as new as the company about me, would point to the lofty proceeding and in rolls of laughter, tumbling over backwards, the scenario once again became good entertainment.

THE HONEY BIRD

The Black Throated Honey Guide (Indicator-Indicator) deserves mention because the bird is legendary among African honey gathers. Brownish gray with a distinctive black throat patch, this bird with its incessant chattering will guide the wandering nomad or even Africa's vicious badger, to honey. Hopping from tree to tree, the pint-sized sparrow waits for the follower to catch up and thrives upon this symbiotic relationship. Often times, when out in the bush stalking game, the hunter is thrown into a panic, as the Honey Guide will arouse the entire neighborhood. So persistent is it's calling, this pint-sized bird seems to grow impatient with those who refuse to follow. Upon taking up the invitation, a bee's hive will surely be discovered.

The Africans also say that when the prize is reached, the gatherer must leave some of the hive behind for the bird. Those who selfishly take everything away, the story goes, will be surprised because next time out, the bird will lead you to a cobra. It seems that this bird is not only a guide for honey gathers but also reeks revenge upon the greedy. It would have been interesting to discuss in their language, the Ndorobo's symbiotic relationship with this bird, since these nomads are famous honey gathers and use the Honey Bird in their quests.

Part of our riverside campsite included a tent not much larger than a telephone booth, which hovered over a hole and used as our toilet. Included in this arrangement was toilet paper, a most appreciated luxury in the bush. Using the facility one late afternoon before leaving for the leopard blind, I found myself in a dilemma. Taking the tissue with one hand and just as I was about to tear off some paper, I noticed inside the roll, a very large scorpion, tail poised and upset at my intrusion. In my comprising position, I was in no way going to disturb the creature since I needed more time to figure out my next movement. We stared at each other in the unfriendliest way. Finally, it was time for action. Slowly turning the roll of paper on one end and raising one foot at the same time, I gave it a violent shake and as the scorpion fell to the ground, I came down on it with a heavy boot. After dinner, I told Freddie the story and we both concluded it was a tale that was best left behind me.

I did have one successful morning with buffalo. Once again, and in the thick of it all, as Freddie and the tracker discussed a herd not very far away, I looked to one side of the clearing, down a long narrow opening in the bush, which for some reason was empty and reminded me of a bowling alley. As I waited for their next move, to my amazement some fifty yards away, a long horn emerged from one side of the alley. A rhino I thought, as I pulled Freddie to have a look. To my surprise the rhino turned out to be buffalo. The animal had pushed out one side of his large spread through the bush and in the distance, all I saw was one horn, which appeared to be a rhino. I felt totally foolish. I did redeem myself, with one shot through the base of the tail as the animal raced away. I made a clean kill. The rejoicing and whooping back at camp certainly made me feel special. No nasty clean up with a wounded animal lying in wait. As a token of their appreciation, the rookie was given the tail, which was fashioned into a flywhisk. I was also given the front hoof, which was later mounted and lined with teak. Freddie claimed the head was a record for Kenya, if not a world-class trophy. The head now sits with me in Canada and according to the documentation I have read, the horns are about one inch or so off the world record. I'm sure buffalo meat was another reason for the rejoicing at base camp that night, since the dancing and singing went on late into the night fortified with full stomachs and pombe. The nearby village was also feasting.

Two Wandorobo boys waited for my return one afternoon, one holding the baby baboon. We were breaking camp the next day and I purchased the sickly animal for six shillings. I knew it had a slim chance of survival out in the forest since it was loosing hair and was scabby and needed professional care. With our gear stowed safely in the lorry, we set off for Nanyuki. The following day, I arrived in Mugoiri with my new addition. Our Siamese cat had not yet come into our lives and so it was only Tuffy, our faithful German shepherd who had to contend with the new arrival. Maeve was delighted with the infant baboon and used makeshift bottles with nipples purchased in Murang'a to feed the orphan. We already had experience, having nursed a baby Dik Dik, a ten-inch high gazelle. My first task was to build a good size wooden cage, complete with fluffy towels wrapped around a wind-up clock for the baboon to grasp at night. Wrapped tightly in a towel, the ticking clock was supposed to simulate the mother's heartbeat. I was told that the little fellow took to it immediately, since I was not present for the next several days.

The baby baboon clinging to maeve's leg

It was while I was banging away on our front porch framing a roomy wooden cage, that I noticed I kept hitting my thumb with the hammer. Now I knew that I wasn't that bad of a carpenter, and after several more whacks, I sat back and called to Maeve who was having tea with our teaching colleague, Breda. I said something felt wrong and was told to join them for a cup. Feeling dizzy, I lay on the bed. It wasn't long before waves of soaring temperatures overcame me and moments later, bone chilling, teeth chattering, freezing bouts took over, only to have the raging fever return. It wasn't too long before the nursing sister arrived, took one look at me and declared that I had contacted malaria. I recall parts of the delirium vividly. A week later and several pounds lighter I resumed nailing the baboon cage, thumb and malaria safely out of the way.

One story Freddie told me around our campfire dealt with a very rich fellow who had come to Africa to shoot a lion. As he told the story, I couldn't imagine why anyone would cross an ocean and pay to kill a lion. Freddie and the client, a Hollywood actor, sat in the blind waiting for the lions to approach the hanging zebra. Freddie had been baiting the pride for several weeks and had them conditioned to feed off his bait. Quite sporting! The client made it clear that he didn't have much time to waste sitting around. As they sat in the blind, peering through the peephole, guns propped up on forked branches, the lionesses approached, followed by a massive male. Now these animals were quite close. As it happened the male, which was to be the trophy, decided either he wasn't hungry or that something was amiss. As the females fed, the lion walked over to the front of the blind and with a mighty expulsion of air, plopped down in front of the peephole, completely covering it. Tension inside the blind was thick enough to serve. Staring into his client's bulging eyes, Freddie seemed to think he could control the would-be lion hunter as he sat paralyzed. The male lion was literally inches away. The unexpected had happened again.

Behind Freddie and his client, knelt the head tracker, a very able and experienced African. Watching from the corner of his eye, Freddie could see the tracker's hand moving slowly towards him, straining in slow motion for his attention. Over the campfire Freddie repeated several times how upset he felt that the 'foolish' tracker could possibly bother him at this crucial, life threatening time with the novice hunter next to him ready to crack and a huge male lion blocking their peephole. After what seemed an interminably long time, the hardened grip of the tracker proceeded to squeeze his shoulder with such strength, he was forced to abandon his staring at the client and the lion and turn slowly to glower behind him. He managed to turn his head ever so slowly only to find himself peering over the tracker's shoulder and into the green eyes of a curious lioness. The female had wandered around the back of the blind and discovered the motionless trio and decided to have a closer look. So they now had a resting lion in front of them and a curious lioness breathing down their backs. Remaining motionless had saved their lives. But how long could Freddie keep the situation under control?

Freddie said had the client seen the lioness all would have been lost and surely they would have been served up as the lions' next meal. He had to risk the consequences and made a decision. He fired at blank range through the peephole. With the sudden burst of gunfire, the resting male lion shot straight up and disappeared into the bush. The female lioness startled as well, leapt away and disappeared along with her feeding sisters who had been enjoying their zebra meal.

Several waiting staff appeared at the sound of gunfire and were told to carry the client away. Freddie and the head tracker had a daunting task ahead of them. They decided to track the wounded lion immediately since the bloodstains were dark and indicated a damaging heart wound. It would be criminal and against ever ethical code to allow the wounded lion to languish in the bush. Also, what would be the consequences if someone unknowingly wandered past the wounded animal? After tracking the blood trail for what seemed to be hours, the lion was discovered in the undergrowth. Gun poised, throwing rocks into the bush and preparing for the charge, both waited. The lion never attacked. The king of savannah had crawled under the bush and died from a piercing heart wound. Upon skinning the animal, it was discovered that the bullet had torn away the bottom part of the animal's heart. Gives a whole new meaning to 'the lion hearted.' Freddie admitted to crying over such a senseless and cowardly act and vowed never again to hunt big game for sport. That was years ago and Freddie Seed, true to his word, became an ardent wildlife conservationalist working for the game department and taking safaris out with clients but shooting game with a camera.

K.C.Jones tells of a conversation he had with George Adamson, Africa's lion man. This man was as gentle as the winds, which blew over his lion camps where he rehabilitated the animals from 'Born Free.' He became the source of lion lore in Kenya. Now George who lived an isolated life, even as a younger man as game wardens are wont to do, had a friend who would visit him at night for a 'sundowner.' George also had one of his full-grown lion as part of his household menagerie. Those who knew George never found this unusual. As the story goes, it was not uncommon for the prodigious animal to saunter into the living room and with a mighty sigh, lay prone at George's feet. These were lion, which were being rehabilitated for the wild, and learning to hunt on their own. One evening, his guest pulled up in his Land Rover, slammed the door, and as he walked up the front porch stairs, gave the lion laying at the door a gentle shove with his foot so he could step over and into the house. Over drinks and conversation of the day, the guest suddenly gasped in horror. George's lion, edged into the room, yawning from a nap. The animal on the front steps was a wild lion, one, which had come to investigate a possible intruder inside the house and possibly even a potential mate.

The legendary Serengeti black maned lion

Visitors to Bwana George Adamson found themselves in a unique position. His camp in Marsabat, after the filming of 'Born Free,' was devoted to the rehabilitation of the lion, which were used in the production of the film. Visitors were ushered into a wire holding cage and the lions roamed about free.

You always had to remember you were in Africa and to pay attention because so often, second chances were not an option. Three lions killed a senior government game ranger in Malawi's Nkhotakota District. A Mr. Waya was traveling by motorcycle from Kasungu when the lions attacked. A lorry driver found his motorcycle with its engine still running, abandoned on the side of the road. Mr. Waya's body was found near the motorcycle and his rifle lay some fourteen feet away. A hunt was mounted and one lion was shot and another wounded. A third escaped.

SAFARI ANTS

Safari ants (siafu) were unknown to me, but like all rookies, I learned the hard way because I never asked the right questions of my African friends. It was Gerald, an African principal at the local Harambee school, who eventually explained to me how in Africa, you must learn to live with nature as opposed to conquering it. (Interesting how our creation myth found in Genesis, tells us that the our world around us was put into place for our exclusive use while harmony with the nature is never mentioned.)

One early morning, before leaving for classes, our dog Tuffy was making a fuss and what I saw on our front yard Kikuyu grass was startling. Tuffy was tied to a long wire run because he had recently raided the school's storehouse and dragged off the hind quarter of a cow. I reluctantly tied him at night knowing full well he was not very popular with the students who had gone without their meat rations. That morning he was barking and thrashing about at the same time, covered with safari ants. What to do? I rushed into the house and returned with the only weapon I could think of and that was a tin filled with kerosene oil to kill off the intruders which swarmed all over him. I gave him a healthy dousing and released him as he strained on the leash. Once released, he shot away like a sprinter off the blocks and was last seen hightailing it through the neighboring pineapple field. Now the safari ants in the millions were milling about the front yard, upset at the being doused with kerosene, and interrupted as they marched to new quarters. In the meanwhile, I was doing the two-step trying to avoid the hordes. A brilliant idea came to me, born out of my enterprising North American mind. I would divert the main column by spreading kerosene in their path and thus keep them away from the house. Safari ants march in a long single file four inches thick, all the while being guarded on their flanks by the soldier or askari ants. These two inch soldier ants assault anything which nears the main column by hurling themselves head first at the intruder. With their enormous jaws, they sink their mandibles into the attack and take a bite, which can only be described as wholesome, sending the victim straight up and shrieking in pain. Funny to see someone, usually a muzungo, tearing off his or her clothing as the askaris, beneath stockings, pants, and other garments, attack with a vengeance, burying their heads in their victims.

Well, I doused the column and retreated with satisfaction at my ingenuity. It was then I noticed that the safari ants began to spread. They spread in their millions all over the lawn, my Land Rover in the driveway and, like spilled ink leaking on a sheet of white paper, they swarmed all over our new house. At one point the entire side of the wall was completely covered. The wall was black and bristling with the creatures. Another nightmare and now what?

Rushing to my African neighbor for advice I was knocked over at the reply. It was simply, 'Go to class.' The safari ants were in no mood to be fooled with. Leave them alone and go away. They will regroup in their column and continue on to a new underground home on higher land to avoid being flooded out during the forthcoming rains. It was all very simple but why did I interfere with them in the first place? I did as I was told and at noon, the ants were gone leaving only a bare, four inch path where they had passed. My question to

Gerard, the elementary school principal and a weekly visitor for his English lessons, was what does a family living in a mud hut do when the safari ants march and the shamba is in their way threatening the sleeping occupants? Once again, the simplicity of it all. Before the rains, merely spread several inches of ash from the fire around the hut because the safari ants cannot crawl over the barrier as they pump their legs and get nowhere in the soft ash. They simply go around and on their way.

Living in the bush and being outside the polite social circles of the few remaining colonialists in Murang'a, it was with some reservation that we accepted a dinner invitation from the local minister and his wife who were unknown to us. We never pursued the social life of the former colonialists, an anachronism after independence, and a lifestyle outside the experience of most North Americans. Also, we felt they were only being polite to the newly arrived and isolated newcomers. We proceeded to Murang'a at the appointed time for dinner and parked the Land Rover in the front yard and were graciously invited in. Not really having a lot in common with our hospitable hosts from England, the sherry before dinner relaxed the atmosphere and we were settling down to a comfortable evening or so I thought. Maeve sat in one of the easy chairs across from me, sipping her wine with her usual dignity when the first spasm hit her. She jerked nearly spilling her drink and tried to disguise the seizure. Wide-eyed, I watched in disbelief as she twitched and twisted in her chair, all the while our very proper hosts, who could not help but to see her contortions, talked politely away without the slightest acknowledgement of her discomfort. I later thought that maybe our hosts felt this poor lady suffered from epilepsy or some other spasmodic disorder. I wasn't as polite and stared open-mouthed when suddenly, with one mighty leap, Maeve drove ceiling high like a basketball player, spun around in mid air and hopping on one leg, hightailed it out of the room leaving a trail of garments in her wake. Later, I rolled in laughter because our hosts carried on with the conversation, half wanting me to believe that this was not unexpected behavior from 'American' guests. Maeve had inadvertently stepped on the vanguard of askari soldier ants protecting the main column as she left the Land Rover, and safari ants as they are in the habit of doing, lay quietly and without warning, until they decide when its time to attack en masse. Burying their jaws and heads in tender flesh leaves the victim few choices. Strangely enough, we were never invited back for drinks and on the rare occasions when I encountered the couple in Murang'a, the most I got was a quick doff of a ministerial hat as they hurried away deep in hushed conversation.

Safari ants could be very useful. Hunting was unofficially on my school timetable making me the main meat provider for our students. I would be out in the bush at least once a week. I would have the skins of the hunt professionally treated in Nairobi but the heads with awesome sets of horns presented a problem. My attempt at boiling croc heads ended up in a smelly mess and a lot of extra teeth. Once I tried to clean the head of a baboon, which had been killed by a leopard. I soaked the head in the bathtub while Maeve was out, only to have a further mess to clean up. I was elbow deep scrubbing away when I called to Mary, our house girl and pointed to the partially submerged baboon head and asked for its name in KiSwahili. I nearly fell over when she said the word, 'Man.' Holding myself up against the wall in tears, I asked if she really thought I had killed a man and was now in the process of cleaning his head. I had always suspected that she thought I was odd. Once again, cleaning the heads of the various animals was solved in a simple way, which I began to find annoying whenever I asked my African friends for advice. Pull up the Land Rover to a safari ant turret and drop the head and return in several days to find the skull bleached Sahara desert clean and odorless.

CHIGGERS AND OTHERS

I never realized that walking around in the dust with open shoes such as sandals would be a problem. Our house girl Mary was very intimidated by my presence being the first muzungo she had to deal with face to face. My long beard didn't help matters. I was told that the Kikuyu mothers in the neighboring shambas would use me as a threat with their children. If the kids acted up and needed discipline, the shaggy muzungo who lived in the white house on the hill, would come down at night and steal them away from their fireside blankets. I was the resident boogey man. I never understood the significance of facial hair and a ten-inch beard, which I learned, inspired fear in the African children around Mugoiri. I always wondered why the young ones upon meeting me during a stroll, would, without hesitation, dive headlong into the undergrowth in fits of screams and terror, looking wide eyed behind them. It made one wonder. And so it was with Mary, who felt very uncomfortable in my presence and therefore, I tried to avoid her whenever possible.

One afternoon grading papers before dinner, Mary noticed me rubbing my toe, which had been itchy for days. Head lowered she approached me and asked if she could see my foot. Well, I thought, this was a start. Leaning back, I lifted my foot which she examined with a 'tisk, tisk,' shaking her head. Without a word as was her style, she dropped my foot, left the room and returned with a needle. Now she had my attention. Taking up my foot again, she proceeded to pick away under my large toenail. I tried to show little of the discomfort I was feeling as I gripped the chair with white knuckles, teeth clenched, brow furrowed. Having dug out a considerably large hole, she dropped my foot unceremoniously and proudly showed me the results of her prodding. In the palm of her hand she held the unbroken sac of a tiny worm, which had burrowed under my toenail and was commonly known as a chigger. It was important not to break the sac since to do so was to supposedly cause all sorts of blood related problems as the wee offspring of the chiggers floated inside you. Unattended elderly Kikuyu who lived by themselves often had their toenails buckled over and bent backwards because of numerous chiggers, which had burrowed underneath them over the years. Chiggers lived in the dust and left large holes under your toenails.

Mary Wairimu a quiet young lady

Besides chiggers, there was a host of other parasites, which left the victim scarred and often deformed. I stopped my Land Rover one late afternoon for an old Kikuyu man, complete in his knee length army issue coat from old wars. He wore a wide brimmed hat, brown and stained from long use. That was all he wore as he eased himself, barefooted into the passenger seat. I was returning from a shop in Murang'a and always stopped for the old, especially the women-carrying spine bending loads. With my half dozen words in Kikuyu, we carried on our one sided conversation because all I had to say was, 'En Ay,' which was a term of agreement and one could use it in any conversation and as many times as you felt like. The upshot of my extremely limited Kikuyu vocabulary was that I had the reputation of being able to speak the language. So with my passenger in tow, and my constant 'En Ays,' he eventually signaled me to stop when we neared his shamba. As he stepped out of the vehicle, he turned towards me for the first time to thank me with a hearty, 'Negwa.' I was stunned at what I saw. One side of his face was completely eaten away and you could see his teeth and gums, down to his throat passage. He was the victim of yaws.

Walking back from class one day, following the path along the driveway, I approached a young boy dressed in a half coat or smock buttoned up to his neck and barefooted. What I couldn't make out was the way his exposed legs and feet appeared. To say they were swollen would be an understatement. Lower limbs were blown up to bursting proportions, with taunt skin ready to split. His toes were so disproportioned, his feet looked webbed. The young man's legs were shapeless, engorged stumps. He asked me for some money to buy food. I had him follow me to meet the head mistress and found out his story. He, along with his whole family, was the victim of elephantiasis, a mosquito born parasite and readily cured in Nairobi for a mere twenty or so Canadian dollars.

A young man with elephantiasis

STONED IN NYERI

There are four types of malaria caused by different mosquito born parasites. Falciparum is known for its severity and high mortality rate while vivax for its tendency to cause relapses. There is also ovale and malriae. Malaria is controlled with weekly doses containing chloroquine, mefloquine or doxycycline or one of the more up to date powerful drugs. All of these have limited effectiveness, since the parasite shows remarkable resistance in a very short time. The old timers in Kenya drank their gin laced with tonic, which contained quinine to combat malaria. Any excuse for a sundowner. Quinine is found naturally in the bark of the local 'fever' tree, a type of acacia with a reddish hue. The problem was that quinine eventually distressed the inner ear, which left one listing to port or starboard over the years. It wasn't difficult to pick out an old timer, as he approached you at an odd angle. It also affected the hearing. A veteran volunteer who had used quinine for scores of years, eventually returned to Europe and to a retirement home. It was during the war and as he rocked away in his chair on the third floor of the home, a bomb blasted the building apart leaving him three stories high with his back exposed to the open sky, still rocking away. Unaware of the damage behind him, his response in KiSwahili was, 'Odi' or 'Come in.' I have no idea the type of malaria I contacted after my Uaso Nyiro experience but years later I was told rightly or wrongly that malaria is a mimicking disease and therefore difficult to diagnose. So one is never sure of the source of an ailment, whether it is a virus, a genetic disorder or a relapse due to malaria, the mimicker.

It was a February afternoon in 1968 coming home in my Land Rover that I felt the first pang of what was to be a long and bothersome affair over the years. It was the rainy season. I awoke around 3 a.m. with a terrific lower back pain. Unable to sleep, I dressed quietly and out I went into the downpour hoping the night air and steady rain would somehow relieve the pain. After what seemed a long walk through fields of pineapple and rows of banana trees, the pain became unbearable and I found myself pounding on the headmistress's door in the hopes someone might drive me to the hospital in Murang'a. As it turned out the monsoon rains made it impossible for the school's car to travel the road and that left my four-wheel drive Land Rover. I couldn't drive so as a last resort, I banged on a fellow Canadian's door, Bernie Butt who had just arrived in Kenya, as my replacement in Mugoiri. Despite his inexperience, I needed a ride at any cost. I knew I had to get medical attention quickly.

I roused Maeve who became very anxious, and with Bernie at the wheel, we made off ploughing through thick sludge towards Murang'a. The road was hazardous at the best of times. At night with the monsoon rains pelting down and further reducing visibility and with Bernie, a novice with four-wheel drive and a Land Rover, the open-sided road, which disappeared into black crevices, was going to prove this an interesting trip. We both offered Bernie constant encouragement, while I lay doubled up in the back. The night was beginning to fade in and out as the pain increased with each roll of the Land Rover.

A TOUCH OF AFRICA

The Mugoiri road during the rains

Upon arriving at the Murang'a hospital, we were not surprised to find it closed. Maeve took off in one direction and Bernie in the other. A male nurse appeared and shook his head helplessly. I remembered the one Asian doctor I knew and after several attempts at arousing the switchboard operator, a call was put through to my friend. Peering at me in a fetal position in the back of the Land Rover, the doctor recommended another hospital immediately. His diagnosis was either a ruptured appendix or kidney stones. I had never been hospitalized and so I was open to all sorts of speculation. After a massive injection of morphine, the darkness was complete and off we all headed for Nyeri and a somewhat larger hospital with nurses and a volunteer doctor. I remember an incredible burst of euphoria and never gave another thought to the road, the rains, or to my lower back.

I was unprepared for what happened next. When I awoke somewhere between darkness and dawn, lying on a gurney with a white sheet covering me and still fully dressed, I could hear groaning and moaning all about me. Peeking from under the sheet with one eye, I was shocked to see a room full of bad tempered African women, tummies swollen and obviously very near to delivery time. I became the object of their laborious stares. It seemed that a male of any color was the last person they wanted to see. Eventually, I managed to get a young nurse's attention and assured her that whatever my problem was, it wasn't what they had and would she kindly get me out of the delivery room. I was wheeled into the only available space, the hallway, and away from their menacing stares.

The next morning I asked for a dressing gown since we had left in a hurry the night before. Now clothes donated from America were always popping up in the strangest of places and once again, this was to prove no exception. The young nurse, proud of herself for finding a make-do dressing gown, handed me a brown herring bone woman's coat, with two large buttons missing and the shiny lining hanging behind like a bridal train. Walking to the bathroom, I must have looked quite the sight, with one hand grasping the open front in an attempt at decency and with the other waving at my fellow patients, my coat lining trailing several feet behind. I could hardly wait for visitors.

The next morning the doctor saw me, and after a brief examination, he was convinced and rightly so, that I had a kidney stone and told me to expect more pain as it passed down the urethra. He congratulated me on my good fortune. Dr. Killien was a Czech doctor who, when finishing up his volunteer work in Kenya, was returning home to Europe to open up a kidney wing at a new hospital. He was a specialist.

The treatment was excellent; the food great, the nurses always helpful and the remedy for kidney stones was awesome. Drink lots of liquid and twist about frequently. I should be able to pass the stone without surgery if I followed this routine. Now my Land Rover was still in Nyeri and so were many friends who had regular parties. Nyeri had electricity and music. It was a simple task to arrange. K.C. Jones would back up to my ground floor open window and I would hop into my Land Rover and off we went to visit one of our many friends. There was always liquid refreshments and of course dancing and twisting to the wee hours was what the doctor had ordered. The treatment carried on for some time without the stone moving but with no complaints from me. Finally, the doctor unable to confirm the location of the stone needed some hard evidence and decided to send me to the nearby African government hospital in Nyeri.

Feeling absolutely fine and in good spirits, I walked the half hour to the government facility at the appointed time to find a winding line several hours long. This facility had an X-Ray machine. The idea was to inject a dye into my arm and take pictures at certain intervals and where the dye stopped, the stone would show up as the culprit blocking the way. Now the line seemed to stretch on and on, snake-like, the sun scorching, and everyone shuffled but a few dusty feet at a time. It was going to be a hot one under a cloudless sky. Kids bawled, mothers soothed and the ever-present African dog scoured the layout in the hopes of finding a mislaid morsel. I refused to use my status and a 'muzungo' and to proceed to the front of the line.

My place in line was behind two men who acted as aides for a man lying on a homemade stretcher. The wretched fellow was swathed in bandages and wrapped up not unlike the mummies we had seen in the Cairo museum. One hand was exposed along with his left eye. I couldn't help but stare at that one eye which never left staring back at me. This went on for the longest time as we dragged forward, several feet at a time. At one point with his free hand, Lazareth as I unconsciously nicknamed the unfortunate fellow, curled a twisted forefinger towards his helpers in an attempt to get their attention. When the lead man finally bent over him, I could make out their Kikuyu and understood a word or two of the hushed conversation. After several minutes, the assistant turned to me and said, 'Mr. Amien, would like to greet you.' I was confused and stared at the wrappings oblivious of whom I was watching. Finally, the one fellow said to me in faltering English, that the patient they were dragging about was none other than the butcher from Murang'a, a fellow I knew well but who now appeared in disguise. He had been in an auto accident and had suffered severe burns. He was quite animated as I showed recognition and his one exposed eye, fluttered rapidly while his finger seemed to be tapping out a tune, twitching in spasms. I never saw him again after that blistering morning in line as he was hauled unceremoniously through the dust.

Finally, getting into the X-Ray room was uneventful except when I was told to undress and put on the button less gown, which I did but backwards. The curious onlookers got an eyeful of muzungo since I was strapped down on the steel table, naked with exposed feet pointing skywards, a needle in my arm. The attendant had left for a late lunch, so I was on my own, or at least I thought so, as I lay bound and helpless. Windows were an open-air affair and for those at the head of the line, leaning inside for a look at the proceedings helped pass the time in line. I definitely heard women's voices and the odd, 'En Ays.' Upon leaving the hospital and passing the long line of women, I was almost certain their conversation in Kikuyu included details about me since a chorus line of 'En Ays' and the odd leer greeted me, as I walked sheepishly through the grinning line of patients.

I have always wondered whether the malaria parasite, that so called mimicking disease, was responsible for my kidneys problems, which produced so many stones over the years. If so, the leopard on the Uaso Nyiro had fared the best. Sitting in the blind, covered with mosquitoes waiting for that shrewd old cat, still leaves me wondering.

IRELAND COMES ABOARD

In September 1966 Breda Sherwin arrived in Mugoiri from Ireland, with an inimitable flourish. Maeve (nee Colleary) and Breda became instant friends. We enjoyed years and tears together. Breda always added a sparkle to any gathering as she sallied about in her mini, cigarette holder punctuating her Irish brogue, and a cocktail near at hand. It was decided that Breda who had purchased a second hand car should brush up on her driving before she ventured onto the African roads, which could be testy. I was the designated teacher and so the first lesson dealt with gears, which she thought was a tiresome task. Our first outing was frightening for any unfortunate who ventured roadside, which included the local farm animals. To say Breda loved to speed would be understated while the conditions could be scary for the most experienced driver. On her first solo she was unable to negotiate a turn in the road, sped through a shamba hedge, ploughed over the garden and finally came to rest in a Kikuyu hut. I rescued the car and unabashed, she apologized to all present and carried on, full of good cheer and eager to get on with it. We never discussed her previous driving experience in Ireland, if in fact she did drive, but I'm sure the roads were somewhat quieter after her departure.

A CHARITABLE BALL

It seemed that since we were all living in isolated conditions with long months between holidays we were always ready for a get-together with our similarly isolated teaching friends. Without a lot of creature comforts, it became necessary to improvise and make our own fun. Improvising was surely the only way to endure the dreary monsoons. Having scoured the school's library with its limited contents, it wasn't difficult to exhaust the shelves. I felt that I really knew Somerset Maugham, having reread most of his work several times. It seemed our friends who also worked under similar conditions, underscored the importance of a well-orchestrated social life.

The Murang'a Country Club had seen better days. The buildings represented a colonial past, which long ago served their purpose for racial segregation when Africans were admitted but only as working drones. As a Canadian and without any knowledge of colonialism, it all seemed archaic and so unnecessary. After Independence, both Africans and the local Asian population were admitted. We were casual visitors to the Club; tennis courts and fading paint told how neglected the club had become. We discovered that for a very minimal fee, the facilities, such as they were, could be rented for a private party. Well, a costume ball was decided upon and every one threw themselves into the planning with gusto. Since Maeve and I lived the closest to the Club, and I owned a Land Rover, a lot of the hands on arrangements were left to us. The music proved to be a thorny issue despite having the best piano player in the land, namely K.C.Jones, the Welsh, 'Iron Lung Basher.' The problem was that the Club was without a piano. Having shared our problem with my friends in Murang'a, it was mentioned that the local minister's wife was a trained pianist and owned a piano but she would be reluctant to share the instrument and even adamant at the thought of having it moved to the Club, despite the fact she lived only a short distance away.

We did manage to wrangle the piano from the minister's wife after a compelling plan was hit upon. If the event had a charitable aspect attached, surely it would be difficult for her to spurn a worthy cause? Thus satisfied, the event was planned, the costumes decided upon and the night approached with excitement. It had been raining for weeks, the days dragged on and we were all ready for a bash. With the aid of several friends, I arrived at the minister's house, subdued in seriousness and filled with last minute trepidation at the very real thought of our being refused in the final hours. Being the spokesperson for the tattily dressed group in their make-believe finery, the piano was tenderly lifted into the Land Rover and spirited away under hushed sighs and gasps. We were cautioned that the precious instrument, to be returned the next morning, should be in the same excellent condition as when it left her very proper living room. We all agreed.

Well it wasn't long before the Club was filled with splashes of colors with costumes reminiscent of a Halloween party gone badly. However, it was K.C. who got everyone's attention as he performed on center stage. Rolling up his sleeves and shouldering his cape, he tore off the top of the piano for a 'better' sound and lived up to his reputation as a first class entertainer. I cringed at the beautiful piece of furniture as the night went on. Quarts of Tusker beer balanced precariously near the keyboard and rocked unsteadily to, 'Great Balls of Fire.'

Everyone agreed it was a first class get-together, ending with first light and the declarations of cooing morning doves. The piano was not in the pitiful shape I imagined, and the luster appeared after we applied some tender loving care. With the various pieces found and replaced, restoring the look of a fine piece of musical furniture was not a difficult task.

Piano returned, we said farewell as we headed south and the stragglers left northwards. It would be difficult to forget K.C. waving to us as he stood on the tarmac road hitching a ride from a passing lorry. There he stood, in his costumed finery as a dazzling cleric. He had managed to 'borrow' a bishop's regalia, complete with embroidered cape and miter, the arch shaped pointed hat, heavily embossed and glittering. Waving his staff and with a flurry of flowing garments, he disappeared into the lorry and was gone. You have to wonder what the African driver was thinking as he stopped for a bishop, hitching a ride in the early morning, unshaven and baggy eyed and with a thick Welsh accent. The road was left barren as the lorry struck off in a cloud of reeking diesel fumes, whisking the cardinal colored hitchhiker away.

WEEKEND GUESTS

Mugoiri was the focal point for our network of friends, and it was not unusual to have four or five guests on the weekend, sleeping in makeshift beds and sharing the food, which everyone would contribute to the cause. Mugoiri Secondary School despite its twelve miles off the main road was the half way point to Nairobi and had the stability of a married couple, which meant food and a welcome mat. We always accepted provisions cheerfully since the availability of most goods was tenuous at the best of times. I could shop in Kahuru, an African village in the foothills of the Aberdare Mountains three miles down the road, but the goods were extremely limited. Kimbo lard with wormy sacks of maize and beans were the staples. So as guests arrived, their foodstuffs were piled up in the communal kitchen to be shared by all. On several occasions we had entertained guests over the weekend and with their Sunday departure, it became clear that neither of us had ever met several of them who had been referred by mutual friends.

On one occasion K.C. arrived with a can of peaches as his contribution. The only problem was the can was impossible to open since it was crimped and caved in. He explained. Hitching a ride from his bush school in Kaheti, K.C. was picked up by an African couple in a Volkswagen Beetle, not the roomiest of vehicles at the best of times. He was stuffed into the rear seat amongst the goods going to market, his legs straddling a sack on the floor. Chatting away with his hosts, he thought he felt the sack move. Trying to disregard the burlap bag, it not only began to stir, it lunged at him and began to gnaw at his leg. Not wishing to appear ungrateful to his hosts, he chatted away with the driver and wife, straining a smile while kneeing the charging sack. Added to his dilemma was a crippling stench, which emanated from the mobile bundle. As a last resort, peaches in hand, he gave the squirming contents a mighty whack, eyes watering at the reeking odor, which now percolated throughout the car, all the while keeping up a polite conversation. Not responding to the blunt smacks of the peach can, he took up a position of defense and gave the heaving mass several weighty blows, fists clenched, legs spread eagle, vision cloudy with the smothering fumes.

As he left the car, gasping breathless thanks, the driver mentioned that he was driving to the market in Thika and expected a fine price for the pig he was hoping to sell. Battered can in hand, K.C. wished him luck secretly hopeful that the animal was still intact and marketable

On another occasion the crew from Kaheti arrived in their newly acquired school Beetle, back window missing with one of the fellows sticking out through the gaping hole, waving wildly as they pulled up. What got my attention were all the footprints on the inside of the roof. Apparently, on their return from Nairobi during the early hours, they were involved in a pile up. Their car turned upside down as it landed in a roadside ditch. No one was hurt and so the occupants up-righted the car, which was none the worse for wear, despite the dented roof and unusual footprints.

Mathew Mathew from Kerala in Southern India joined the staff at Mugoiri as a science teacher. Tall and mustached, with shiny black hair, his infectious grin was sure to be a winner with the students. He moved into the house below us and I looked forward to tasting authentic southern curry. We were becoming a confederacy of nations at Mugoiri, with Europe, the sub continent and North America represented on staff.

OCEAN SAFARIS

Together with some 'bush teaching' friends, we decided to travel to Malindi just north of Mombasa on the Indian Ocean. Maeve and I had been to Mombasa and had heard about the sleepy village called Malindi nestled on the seashore, a little known destination at the time. We rented a four-bedroom house on the beach, next to the Adamsons' of 'Born Free,' for the tidy sum of about $12.00 per day. With my Land Rover jammed with bodies and luggage we made the 325-mile safari from Nairobi to the Indian Ocean on a leached mud road where the elephants having dusted themselves with the reddish soil looked garish and used the 'road' as a convenient thoroughfare. Needless to say, the elephant had the right of way and as we waited for them to pass, sang a popular tune, 'A Whiter Shade of Pale,' where one line in the song tells of a sixteen vestal women, heading for the shore.

The crew in Malindi

Malindi was best known for the column left behind by the explorer Vasco da Gama who in 1497 was the first European to circumnavigate the world. The marker stood in an overgrown field a short distance from the water. There was little else for the tiny village to offer except the few tourist hotels where the menus were in German and a small open-air market which offered local provisions. A few miles outside of town where our secluded beachfront house was located, the beauty of the Indian Ocean and the forest cover that hinged the seashore was nothing short of spectacular. The house was built on the sand with a wide porch and inside a large kitchen next to a spacious living room led down a hallway with bedrooms on either side. The walls in these rooms only went up to about eight feet to create an open-air affect so the slightest breeze could pass through unobstructed. Kitchen help was included in the price of the rental and so we had a gentleman on board who would sort out the fresh catch the fishermen would dump on our porch early each morning for our daily meals.

Delivering our fresh fish each morning

Despite the daily catch we were offered on the front porch, it was still necessary to shop in town for fresh produce and the like. We teamed up with a cooking partner whose name we drew from a hat and we were then responsible for that day's shopping and cooking. Off to town we would trek, baskets in hand and with a list of the items we would usually find in the African market. Dress was informal to say the least since swimsuits seemed to cover most occasions except when we were off to town and the marketplace. Then it was appropriate to wrap a kikoi around the waste and barefooted, top it off with an Arab fez. On one such jaunt along with my cooking partner, we headed down the baked road and once in town crossed the field where da Gama's etched stone column recorded his achievements. As I passed by the marker I could distinctly hear an English speaking voice declare, 'Here's one now! Quick take a picture before he sees us.' There before me was the ubiquitous zebra stripped mini tour van with tourists from Nairobi hiding behind enormous zoom lenses. Now, besides my waste bound kikoi and colorful fez, my full beard was out of control and so I must have appeared unusual and fit the description of the local inhabitant. As the cameras clicked away, the guide would hasten to tell his charges to be careful in the event I became aware of the photo shoot and become upset. I might even demand money. And so I decided to have some fun as I stroked the column in wonder, tugged at my beard in consternation and suddenly turn to face the mini van and grimace a fearful scowl. The cameras would disappear and the passengers would look sheepishly about, while some busied themselves with a bothersome fingernail. No sooner would I return to my examination of the stone marker, than the cameras would once again zoom in and click away. I did this several times until my partner who had walked ahead, waved me on to follow. The equatorial sun was hot and the mini van was soon off to capture more of the indigenous creatures of Malindi.

Maeve and Bert on sands of Malindi

The golden sand we walked each day, stretched for miles, unbroken and untouched. We were alone except for the chattering forest monkeys and the occasional leopard track we spotted on the beach. Monkey is a favorite of the leopard. One evening, after our nightly entertainment hour, which everyone took turns providing for the group, we spotted a huge marine turtle on the beach just outside an open window. She had dug a hole and deposited at least seventy-five oval shaped leathery eggs which she then laboriously struggled to cover with her hind legs. Her eyes teared over in an effort to keep them from drying up. It was decided that she needed help on her return to the water, so we all heaved and pushed and led her to the sanctuary she called home. The next morning we noticed that the entire beach was heaving with these mounds of covered eggs. It is sad to note only a desperate few of the newly hatched turtles will ever join their mother in the vastness of the Indian Ocean and to return one day to the very same patch of sand where they were born and deposit future generations of marine turtles.

It was on a return trip from Malindi that I found K.C. Jones alongside of me as my sole passenger. We planned to travel Kenya's remote N.F.D. where we would meet up with Maeve. She would leave Malindi in several days and once in

A TOUCH OF AFRICA

Nairobi, catch a ride to the north with the Flying Doctor organization that left on weekly missions to Kenya's isolated northern province. These same doctors told us tales of performing operations in the bush using only the lights from a nearby Land Rover. Since it would take Maeve only hours to fly from Nairobi to South Horr, K.C. and I had to leave two days earlier to be present on her arrival with the doctor who would drop her off and carry on to another outpost.

When K.C. and I arrived in Nairobi we decided to eat before carrying on with our two-day safari north. We ended up at a pub called the 'Dambusters,' named after the famous sortie during World War II. Once inside and to the delight of K.C. there in one corner was a piano, covered in dust and waiting. Without the least hesitation, K.C. the 'iron lung basher' from Wales was soon hammering out a tune as the seated customers forgot their meals and joined in the raucous song. The owner of the pub, a Scotsman called Ian was over in a flash with a hardy handshake and frosty beer to welcome the piano player. K.C. indicated to him that I was his 'mate' and we soon had food and beer flowing on behalf of the delighted bar owner. Ian was an original and one of the remaining famous R.A.F. fighter pilots who wrecked havoc on the German installations during one of the wars most daring bombing missions.

Over the years we all became friends with Ian and his son and on weekends, when it was possible to get out of the backcountry during the dry season, we would head for the Dambusters. Ian who was always gracious made accommodations available for us in a converted granary of sorts, where beds were available on a first come basis. We met many remarkable travelers who decided to stay awhile in Nairobi as they trekked across Africa. One young fellow stayed for two years and when he finished reading 'Gone With the Wind,' he left the book on the table and disappeared without a trace. This was the time of the Beatles and Nairobi and the Dambusters rocked with an eclectic crowd and our English buddies, most of whom were musicians, some from Liverpool, held their own with even the most famous groups of the mid sixties. Upon their eventual return to London, one band had a serious following of groupies. It was a time for music and friends and the Dambusters was a welcomed relief from the isolation of the lonely backcountry.

A LADY FROM YORKSHIRE

I struggled with indecision as to whether to include in my story, our time with Maureen Thompson from Yorkshire, England. It is a tragic one. Maureen arrived as the new teacher at Mugoiri and with Breda Sherwin, moved into the other half of our attached house on the hill. A stunning blonde with a distinctive Yorkshire accent, Maureen was an instant celebrity. Her wit won her over with everyone she met and her kindness and dedication as a teacher was evident to all. She was a welcomed addition to Mugoiri and for Maeve and Breda. Many a night we spent sharing stories and good cheer. One weekend, our staff attended a conference in Nyeri. Our group was joined with other 'bush' teachers from the area and we all sat around in a circle under the shade of a spreading flame tree while the guest speaker droned on and on. I sat next to Maureen. Across from us, an extremely large and corpulent fellow, stuffed into a pair of khaki shorts, bulged and heaved, sweat everywhere, leaving map-like stains all over the poor fellow's shirt. It was obvious he had made the supreme effort while struggling to get into his bursting pants, which revealed his every contour, with the most unfortunate clarity. We all tried not to stare, as our colleague in front of us appeared to be melting in the stifling heat, his color deepening before our fixed eyes. This gargantuan was impossible to ignore as he sagged like a melting candle, lower and lower. Maureen could no longer resist the temptation and with her dry sense of humor, leaned over and whispered, 'I think I'm going to have a bad thought!'

Our Dutch contingent of friends had a house in nearby Murang'a town where two nurses and Gerard, a volunteer engineer lived together. It was Gerard who was responsible for our murky water coming from the upstream coffee factory in the foothills. Gerard was single and it soon became apparent that he and Maureen were a 'number,' as Breda would say. Our times together were always an event and the couple announced their intentions to get married, surprising no one.

One weekend, our guest was K.C. Jones and after a late night with Maureen, Gerald, Breda, and Maeve, I remembered on the Saturday morning, that I had chores in Murang'a. Meanwhile, the engaged couple was preparing to take off to Nairobi to decide on outfits for their upcoming wedding. I offered a ride to K.C. as the Nairobi bound Beetle disappeared ahead of us with Breda in the back seat. Maeve decided to stay behind in Mugoiri. Cruising along the dusty Mugoiri road with K.C., I approached a rise. There had been a mishap. On a small hill a crushed Volkswagen Beetle was off to one side twisted and silent. In the middle of the road, a Land Rover sat steaming with front-end damage. Gerard was pacing back and forth, a huge lump rising from his forehead, eyes glazed, all the while talking gibberish.

Breda, along with a young African boy they had picked up on the way, sat very still in the rear seat of the car. On the side of the road, Maureen lay motionless and bruised but looking peaceful with her long hair falling about her shoulders. She was dead.

The next few days were traumatic for all of us. Gerard was hospitalized in Murang'a, and remained incoherent. Breda with a broken pelvis and nose suffered quietly in her bed, and the African boy they had picked up on the way, died of his injuries. The headmistress and I made the funeral arrangements, which included a hasty trip to Nyeri to pick up a wooden box. Maeve kept Gerard who was delirious, under control while she worked with the doctor in realigning Breda's nose. The niceties, which take place after death in our society were absent. There was no funeral director to assume responsibilities. Death in Africa is raw and bleak. A funeral mass was said the next day in the local church at Murang'a, a church depressing and shadowy, surrounded by towering trees, a church which had lost the battle for sunlight.

Maureen was buried in the gloom, a graveyard in a clearing of dense vegetation. Now the story continues as Gerard, weeks later, chisel in hand, chipped away at a piece of stone in an effort to make a worthy marker for his beloved Maureen. Being a man of conscience, he felt it necessary to fly to Yorkshire, England and visit the Thompson family, in order to give them an accounting of the accident. The following was told to me. Gerard arrived, found the house, and knocked on the door, which was opened by an elderly gentleman, Mr. Thompson. He was Maureen's 'most favorite person in the world,' as she would often say to us about her dad. Gerard introduced himself and immediately found he was standing alone on the front porch, door closed in his face. The next morning, Gerard thought he should try once more before he returned to Kenya and when he approached the house for a second time, he noticed a wreath on the door. Mr. Thompson had died during the night, suffering a fatal stroke.

Weeks later, Mrs. Thompson arrived in Mugoiri from England. The headmistress introduced me. Maureen's mother was in Kenya to make proper arrangements for her deceased daughter. She rejected both Gerard and the handmade gravestone. She would do it right and proper.

TARZAN

Several miles before Nairobi, near the town of Thika was a relaxing stop for travelers. An English inn called The Blue Post Hotel, just off the highway, was quaint and correct. Drinks were served on the outdoor patio and we could watch the traffic to Nairobi in front of us and wonder at the thick undergrowth in the back. Behind this undergrowth, a noisy waterfall spilled over a rocky ledge. In fact, there were several falls next to one another. It was a picturesque setting for a picnic even if it was a long drive from our school in Mugoiri. We had memorable times together with friends, eating our sandwiches, while we lay on our blankets, watching the water tumble and fall before it turned into mist in the eddies below.

The innkeeper told me that several Hollywood Tarzan movies were filmed here, using the falls as a backdrop. It was here that my childhood hero had wrestled crocs and swam beneath hippo, only to be confronted with a twenty-foot water python, his dagger slashing away. It was here that the African porters, under heavy loads, crossed the treacherous currents as the white Bwanas shouted their orders. Meanwhile, Cheeta swinging from branches was always getting into mischief, whilst Boy and Jane were secure in their tree house with Tarzan keeping their world warm and safe.

The setting used by Hollywood to make Tarzan movies

Looking at the serene setting, I was unable to see the crocs or hippo of my youth, while twenty-foot pythons were only on celluloid and the African porters were now serving tea and the heavily loaded elephants were the fuming lorries on the tarmac, racing for Nairobi. The tree house was nowhere to be seen and most of the Bwanas had left Kenya long ago. I was to find my childhood Africa, in the years ahead. I found my crocs and my hippos, my elephant and even a sixteen-foot python. I also found vestiges of the Bwanas, still shouting humiliation, as they desperately clung to their yesterdays.

A SINGING SHEPHERD

Part of my teaching duties at Mugoiri was to invigilate exams at the end of the school year. I was asked to supervise at an elementary school where students would, under a tremendous amount of pressure, write what amounted to an exam, which would determine their path for the rest of their lives. Without an honorable pass, secondary school and further education would come to an abrupt halt. It was the 'Russian Roulette' of the academic world at a very young age, a do or die situation. Parents, siblings, relatives and neighbors all played a role in the students' formation up to this crucial entrance exam. Tension hung like the humidity, as I pulled up with my Land Rover, sealed exams in my briefcase fresh from the District Education Office.

Students, teachers and family members standing in silent groups eyed my briefcase as I left my Land Rover. The school so typical of the countryside was built by the local people from their lean resources upon heeding the cry from their President for 'Harambe' or a pulling together as one. Walls of mud enclosed a wooden frame, topped with a corrugated tin roof. Education was the vehicle out. A teacher was hired or fired by the parents since tenure depended upon the results of this decisive final exam. The stillness of the gathering left me feeling awkward and for some reason, responsible for the tension. As I walked by the small groups, several familiar faces nodded, eyes, all the while, fixed on the exams. Inside the school, the mud floors were damp with water to keep the chiggers at bay. Students had their compulsory Kimbo lard can filled with water sitting at their desks, ready to sprinkle the dusty floor as the day wore on. Without the benefit of electricity, long shadows filled the anxious atmosphere. It was an edgy place to be. The expectant students, like the shadows on the walls, filed in behind me, silent, heads down, eyes darting and fretful. Once seated at their homemade wooden desks, pencils poised and erasers ready, the exams were handed out, the cards for their future having been dealt.

As the students wrote away, I found myself in a dreamy state, fully relaxed and drowsy, windows open, an occasional breeze quaffing in the smells of Africa, while listening to the rubbing of busy insect wings, telling of their presence beneath patches of green. The passing of the occasional shepherd, who tended his bawling flock, singing a doleful requiem, completed the day. This herder and his drifting refrain sent melodies through the room. This was Africa, and what a woeful dirge, the herder sang. Oh, to understand Kikuyu I thought, as I mused at the echoing refrain.

Some months later, I recounted that dreamy time in the foothills of the Abedare Mountains, remembering the serenity of the day, listening to the soul of Africa. My Kikuyu friend Gerard, listened to my reminiscing and asked me if I recalled the shepherd. I thought it a strange question since I didn't even remember the name of the school. The shepherd was well known to everyone in the area except me. He was non other than the school's principal, who in his laments for tenure that afternoon had been singing out the curriculum to the eager ears of his students, as well as entertaining the dreamy muzungo, who languidly waxed in the splendors of Africa. The fellow was desperate to insure his job.

BUSH TELEGRAPH

A truly amazing phenomenon challenged my beliefs...bush telegraph. Simply put, bush telegraph is magic. Messages are transmitted over long distances without the benefit of mechanical means or so I was led to believe. As a normal skeptic, when evidence becomes a trade off for common sense or tangible proof, I was convinced that I had clearly missed the obvious and spent a lot of time looking.

A few examples of bush telegraph should be enough to illustrate the point. Maeve and I, alone in our house on the hill and late at night ready for bed might decide to make a spontaneous and unscheduled safari to Nairobi early the next morning. Up and out of the house at seven or eight, I would find several local Africans packed and ready and asking for a ride to Nairobi as we drove down the driveway to the dusty road which lead to the Nairobi tarmac. I never thought much of this but the pattern repeated itself several times, and then many times thereafter. I began to take note. City clothes, goods packed in reed baskets and wearing one's best shoes was not a coincidence. On other normal mornings, walking to class, I never saw a group waiting for a ride.

It was decided that we would hire a house girl to maintain our lives with some semblance of normalcy. On the day we decided to interview help, the applicants were lined up outside our front door. Maybe we had inadvertently mentioned our intentions to the other staff members or the headmistress. We do not recall saying however, when we would hire.

South Horr and an isolated river laga, is a distant place. It was in such a laga that we encountered a pride of lion and were very fortunate to have avoided a serious mishap. Now we were back to Kikuyu land and to Mugoiri, without any means of communication having taken place. Our first chance meeting was with a friend who enquired about our near mishap with man-eating lion in that remote part of Africa. He shrugged off my question when I asked how he had heard about the ordeal. He had heard the story from a local African.

I am still baffled at the series of coincidences and at the same time frustrated to have missed the obvious and what was probably a simple explanation to bush telegraph.

THE SERENGETI

Deep inside N'Goro N'Goro crater, adjacent to the popular Serengeti Plains in Tanzania, animal spotting was effortless. Inside this sunken volcano top, encircled within a two hundred mile rim, many hundreds of meters high

A TOUCH OF AFRICA

roamed rhino, zebra, all the plains animals, gaping hippos, wild hunting dogs and the ever-present slinking hyena. Also present were the big cats. Over forty thousand animals call this home. I had guests from Canada on a two-week safari and the caldera was one of our destinations. A Land Rover was necessary to climb over the sharp edge and into the world's largest unbroken crater. Now as a Canadian, I knew how to drive on icy pavement but nothing had prepared me for the unassuming black cotton soil of East Africa. Black cotton soil seduced you until you were hopelessly bogged down.

It wasn't long before I was thoroughly stuck, having paid too much attention to game watching and not enough to the trackless plain. I abandoned my guests in the Land Rover and crawled under the vehicle and settled on my back into the oozing muck. This was not a wise move since I knew better than to leave the safety of my vehicle but predators do not associate gasoline and other fumes with an eatable meal, so I believed. While under the Land Rover, pushing branches and rocks under the wheels for traction, I noticed a shadow pass over my protruding legs as I lay sprawled on my back. All I could see were the powerful legs of the legendary black maned Serengeti lion as he passed by, pausing momentarily, before carrying on. Two miserable boots covered in mud did not appeal to him. The lion becomes all the more awesome without the protection of steel bars or a cage. This animal deserves everyone's attention.

Lion on a kill under Mt. Kilimanjaro

When I finally got out of the sticky mess, I continued on with my tour around this amazing Eden, guests safely sitting in the back of the Land Rover, cameras clicking away. Now the rhino, second in size only to the elephant, snorting in the wind, a stabbing horn of hardened hair announcing an ever-present challenge, was always worthy of a picture of two. Here lives the prehensile lipped black rhino that dines on thorn bushes, which no doubt accounts for its nasty disposition. There is also the enormous white rhino, males tipping the scales at four thousand pounds or more. The white rhino named for its wide mouth used for mowing vegetation, is a misnomer because the Boers of South Africa referred to the animal as 'vide,' an attempt at the word 'wide' and in turn misinterpreted as the word 'white' by the British.

Spotting a female rhino called Gertie, who was well known because of her enormous horn, standing with her blunt faced calf, I approached as my guests in the back readied their cameras. It seems I got too close and kicking up the turf, she charged like a freight train that was already late. I spun away, quite confident that I could out distance her as she jerked her horn upwards, trying to hook the back of the Land Rover. My guests squealed in excitement. As the irritated female pounded closer, my speed became noticeably slower and my guests, noticeably quieter. I was being forced into a swampy area, losing speed as I prayed that it wasn't black cotton soil. It was tense until suddenly, the rhino gave up as abruptly as she had started, wheeled around, and ponderously high stepped away, her blunt nosed offspring nudging her side. My guests found N'Goro N'Goro crater exciting.

Inside N'Goro N'goro crater with an angry rhino

Crawling in four wheel drive out of the crater, you immediately became aware of the unending expanse before you, leaving the fabulous Serengeti Plains far behind. It was on a previous safari that the jarring of the Land Rover, at least I like to think so, caused one of my fillings to loosen. I spat it out, leaving a gaping hole in my back molar. Only later did I laugh at the incident since I realized I was in Dr. L.S.B.Leakey territory, and the fossil rich area of Oduvai Gorge, where this famous paleontologist and his wife Mary set out the ground rules for man's origin with their spectacular discoveries on early man. How would the scientist ever explain a filling from a molar nestled amongst the fossil rich rock and where would it fit within the framework of evolution?

JACK FARREL

Nanyuki was renown for several reasons, one being the sign, which read, 'HIPPOS HAVE THE RIGHT OF WAY,' as you neared the town and another indicating you were on the equator. William Holden, whom I had refused water in the N.F.D, owned the world's most exclusive and private resort, 'The Safari Club.' It was said that the Club admitted only five members, one of whom was Sir Winston Churchill. Sun glassed celebrities paid dearly to roam the manicured lawns and eat in five star dining quarters, while it was not uncommon for guests to be invited out on an elephant hunt under the suntanned, scrutiny of a 'white hunter.' Such was life of the rich and famous.

I was most intrigued by a particular establishment on the side of the tarmac, which sat opposite the colorful sign, which read, 'THE EQUATOR' showing the world with a red line circling the center of the globe at zero degrees. Inside this popular inn filled with locals, was a bar across the back of the room, behind which a not so friendly bartender served his brews. It was the white painted line, which was most conspicuous, however. From the front door as you entered, across the floor, up the front of the bar, across the top and over the bar, down the back and up again on the far wall, this white line indicated the two hemispheres. In other words, one could stand at the bar, order a drink in the southern hemisphere and have it served from the northern hemisphere. A long way to go for a drink, the uninitiated might say.

It was Freddie Seed, professional hunter, sometime game warden assistant, who lived in Nanyuki who introduced me to Jack Farrel on our way to the Uaso Nyiro River and our camp. Freddie had suggested a brief visit as we passed the Farrel homestead, a piecemeal timbered dwelling, which had long since felt the caress of a paintbrush. Bleached and tired, the building sat in the full glare of the equatorial sun, far from the disapproving eyes of the former colonialists.

Hearing our Land Rover pull up, Jack Farrel pushed open the remains of a screen door and stuck out a weathered hand. He cut a remarkable figure. Overalls, with one shoulder strap dangling down, stretched over a lean frame of six or more feet. Pulled over his head was a well-used russet colored felt hat, round on top with a stained and drooping rim. I think these hats were popular with the Hatfields and McCoys from the Ozark Mountains in the southern U.S.A. It was his beard, however, that got my attention. It was surely the most unruly growth I'd ever seen. This crop of hair, having been left to its own devices, hung nearly two feet, ending in wispy strands. Warm blue eyes, welcoming and alert, were also a distinguishing feature and difficult to ignore.

We were ushered into the cabin and seated at a rough table. Beer was set down before us and I was offered a drinking glass. This vessel was unique since it was missing a large V shaped chunk on one side and only a third of it could be filled, not withstanding that a drink from the wrong side could cause a serious lip injury. Jack had begun his travels as a young man from New Zealand and throughout the years found himself in the British Calvary, saddles being a favorite topic, and eventually road building and prospecting in Alaska. Kenya had become a permanent stopover.

The house lacked partitions and leaned toward the open concept look. A long legged bed was fixed against one wall and to my left was a collapsed chesterfield. A woman, with her back to us, worked over a sink, which was held up by a rusty drainpipe. She stood quietly over her chores and I recognized her as Masaai. During our visit she never approached the table nor did Jack feel the need to introduce her. I had noticed several very handsome young boys outside as they shouted after a heavy bottomed honking goose. At the time, Jack had been married for many years, happy and settled and ostracized from the 'white' community.

He told us of his efforts at cattle ranching and the conversation turned to the marauding lion of the area causing constant grief with their nightly prowling. The lion had recently killed two of his steers. Jack talked with ease and with an assurance of a man who fit into the place he found himself in. He was rich in the goods he could do without. He talked of elephant and the buffalo, which roamed the Uaso Nyiro River area, our camp for several weeks to come. He for one was unconcerned about the buffalo competing for grass with his herd. He never mentioned leopard. Jack recounted a hilarious story for us, which took place several nights previously.

Jack's neighbor needed subduing. (I was amazed that he had neighbors at all since his cabin looked like the last chance motel.) Alone, with only the assistance of several Africans, lived a wealthy Italian bachelor in a grand house secluded in the bush, not two miles away and rarely seen by outsiders. His drinking habits were notorious and completely out of control and his wealthy industrialist parents had bought him seclusion far away from the gossiping crowds of Europe. He was maintained with a handsome allowance on the condition he stayed away, far away. This gentleman had the reputation for running wild and shooting up the 'neighborhood' while naked and gloriously drunk. Upon falling to the ground, he would be the object of still another search party, dragged home and put to bed. His recent drinking spree was more of a concern than usual and his bodyguards turned to Jack for help. Jack found him, heaved him shoulder high, and carried him home and to bed under the watchful eyes of his anxious staff. Freddie Seed and I thanked our host for his hospitality and headed off towards our Uaso Nyiro camp, richer for having met Jack Farrel.

Several months later, I was invited back to Jack's homestead to hunt Impala for my African students. It was a weekend affair and I brought my friend K.C. Jones along. Not wanting to arrive in the dark, K.C. and I pulled up to the cabin, one late Friday afternoon. I remembered the lone bed and brought my own sleeping gear. I needn't have bothered. A teenage lad walked up to my Land Rover and directed us to his father. After several wrong turns, we found our host in the lower pasture. Jack who sat in his Land Rover welcomed us, hat pushed high and relaxed. His blue-black rifle barrel lay across his lap. In front of his Land Rover, milled a herd of cattle, enclosed in a thorn bush boma. Outside the boma, several warriors sat around an open fire, spears pointing skywards. It was dusk.

Jack in his astuteness answered our curious looks. He couldn't remember the last time he had slept indoors. The Land Rover was his bed and his cattle and warrior ranch hands were his company each night. He invited me to pull my Land Rover along side and get comfortable. I had ceased to be shocked in Africa and getting comfortable, settled in for a chilly evening, wrapped in bedding. K.C. was somewhat concerned about the sleeping arrangements, but managed to keep warm as he wound himself in blankets.

Jack was at his best that evening. He told tales of foot safaris and the N.F.D. to which I could now relate. Chilling tales of stalking lion ran far into the night driving home the fact that we were there supposedly protecting his cattle from those very same cousins in his stories. At one point, I remember a lull in the conversation and Jack disappearing under the folds of his old felt hat. I also remember Jack asking us to listen for lion during the night. I decided then and there, that's all I would do, listen.

The next morning, burnt coffee and a brisk handshake with pointed directions, saw us off. I managed to get two Impala for the school and one for Jack's pot as he requested. One memorable event was how I inadvertently left K.C. in awe. As a resident of Kenya, I qualified and passed a rigorous examination for my hunting license taken in Nairobi after weeks of study. And as a resident, I was issued a book, wherein was recorded, the restricted number of bullets I was allowed each year. The government demanded strict control. Bullets were precious and not to be wasted. Early that morning with K.C. in tow, I approached a waterhole and spotting a large herd of male Impala took aim. When the dust settled, before us lay two male Impala. K.C. rubbed his eyes and I did my best to keep a straight face. The Impala were standing in line with one another and appeared as one. Without the benefit of any explanation, I muttered something about ammunition being rationed and that one had to conserve each round. I tried hard at keeping my composure and a poker face. My reputation soared amongst my friends as K.C. told and retold the story as I quietly went about my business, furthering my reputation still as my modesty forbade discussion about my awesome abilities in the field while conserving ammunition.

An Impala male

THE PEACE CORP

Don Carr was an American Peace Corp volunteer. He had heard about the Canadians and one Saturday morning, accompanied by two Kikuyu boys from his secondary school, paid a visit. The trio had walked some dozen miles, a route which took them over several rivers, and one that required them to straddle a shaky log, the other leaving them wet, waist high. We were pleased to welcome them and it was obvious, Don was a very lonely young fellow. Peace Corp volunteers were forbidden to own a vehicle in Kenya and usually lived in the most miserable surroundings. The Africans wondered why these rich people from America lived so poorly, since they themselves strove to live like Americans and consequently, were suspicious of them. We wondered at this apparent contradiction, too.

It was Don who told us the story of a fellow volunteer who had vacation time coming to him but was stuck with his pet, a ten-foot python. I imagine he was looking for a snake sitter, the thought of which made me recoil. Unable to find a sitter for the snake, and not wanting to miss a safari to Mombasa, he decided to solve the problem himself. Emptying his propane fridge, he stuffed the serpent inside and off he went for two weeks. Upon his return, he removed the well-chilled reptile, placed it in the sun and by nightfall his pet was ready for a live mouse. (Another tale we heard was about the Kikuyu family whose ceiling collapsed and a very large constrictor fell to the floor. Apparently the python had lived in the rafters for some time, feasting on bats and had grown fat and eventually too heavy. It is rare for Kikuyu huts to have ceilings). I had a soft spot for the Peace Corp volunteers who always seemed to be unappreciated while doing tremendous work without much trust from the local people. Our two African teaching colleagues kept Maeve and me at a healthy arm's distance in the staff room upon our arrival in Kenya. It was only after we were identified as Canadians that the atmosphere became relaxed and friendly. Living amongst fields of corn and banana trees, dotted with mud huts, didn't seem worthy of any covert operations.

IT'S A SMALL WORLD AFTER ALL

We met Stephen, son of Chief Ignatius our neighbor in Mugoiri, on a dark and blistery night. Stephen tumbled into our living room, muddy, soiled and very wet. Introducing himself as our neighbor, several shambas away, he proceeded to recite a soliloquy from, 'The Merchant of Venice.' Stephen was very drunk. He likened his father to Shylock and stammered away, telling us of his misery. His unhappiness it seemed was because he had been trained for anything but to assume responsibility of the Chief's extensive land holdings. Stephen was nearly asleep in the puddle he brought in. He was bitter, cared little for himself, and beneath the portrayal of an angry young man was a sensitive and very humorous character.

Over time he became a frequent visitor. Chief Ignatius was a kindly old man and was at a loss with a son he never understood. Stephen regressed steadily and near the end was caught sniffing gasoline. Stephen had been an overseas student and held an excellent degree from the University of Toronto, some ninety miles from our home in Canada.

WANDERING IN LAKE NAKURU

I had no idea why I accepted an invitation to a buffalo hunt given the state of affairs at the time. Having contacted a 'bug,' I went paralyzed. Exactly one half of my body went numb for six weeks. The ailment affected me right down the middle, and a line from head to toe marked the boundary. It was amazing because even half of my nose was numb, while the other half was normal. Some diagnosed it as black swamp fever, others, a disgruntled neuralgic nerve. I do remember pulling off numerous ticks I had picked up in the long grasses because the hair on my legs made it easy for them to cling on and get a firm hold as they burrowed inwards. The Africans' hairless legs were a distinct advantage. I was treated with a case of cortisone, which I obtained from a bush dispensary and took daily injections for six weeks. At the time, I never knew the serious consequences of stopping cortisone injections abruptly.

Arriving at the designated meeting place, a rancher who had offered his expertise as a hunter of big game, greeted us with a no nonsense attitude. The Game Department had given him permission to cull buffalo on his land. A mutual friend had invited us along. Out we marched into the low bush. I can't imagine the picture I presented since in order to see down the gun barrel, I had to close one eye. However, due to my paralysis, I needed help to keep that one eye closed. Taking a long black scarf, I wrapped it around half of my head, covering the open eye and using the other one to see. A swash-buckling sword would have completed the picture as we marched off through the heavy undergrowth, all the while dodging fresh buffalo droppings.

Once again, and still a rookie in Africa, our trusted leader took us into buffalo lie ups and once again we survived without a mishap. We saw evidence of recent activity all around and knew we were on the right track but returned late that day, empty-handed. It was just as well since the excitement was in the tracking and the suspense of the African bush. You never knew what was behind the next turn. I think back and have come to the conclusion that it was probably my appearance that frightened off the game. It would have been most interesting to see our host use his rifle. The poor man had had a misfortune several years back. He was cleaning his rifle and accidentally blew his right arm completely off. I wondered the whole time how he would manage a charging Cape buffalo. So there we were, me with my head wrapped like a dauntless pirate and our one armed intrepid leader pushing his way forward and ever onwards.

JOHN THE COOK

K.C. Jones and Tony Smith were the two main characters at Kaheti, another bush school, located close to the one bus-stop village and some five miles off the tarmac road. Kaheti Secondary School was the main attraction. Living the bachelors' lifestyle had its obvious advantages but the solitary household in Kaheti needed serious attention. One of the immediate problems was the need for a steady source of protein and someone to cook it. Secondly, the house itself was a calamity and in great need of a thorough overhaul. The living room still contained remnants of a recent open fire where a party got out of control and ended up with the local administrator and his wife, roasting a goat. Even the neighboring beasts of burden claimed a familiarity with the dwelling. Having taken refuge in a bedroom one afternoon, I was just about asleep when behind me, through the open window, the enormous head of a Jerusalem donkey materialized, gave a mighty bray followed with a stifling wave of bad breath and disappeared. Needless to say sleep was somewhat tenuous after that. It was the kitchen, however, which was in need of an urgent refurbishing.

There was a stove somewhere under a pile of paraphernalia, next to a shaky wooden table and a couple of chairs, which looked dangerously in need of repair. A box-sized fridge, which was often used to store non-perishables long forgotten, door open, was against the wall. Taking a look at their deteriorating surroundings, decisive action was called for immediately. K.C. and Tony let it be known that they were in the 'household help' market, namely looking for a cook who would facilitate their return to a level of subsistence needed for their continued well being. Applicants arrived and one gentleman was selected.

John the cook presented formidable credentials. He had previously been in the employ of the former Governor Barring, the British representative of the Queen in Kenya before independence. John won the cook's job without a challenge. He also accepted the local salary much to their amazement. The much anticipated day arrived and John began his duties with a flourishing command. The purchase of a 'cock-hen' for eggs was urgent. He returned from market with a bird in hand and proceeded to secure it to the kitchen table leg with a long cord. His uniform, which consisted of an abandoned hat he picked up in his travels and the ubiquitous floor length army coat over knee high rubber boots, should have been an early clue for the bachelors. The resident chicken in the kitchen should have also raised some doubt or at least an eyebrow or two.

At first, dinner was eagerly anticipated according to K.C. It soon became evident however, that eggs cooked in a variety of ways, most days of the week, was going to be the rule. Meat on the menu was a rare commodity and often recalled with fond memories. What seized everyone's attention however, were the napkins. Now meals were always taken in the dining room, which was an area off to one side of the main living room. Each evening, the table setting was bejeweled with artistically folded creations. As the days wore on and dinnertime approached, the conversation invariably turned to table napkins. Could John possibly come up with still another creation? K.C. admitted that the butterfly was his favorite while Tony seemed to favor the swan. Each evening, John would surprise them once again with his seemingly inexhaustible command of the napkin.

It was a weekly routine for John to submit the household bills and each week, money was doled out to pay them. It was only after the charges rose to suspicious amounts that the items on the bills were scrutinized. Foremost charges were for the great quantities of meat they were paying for on a regular basis. It appeared that the bachelors were keeping at least on local butcher, fully employed. Other household items, which never passed the chicken or the kitchen stove, were brought to John's attention. It was fiscally imperative that John should be released before funds gave out. I have no idea how it was discovered, but John's duties for the former Governor General of Kenya came to light. Apparently, his sole responsibility at the mansion's table was confined to napkin preparation, a chore in which he had learned to excel. His reputation in the Governor's house went unchallenged. Colleagues held him in awe. My subsequent visits to Kaheti were never quite the same after John departed with the cock hen. The string however, remained as a reminder, dangling from the kitchen table leg, a memento of what could have been.

A PLACE TO LEAVE YOUR HEART

Years and years before the 1994 genocide, I found myself in Bujumbura, the capital of Burundi in central Africa. I recall having flown from the new airport in Tanzania called Kilimanjaro, with a gentleman from former Rhodesia, now Zimbabwe. He was interesting and knowledgeable in African affairs. I had been stranded at the airport while one aircraft was being cannibalized for parts in order to outfit the second. My destination was Kenya but because of the border issues with Tanzania, the two countries were not on good terms and so I had to fly into Nairobi from a neutral country, in this case Burundi. I was greeted at gunpoint in the Bujumbura airport and the film of my camera was unceremoniously ripped out of my camera. Not an auspicious beginning. I was planning to stay with a group who had a house a few miles from the capital. Despite my being sent by a friend of these people, the fellow in charge turned out to be weird. He left me standing in the sun while he scrutinized my passport and at the same time decided how much to charge me. I was forced to leave the house for a downtown hotel, riding in the back of an open truck, only after being embarrassed over my lack of interest in soccer and my likewise scant knowledge of Italy's winning of the World Cup. So far, Bujumbura was not very promising.

The Meridian on the Nile was the only hotel available, and although it was expensive, I was glad to be there. I bumped into my friend from the airplane and had coffee with him. It became clear why he was on such good terms with the military government and why he was whisked through at the airport, grinning broadly as he waved goodbye. He sold weapons. It would be several days before I could arrange a flight out to Nairobi and so I was fortunate meeting up with a young fellow, a self proclaimed guide, who assured me that he was the best in Bujumburu, an indication of his entrepreneurial enthusiasm. We left in his car, one held together by good will. Smiling at the eagerness of this young man, he turned out to be a treasure of knowledge and we had many laughs together.

We traveled the torturous route of the Arab slave traders, now a paved highway. This was a road, once lined with Africans, tied together and dragged from the heartland of the continent to the shores of Lake Tanganyika, a temporary stop on their way to far off fields of misery. Families were corralled in camps near the Lake and sorted out by the traders. Mothers would have children yanked away, while fathers watched helplessly as wife and offspring were separated and chained for the final march to the coast on the Indian Ocean and to their doom. The new world flowed with this disposable labor that was replaced from the seemingly inexhaustible heart of Africa. The Americas built empires on the backs of Africans. Besides the U.S.A., Brazil was a major importer of slaves who were used to fuel the sugar industry and still later the gold mines right into the nineteenth century. The plundering in human merchandise will forever be blight on the 'civilized' world.

I took a picture of the famous boulder, which marked the spot where the journalist Stanley meeting up with Livingstone proclaimed, 'Dr. Livingstone, I presume?' As I look at the photo before me, I can clearly read the inscription:

LIVINGSTONE
STANLEY
25-XI-1871

The rock where Stanley and Livingstone met

Some time later and on the other side of the Lake Tanganyika, in a remote settlement on the coast of the Indian Ocean, I came across a gazebo fashioned in marble, all mossy and rich in mould from the humidity. Lush undergrowth was choking the monument to Doctor Livingstone, who spent his life in Africa and survived crippling bouts of malaria and other fevers in addition to being dragged off by a lion. He had often told his African devotees that his heart would always be in Africa. Upon his death, the body was summoned to London for a national burial in Westminster Abbey. His faithful porters carried his body, wrapped in skins, across Africa, and many months later, they arrived at the coast across from the island of Zanzibar. Before they reached the coast however, they fulfilled the wishes of their beloved Doctor. They left his heart buried in this moss-covered gazebo, in a place called Bagamoya, 'a place to leave your heart.' It was also from 'a place to leave your heart,' that many African slaves saw their loved ones for the last time as they were being dragged off into the bowels of leaky, rat infested ships to suffer the horrors of slavery in a world distant, cold and foreign.

AND TODAY?

The Padre, Fr. Joseph Polet, who became a friend over the years, requested assistance in outfitting his secondary school library in Wamba, N.F.D. It was on a return visit to Kenya, that I was shown the empty cement block room escorted by a teaching Sister, Ivana Gay. I returned to Canada in September and managed, over the months, to beg a cargo container filled with suitable used text books, donated by a local school board. The plan was to return to Kenya the following summer as a family with Katharine and Christopher. The children had grown up listening to stories about Africa, so they were excited and the Padre was anxious to meet them.

It is an interesting story to relate how I obtained the books for the library in Wamba in the remote N.F.D. I returned from Kenya and in early September back in Canada, sitting in my kitchen when the telephone rang. A teacher who knew my brother Bob enquired if I had any use for an undisclosed number of secondary texts. Her son worked for a school board near Toronto and told her the board was about to shred thousands of books in order to purchase the latest editions. I seized the opportunity, and on the appointed day, drove to the board warehouse, met the son who graciously escorted me through rows upon rows of nearly new texts all neatly stacked on skids. I was to take as many as I needed since the remainder would be shredded. There was one condition. Since the books were stamped with the board's logo, I must promise not to dispose of them in a public dump where they could be traced. It would be political suicide for the board members if the tax paying public knew about the horrendous waste. Some of the expensive hard covered texts were brand new but not latest edition. The young man who also owned a pickup truck marked the texts I could use for Wamba and promised to deliver them to a friend's garage in downtown Toronto. Well I had the books, the first step in a long journey to the N.F.D. Back home the school semester began and as I was leaving the principal's office, having discussed my recent trip to Africa, a parent who was waiting outside the open office door recognized me as a teacher of one of her children. After a polite greeting she said she had overheard my conversation with the principal and the need for overseas surface transportation for the library books that were sitting in Toronto. Well her husband was in the freight forwarding business and getting the books to Mombassa would not be a problem. There would be no charge either since containers were readily available and the books were for a non-profit cause. I only had to get the texts to a particular warehouse on Toronto's waterfront. I immediately called my Toronto friend who said he would have the books transported from his garage the very next day. Several days later, he confirmed the delivery to the warehouse and said, as he was about to unload the books, several of the dockworkers recognized him and filled a container for him with the Africa bound library books. Now the port of Mombassa on the coast of the Indian Ocean is a formidable distance away from the N.F.D. Getting the texts inland would be a daunting challenge. I wrote to a friend in nearby Dar es Salaam in Tanzania and asked for suggestions regarding transporting the goods that would arrive in several months time. He wrote back and requested the arrival date and the relevant paperwork for the books. He had an Asian friend who owed him a favor. Delivery to Wamba would not be a problem! The entire episode went without a hitch and I sat back in amazement as each step fell effortlessly into place. I had to wonder at the generosity of people some who were complete strangers. I sure the Padre would have some thoughts about it.

I received the telegram in early December along with several follow up letters about the accident. Both the Padre and Ivana Gay, who were looking forward to the library books and our summer visit, were returning to the N.F.D. after shopping in Nairobi for their students' Christmas presents. Outside of Nanyuki, on the equator, a heavily loaded lorry swerved to avoid a pothole and crashed into the Padre and Ivana Gay. Both were killed instantly. Christmas presents for their students at Wamba lay scattered on the road. Katharine and Chris, Maeve and I, arrived in Kenya five months later and as promised, I set up the library in Wamba. I visited the gravesite and also saw the remains of the mangled Land Rover I had traveled in so often, twisted and caved in. With the Padre gone, so was a piece of my Africa.

The Roscoes, Adrian and Janice have a family of four, three beautiful girls and a handsome boy. Wilma and Julian have followed their parent's lead and have made their home in Africa. When I first met Adrian in Canada, he had just arrived from Nigeria with Julian their infant son and Janice, his wife, who was down with a dose of recurring malaria. Africa became a reality. Years later, after their tour in Kenya, Malawi, and New Zealand, and then back to South Africa with a brief stint at an American university, the family continues their worldly adventures. Today, Adrian lectures in Oman and maintains his reputation as a scholar and a prolific author. He is also a catalyst for budding writers. During one of their stints in North America, the Roscoes became godparents to our son, Christopher.

K.C. Jones, our Welsh piano basher ended up on the Costa del Sol in Spain after he said goodbye to us as we boarded our flight home from Nairobi. He managed to survive robbers and bandits and was detained in Angola during their civil war as he hitched hiked around the continent. Once in Spain, he met up with several of his countrymen and enjoyed life on the Costa del Sol for two years. Finally home in Wales, he met Heather and had a family of four who like their dad became travelers. We have had reunions in Wales, and

Ireland, Canada and Spain. Our Welsh piano basher eventually left Wales and played the world. He entertained across Europe, the U.S.S.R., America and Hawaii. In Toronto, at a local pub, he increased business so much that the owner called me for months, hoping I could convince K.C. to return.

Alan Butler, alias 'Cumberland Al' from Cumbria, remained in Kenya after us. He met up with Eleanor and upon his return to the U.K., made his home in East Finchley, London. Upon retiring, Al returned to his roots in Cumbria and following his passion, became a playwright and has successfully entertained on stage while one of his achievements was the translation of 'MacBeth' back to its original language of Cumbrian.

Tony Smith the principal from Kaheti School met Teresa in Kenya. They came to Africa from the U.K. They married and migrated to Canada. Tony completed his graduate studies and made a successful career in the telecommunication industry while Teresa pursued her keen interests in anthropology. They reside in Allen, Texas and will soon be retired. They will return to Canada and live near their daughter in British Columbia.

Gerard our Dutch engineer and coffee man eventually returned to the Netherlands and married. He sent us a wedding invitation, which startled me. There was a photo of Gerard and his new fiancée, holding hands, and running through a garden. The likeness to Maureen was startling, and I found it difficult to imagine it wasn't her. With a grown family, Gerard has stayed for the most part, in the Low Countries, and although I have never seen him since our days together in Kenya, my thoughts go back to that fateful Saturday morning on the dusty Mugoiri road.

Breda returned to Ireland and we have kept tabs on one another over the years. We have exchanged visits and remember Kenya fondly, despite the tragedies we shared. She retired as a French teacher in Dublin after marrying Frank, a gentle man and have one son, Patrick. Breda became our daughter Katharine's godmother and over the years she has remembered her with gifts and kindness. Katharine has developed a close relationship with Breda and they exchange visits, Katharine to Dublin and Breda to Barcelona.

Greg Filo, from Murang'a who showed so much patience with me as a rookie and who had given me a traditional African send off of roasted goat, died after a serious car accident soon after we left for Canada. On his way to Nairobi, the most treacherous of roads, he was taken to the hospital with injuries. Apparently, during the night, and without the benefit of a blood thinner, a clot loosened and he died of heart failure. I have his gift on my mantle to remember a friend.

The students of Denis Morris High School took up the challenge. Upon my return to Canada, it was difficult to forget friends with their needs in Kenya. I also knew that the students wanted to be involved. Each year, I held a Starvathon with a specific project in mind. The students would sign up pledges, to be followed by a twenty-four hour awareness program where invited guest speakers would share their expertise. For over twenty-five years, students knocked on doors and signed up donations. Windmills for pumping water, dispensaries, classrooms, famine relief foods, tractors and a truck, tuitions, bridges and warm blankets were all funded by the students, several of whom even went to Africa as nurses, some to India, and others to Central America as volunteers. Their involvement in Starvathon gave them a clearer understanding of international needs and cooperation. Hundreds of thousands of Starvathon dollars were spread out in Canada, Africa, Nepal, India, and Central America and even in the Brazilian jungle, the Amazon.

Samburu recipients of Denis Morris High School Starvathon

The Boran raiders who were plundering cattle and food caught the Old Rendille who had survived famines and tribal wars. The ruthless terrorists slaughtered the old man along with twenty-five school children as they held the N.F.D. ransom. He was a wonderful old icon who delighted in the small gifts of tobacco. I was saddened by the news and angered at the senselessness of the deed. It was John Donne in Meditation 17 who wrote, '*No man unto himself is an island.*' I felt diminished by the Old Rendille's death.

After many years without any contact, I was so surprised to receive the following letter, just as I was finishing up this manuscript.

A TOUCH OF AFRICA

St. Joseph's High School
P.O. Box 485
Kitale, Kenya
17th, September 2004

Dear Bert

Greetings to you and family. I write to you today after such a long time. I hope you are well. There are times I flashback to remember 36 years ago, when you brought me out of the dry and hill country of Samburu to take me to school in order to build up my future. I am mostly grateful for your kindness.

I am still teaching in this school. My other involvements are matters related to persons with disabilities. I am the district chairman of the Kenya union of the Blind, I represent people with disabilities in the national council of Kenya. I am also a committee member of an organization called, 'Edan' that essentially advocates for the disabled in our country.

My children are in school----Damaris 10 in class 5 and the son Baraka is pre-unit next year class 1.

How are your children doing? The greatest day is when we shall meet again. Give me Roscoe's contacts that I may write to him.
Peace be to you, I will write again. Thanks.

Yours,
David Epurr Lokwaro

Epur, our blind Turkana charge who we found on that dark evening in South Horr, graduated from university and became a secondary school teacher in Kitale, Kenya. He is married with a family and continues his very successful career in the classroom. He is looking forward to investing in a small plot of land to grow food for his family and a place to retire. I never knew if he ever found his roots in the remote N.F.D. I doubt it.

Epur enclosed several pictures, one of himself in a gray suit standing in front of a banana tree, which is probably in his shamba. The second photo is with his wife and two children, standing on the side of the road. The children appear to be heading for school, backpacks loaded, and their mom beside them looks on lovingly.

Epur today as a secondary school teacher

The leopard got away. The head tracker on that safari told us what had happened on the lush banks of the Uaso Nyiro River. Each evening at dusk, as we crawled silently away from the blind and inched our way to the Land Rover, the leopard who had already taken his position, which was directly behind us, watched our backs and waited for us to leave. When we were safely gone, the cat would steal past the empty blind, leap onto the rock and tear away at the dinner we had left for him. So we fed him for weeks with choice, well-hung meat. The tracker found his furrowed scratch marks on the tree behind the blind, which he had been using to sharpen his claws in anticipation of his nightly meal. The scratch marks were unusually high and the pugmarks he left were as large as a lion's, so we were not only dealing with a stealthy goat killer, but one very large African male leopard. In the end, the leopard had his nightly meals, while I ended up with malaria, a sickly baboon, and a sore thumb.

Twenty years later, on a subsequent fact finding trip to East Africa, I made a stop in Murang'a, Kenya to visit the gravesite of Maureen Thompson. The site was even denser than I had remembered and it took me a while to locate the exact area. After brushing off the pine needles and debris, I uncovered a large flat, black marble slab. The inscription read, MAUREEN THOMPSON / MR., ROBERT THOMPSON. Maureen lay next to her dad, her 'most favorite person in the world.' Mrs. Thompson had made it right after all and brought the two together again.

Katharine, our very beautiful daughter, developed an incredible ear for languages and teaches at a university in Barcelona, Spain. Her timetable includes International Studies and so she travels about Europe placing her students in exchange programs. Christopher graduated from Carleton University in Ottawa, and works for the Solicitor General of Canada. As a senior policy maker dealing with anti organized crime, and then national security, his career also includes traveling about the world. As young children they visited Africa with us and saw first hand, the settings to all their bedtime stories. Maeve's passion for theatre made her very successful with the local companies and with her students. Today, her drama projects deal with inter relationships and social issues, while she uses masks very effectively in her presentations. She is involved with Amnesty International through her workshops.

Katharine and Christopher D'amico, two great inspirations

My teaching career has taken me from the classroom to Africa on many occasions. With a passion for cultural anthropology, my travels eventually led me to Brazil and the Amazon rainforest. With an anthropologist friend, Dr. John Saffirio, I studied the Yanomama Indians who call the jungle their home. These are primitive, non-technical people and their environment is the antithesis of my nomadic friends from East Africa. The Amazon jungle is in reality the 'dark continent' ……but that's another story.

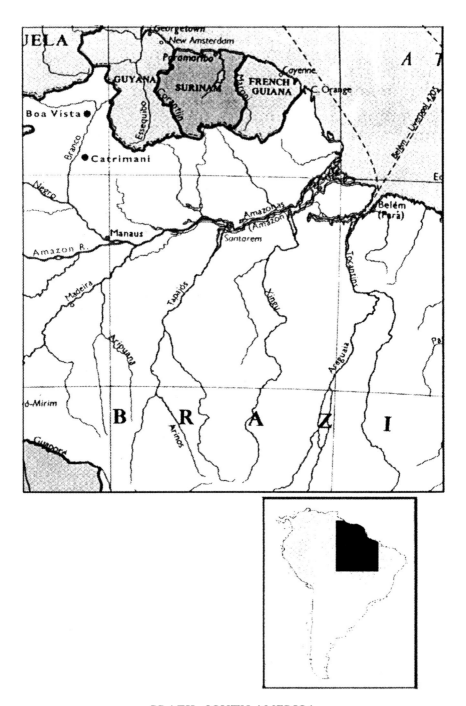

BRAZIL, SOUTH AMERICA

PART II

ONTO THE AMAZON

MANAUS

The Amazon always held a fascination for me and as it happens so often in life, I was made an unexpected offer to visit a very primitive tribe of Indians living in the jungle. These Yanomama Indians were written up in the literature as the 'fierce people.' As it turned out, these people, one of the world's more unusual tribes, had displayed some very hostile characteristics in the early 1960's. The Yanomama are labeled the largest, isolated group left in the hemisphere and represent a continuous link with the culture, technology, and spirituality of the Paleolithic age. Their indigenous knowledge of herbal and spiritual healing is of inestimable wealth. They live in the humid tropical rain forest of the Amazon, which has an average of two to four meters of rain annually. (The term jungle is used to describe a wild, overgrown tract of dense vegetation, often nearly impenetrable; a tropical rainforest is synonymous with jungle and I use the two terms interchangeably.) Arrangements were made here in Canada and with a friend Loy, we departed for Manaus, Brazil via Miami in 1986, the first of several in the years to come.

We landed in Manaus, a large Brazilian city at the headwaters, where the Solimoes and Negro rivers meet to form the confluence of the Amazon River. What is interesting about these two rivers is that they maintain their distinct colors for several miles before they mix into what is known as the Amazon River. The Solimoes is a light grey, limestone color, while the Negro is very dark and the two keep this distinctiveness clearly before they become one. Also, at the confluence of Manaus is Lago Januario, an attraction where one can take a boat ride across the Amazon to the lake and see the incredible vegetation, which grows mad in the surrounding area. Mammoth rainforest trees sit on exposed roots not unlike enormous tripods, which anchor these monstrous trees into the shallow soil. Overwhelming these giants are the air plants (epiphytes), which droop down from lofty branches of their hosts and spread their tentacles downward like dripping, twisting candy. Everything seems to be of outrageous proportions.

The main attraction at Lago Januario is the Victoria Regis lily pads. Seems commonplace until you are in and among these leathery plants with three inch rims and bouquets of white flowers sending out a perfume, which floats over the water. These are not your ordinary lily pads but a variety found only in this part of the world and named after Queen Victoria. Each plant stretches three or more feet across with rims, which fold and unfold each day. The setting is pure jungle and the fish, which swim in and around the plants, are long toothed predators and swarm in a variety of colors and shapes, large and small, as they viciously pick off the bread crumbs thrown into the water. The garishness can only lead one to believe that someone had a sense of humor and let the whole lot run amok. The spectacle just inches below the surface leaves one imagining the

ONTO THE AMAZON

horror of horrors. Piranhas were only one of the fearsome predators and they were not on top of the food chain.

My anthropologist friend in Brazil told the following to me. An American engineer was assigned to a project in Manaus and as required, moved his family to this metropolis at the head of the Amazon River. As a welcoming gesture during his orientation at the job site, the company took his wife and infant child to Lago Januario to see the edge of the jungle and the rare Victoria Regis lily pads. There was also a restaurant stop, which was part of the tour. As the wife and child were being escorted through the lake, she decided that the folks back home would appreciate a photo of the baby on one of these sturdy lily pads. They were certainly strong enough to hold a small person, so the baby would be safe from sinking into the water. As she set the infant on the pad, she leaned back in the boat, focused her camera and snapped what she thought would be an unusual picture. No sooner had she focused and pressed the shutter button when from behind the lily pad, a huge alligator (caiman) appeared, mouth agape. With one horrifying snap, both the lily pad and the infant disappeared below the water. As the tour guide paddled me about, it was difficult to imagine the horror, which had taken place in this serene setting on the edge of the rainforest.

Manaus deserves comment since the history of the city is fascinating. It was the rubber industry monopoly that made the city home to a very wealthy population at the turn of the century. Rubber was the product that Manaus claimed as its own and enormous profits were made by exploiting this rare commodity. Severe penalties were imposed on the unfortunate who was caught attempting to smuggle out a rubber plant. (A similar monopoly existed in Zanzibar with her cloves.) Homes and monuments attest to yesterday's wealth. The ruling classes sent their evening clothes to Europe to be dry cleaned, a three month round trip affair. The architecture of the city, where lepers roam unheeded, had a distinguishing feature, namely the influence of one Mr. Eiffel, known for his famous tower in Paris. His iron works and buildings bear his trademark and further attest to the city's past glory. Today, the city is tired and worn, with the tropical sun aging the old beauty.

The crown jewel of the city however, was not the influence of Eiffel but rather a most impressive structure, surrounded by the outlying tropical rainforest. The Manaus opera house is a piece of work shaped out of Italian marble, by Italian sculptures and adorned with an expansive entrance area of mosaic and marble columns depicting the Americas. This front view stretches several football fields wide and leads one to the main doors. Unfortunately, the building remained closed for years after the demise of the rubber industry. Once inside, the grandeur of the opera house's history surrounds one like a cloak. Dark shadows, exotic woods from the jungle, and crimson velvet drapery ushers one into a glorious past of flowing gowns and starched collars. There is heaviness about the place. From the stage, now hushed with time, one can only imagine the arias of Puccini, as the orchestra pit filled the house with his romantic tales of unrequited love. Velvety covered seats, empty and waiting, had curious pouches sewn in the back. These pouches I later discovered, were filled with ice to cool the patron during the performance, air-conditioning being unknown at the time.

A friend and an amazing world traveler, Ed Arroyave, told me about the opera house as the place to see when in Manaus. He had visited the theatre many years ago and was told the following story. An adventurer who wandered into the opera house, then long vacant and unused, was busy exploring the marvelous interior when suddenly from beneath one of the seats, a venomous snake struck out and bit him. The man died in the aisle. Needless to say, I was quite wary of sitting and enjoying the posh seats in the awesome setting. Somehow, the thought of that unfortunate visitor years ago, left me looking down as much as gazing around. Today, Manaus has regained some of its former importance with the opera house restored and remains the major deep-sea water port at the headwaters of the Amazon. It is also a 'zona franca,' or the major duty free city in Brazil.

The Manaus Opera House restored

ONTO THE AMAZON

Loy and I were surprised upon our arrival at the airport in Manaus. My arrival date was forwarded from my friend in Addis Abba, Ethiopia to his contact in Manaus and we were pleasantly welcomed and ushered through the Portuguese interrogations without a hitch. Outside, in the cool darkness of early morning, he had a Land Rover and driver who was to take us to our pre arranged accommodations, once again made possible through my friends in Africa. Through the shadows of dawn, we sped along, grateful for the ease of it all, since we had been delayed in Miami for ten hours and looked forward to bed. We turned into a darkened lane, continued on through winding alleys and narrow passageways and arrived at a gated entrance. Inside, was a large two-storied villa, and in the haze of dawn, I could make out the silhouettes of tropical palms and other exotics. We later realized that our lodgings were located in the middle of a barrio called Santa Luzia, a place where we discovered, even the taxies refused to enter because of the eminent danger. That first night, we were troubled with wee creatures in our bed. No matter how fresh or crisp the bed sheets, it seemed we always had plenty of visitors. Spraying the sheets with something called, 'Black Death,' seemed a poor option and only after several sleepless nights, did I finally succumb to the deadly potion. The air hung heavy with the noxious smell for days and so scratching gave way to gagging, red eyes and a lot of misgivings. The can with its deadly warnings was finally hidden away to avoid future weakening of the flesh.

After a warm welcome from our hosts, Loy and I had a week to explore Manaus before flying to Boa Visita and onto Catrimani in the jungle. Manaus was an adventure. It is not a picturesque city but one that harbored individual neighborhoods, each much different from the next. Downtown was bustling and filled with every item found in any large city, along with all the upsets of overcrowding and poverty. Taking out one's money was scary since street urchins roamed in large gangs, surrounded you, and in the confusion of it all, one was robbed. One street retailer even left his shop and came over to us and warned Loy to take out his money in private.

The waterfront was most remarkable since not only did one see the flotilla of boats, which plied the Amazon River, but also the markets showcased all the fruits and vegetables of the jungle and even more, a fantasia of fish from the River. Never did I witness such an astonishing display of the strangest looking creatures that called the river home. Some fish had ludicrous stripes, while others donned long, whiskers with gaping mouths, garish eyes, now clouded and unseeing. It was soon obvious that the fish were generally predators since the teeth they exposed were only useful for ripping and tearing. The 'dog fish,' with two-inch fangs made the piranha look pathetic. The pirarucu weighed in at hundreds of pounds and their dried scales were sold as nail files while their raspy tongues were used to grind an aphrodisiac called guarana. The Amazon River contains more variety of fish than all the other waterways in the world.

Numerous researchers have written volumes on the prolific creatures that swim below the surface, and on those, which call the jungle home. An example would be the butterfly population around Belem, a port city, downstream and at the mouth of the Amazon, thousands of kilometers away from Manaus. Belem, Portuguese for Bethlehem, has more species of these flying beauties than the rest of the world combined. Cousteau who did extensive study of the Amazon region, fills pages with superlatives, the only way which one can describe the world's most prolific region.

Black vultures guard the market place, hunched and bleary eyed, perched atop rotting timbers, waiting for discarded fish entrails. During the heat of the day, young children, of every color, swam noisily in the floating debris around laden boats carrying overflowing heaps of produce from far off river settlements. Roughly hewn tree trunks served as gang planks for the endless line of somber porters, bodies glistening, as they staggered under loads balanced on their heads, veins bulging, eyes downcast. So the market at Manaus, with its bananas and oranges, pineapples, watermelon, tangerines and tangles of greens, mixed in with strange smelling fruits with splashes of dripping flowers, all housed inside the iron brocade works of Mr. Eiffel, was a setting unto itself.

SANTA LUZIA

It was always an adventure to walk the narrow streets to our accommodations in Santa Luzia. The open sewers ran darkly with suspicious creatures, some long dead. Narrow lanes with dwellings leaning on one another, were painted outrageous colors. Street kids dressed in ragged shorts, raged over their homemade soccer ball and held off any local traffic until disputes were settled and tempers cooled. It was necessary to pass this one particular house whose owners fussed and pampered over a large pink pig, which made gurgling noises as it fed from the open drains. This swollen beast always seemed to leer at us as we passed. We made friends with the local pub owner, Joseph and his wife Louise, whose open aired corner establishment bordered the stagnant sewer, and became a regular stop on our way home. The drinks were always cheap, cold and a welcomed treat as we sat and watched the neighborhood come alive before us. The owner blared his favorite Brazilian tunes, which made normal conversation nearly impossible. At times, with his open mike on full volume, he would call the neighborhood together and with Loy and I as guests of honor, he would point to us and ramble on about the two Canadian gringos and how he had come to consider us as friends. Of course, most of this was surmised since we knew little Portuguese at the time and used the audience before us as a barometer. We guessed most of the comments were favorable since everyone in the barrio treated us warmly no matter what time of day or night we passed by.

The author enjoying the Nova Bar

It was the way people lived outdoors that was most noticeable to me. Wooden tables, rickety chairs, homemade stools or any other handy piece of furniture was used to enjoy the outside. Of course it was hot and the mosquitoes at night with the stifling humidity got your attention along with the fleas and lice. It seemed to me this was a genuine out of doors culture that came naturally to the people in the barrio of St. Luzia. Shouting faces leaning out of open windows and calling across to neighbors and passers by were lost in the throbbing cacophony of raging soccer fans and screaming youngsters. Lean dogs sprawled on the road taking a midday nap in the heat of the day, while wretched cats and the odd pig were not an unusual sight as we walked the narrow streets, amidst blaring Brazilian rumbas and wannabe Peles screaming at a missed soccer goal. The laughter and infectious grins greeted us as we passed. All in all, it was a lively place to be, a setting fit for a Rockwell canvas.

Lodivico, a guest of our host in Santa Luzia, who was visiting in Manaus, asked me if I was a fisherman and subsequently invited us to his Amazon River settlement, Lago do Aleixo. I was excited and waited impatiently for the appointed day. The date was set according to the moon or the lack of it since, it was determined that a full moon gave too much light and the fishing would be poor. Lago do Aleixo was a leper colony and it would be lepers who would be our companions on the fishing trip. This got our attention. Our host lived in the settlement. One Dr. Silvano, who was sponsored by the World Health Organization and recently arrived from a leper tour in Ethiopia, told us that one of the best places to avoid leprosy or Hansen's Disease, was in a leper colony since the infected residents were tested monthly and all aspects of the disease were contained. Roaming the streets in Manaus and breathing in confined places such as a bus, was much more dangerous since leprosy is said to be an air borne disease and also transmitted in mucus. Leprosy attacks the extremities, reducing the fingers, toes and nose to mere stubs and depressions and leaves the victim deformed, grossly disfigured and often unrecognizable.

Dr. Silvano gave me the following statistics. The colony at Lago do Aleixo had 180 lepers, with only 3 who tested positive. Blood tests were taken every three months and then every six, while treatment was readily available if needed in the form of a tablet. In Manaus, there were 12,000 lepers; 7,000 were positive and lived in the streets. In the Amazon region, it was estimated to have 40,000 lepers, an unofficial count.

LAGO DO ALEIXO

Our arrival in Lago do Aleixo, as one might expect, was filled with some anticipation and curiosity. The settlement was carved out of the banks of the Amazon River and sufficiently secluded to avoid outside contact with neighboring communities. I wondered, if the colony was so safe from the disease, why it was so isolated and hidden away? Only when I realized that leprosy was much more a social disease even today, did I understand the isolation of Lago do Aleixo. The homes of the lepers were scattered about and raised on stilts to avoid the high waters of the Amazon. The central feature was the schoolroom, neatly framed with wooden slats and built high above the flood line on stilts. Once unpacked in our host's house, with our beds located behind a curtain off the kitchen, I was asked to meet the school's principal.

The school house for leper children

Being ushered into the one room narrow building, the headmaster who was expecting our arrival stuck out his arm in a warm welcome. Without taking my eyes off the man, I gave him a hardy shake and told him I was pleased to visit his school. I survived the first test. The man's fingers were missing leaving only a stump and since I never withdrew in horror, I became an instant friend. Leprosy had taken its toll on the fellow. I was told it was not contagious by mere contact. You had to believe it was true. The student population was a blend of colors and great smiles. Clear skinned youngsters giggled and squirmed as I was taken up and down the aisles. These were the children of lepers and lived free of the disease since they had been given proper medical examinations, in anticipation of any early signs. They were a happy lot and were eager to have their pictures taken on the front steps of their one room school.

Children of the colony

I discovered an interesting relic just outside the schoolroom. Exposed ever so slightly in the baked ground, was a curious circular rim of a very large earthen pot or urn. I gently scratched away and uncovered the perimeter of a fired vessel, which was at least two or more feet across. I was at a loss and scraped off more of the crusty soil and wondered at the curious artifact. It was many years later that I read about a very ancient people who had once lived on the edges of the Amazon and one of their interesting habits was burying their dead in very large earthen urns.

Next stop on our tour of the leper colony was the chicken coops. Our host was responsible for developing a very sophisticated egg producing industry operated by the lepers. Neatly arranged enclosures, scrubbed clean, housed the hens. The eggs were collected daily and sold in Manaus and earned enough income to afford the colony its economic independence and social isolation. Supplementing the egg industry were pens of fuzzy piglets, all spotted and squealing. Our tour guide was Oswaldo, who like all the lepers, was self-conscious and avoided eye contact. His nose was a mere bump, while most of his fingers were reduced to stumps. Our host told us how he had noticed him limping several days previously and upon examining his foot, he pulled out a two-inch nail from his instep. Oswaldo had been walking with a limp for several days. Leprosy not only diminishes the extremities but also leaves one numb and desensitized. I took several pictures of the community being very discreet and aware of the peoples' feelings. I took one picture of the raised houses and it was only after my return to Canada and developing the film that I noticed a crouching figure on the porch hiding behind a bamboo curtain. Unbeknownst to me, a leper woman was on the front veranda, saw me point the camera, and dived behind the bamboo curtain, hiding herself in shame.

The people of the colony were forced to live a life outside the regular Brazilian community but they still longed to take pleasure in all the amenities of the wider, outside society. There were obvious limitations but when it came to important festivals, the lepers whooped it up and enjoyed their time as much as anyone. Our arrival coincided with an important national Saint's day and so there was an air of festivity in the secluded community. One of the main events was a boat ride on the Amazon, filled with lepers, food, and music. We watched one such boat, all decorated with ribbons and flowers arrive with the partiers. Our host had hired the large vessel, which took out the lepers for an afternoon's excursion. We were also invited for a boat ride, which would take us to the main channel and through the lush jungle as we motored along. We waited for several other visitors to arrive, including the leper Doctor from Manaus and Oswaldo, and after an hour or so, we left the flimsy, half submerged dock

Once on our way, I noticed several frond woven houses along the shore as we drank a cold beer leaning over the railing and taking in the sounds and sights of the Amazon jungle. These raised, palm-covered huts appeared vacant. Our host told me that they were homes of those lepers who refused to live in the colony and were extremely grotesque looking since they were without the benefit of any medical attention. They considered themselves loners and outcasts and choose to live a life of abandonment and utter despair. They also disappeared in the undergrowth at the mere sound of intruders. It was a ghostly scene, one stricken with the worst of social diseases where lepers lived out their time in Biblical condemnation. These people were filled with self-loathing and were reduced to forbidden creatures of the jungle. *Struggle*, a million voices from the jungle chanted, *it is the Law!*

Bush lepers who refuse to live in the colony

It was on this boat ride that the captain took us for a very close look at the two colors of the Amazon waters before they merged into one. The contrasts up close were as clear as if one used a paintbrush to separate the two rivers, one dark and the other ashen gray. Meanwhile, Oswaldo kept to himself at the front of the boat. Lunch of fried chicken, rice, manioc farina, spaghetti, guanana, and cold 'cerveza' was laid out for us. I never saw Oswaldo eat. Our lack of Portuguese was a further obstacle in getting to know the lepers. A splash in the water and the lot of us were all pointing at the pink dolphin that decided we needed company. These fresh water dolphins are unique to the Amazon River, and appear raw and unfinished.

I was at a loss regarding the how and when of our proposed fishing trip. Our host seemed to have a plan but he was vague about the details. We were supposed to leave for Manaus the next morning and it was already late afternoon and we were still on the water enjoying our outing. When we docked and drank dark coffee with our host, it was dusk with long shadows looming about us. I was confused. Around early evening, there was a thud on the door and our host, after a brief conversation in Portuguese, turned to Loy and I and asked if we were ready. Ready? Off we marched into the dusk behind two silent shadows.

We were led to the marshy shore. All I could see was a narrow craft ten or twelve feet long. Our companions beckoned us to embark. Well I thought, here we go again. I balanced myself near the front of the boat, Loy got in behind me and the two lepers took their positions, one in front of me, and the other behind Loy.

Our fishing craft to cross the Amazon River

The lead man turned out to be Oswaldo, who donned a miner's lamp strapped to his forehead and off we chugged into the inky night, the outboard coughing and spewing deadly fumes in our wake. The sights and sounds were eerie. We had some distance to go before we entered the main channel of the Amazon River. I had no idea where we were going. The blackness was thick. I noticed we were veering off to the right towards a reedy shoreline, which could be seen because Oswaldo had turned on his miner's lamp. As we approached the beds, he stood up in our shaky craft, his light silhouetting the grasses ahead of us, casting gloomy shapes while in one hand he grasped a long spear, a trident with sharp points. All the while he had been emitting a throaty, 'Mm'm Mm'm,' as we ploughed through the waste high vegetation. Loy, who was as curious as myself, asked if our leader was getting sick since the sounds were getting more frequent and not unlike someone ready to lose their dinner. They were not only getting louder, but more desperate. We could wonder out loud to each other since our friends had no knowledge of English and we, likewise were at a loss with their Portuguese. I was squirming since Oswaldo was only inches in front of me and my movements were restricted as

I anticipated a mighty rush of dinner about to usher forth and spray me all over. It was then I saw dozens of tiny lights reflecting in the water…beady eyes. I immediately put things together. I had heard the same distress calls being made, years ago in Africa. It was the call of a mother crocodile, or in this case alligator, beckoning to her young. The youngsters were heading towards our boat, answering the calls. Without hesitation, the trident was flung headlong into the reeds nearly tipping the boat and came back with a small creature squirming for its life. It was dispatched by a knock on the head with a hammer and thrown down in front of me, still wriggling and slashing about with its tail. It was starting to get crowded. Alligator was to be added to the next day's menu.

We were soon in the main channel of the Amazon River, a stretch of water so far across, the opposite shore could barely be seen, even in daylight. Our craft with its four passengers plunged ahead, straight for the other shore. The waterline was only inches away from our being swamped and I couldn't help but think of all the predators I had seen in Lago Januario. On and on we went and at one point I thought I could see an ominous black iceberg fast approaching our starboard side. I was mesmerized as the shadow as large as a train came closer and closer. Swallowing hard I strained to recognize the apparition in the inky night. It was probably only fifty feet away when I shouted to Oswaldo, pointing at the on coming disaster. He flashed his headlamp to warn them off. With deft strokes our two fishermen with oars cradled against their chests, added their backs to the spitting engine and our craft lunged forward, leaving a dismal wake. It seemed only seconds before the throbbing of the powerful engines passed our stern. The deck was strung with hammocks with the crew fast asleep. A commercial fishing boat, without lights, was on its way to cast their nets. I was to learn that boats on the river like the taxies in Manaus, never used lights since it was considered a waste of power. I felt cold and shuddered at what could have been, my worst nightmare even to this day. For a long time our boat was silent, the fishing vessel's droning engine lost in the mists like some watery creature retreating to its lair.

Once across the river, we were immersed in a treetop jungle of vegetation. Each year, the Amazon floods and rises as high as sixty feet. Trees are submerged leaving lofty crowns exposed above the water. It was amongst these treetops, we now cruised. A lone iguana was spotted in its dry perch and was quickly added next to the alligator between my feet. A long line was baited and strung out between the treetops with shiny hooks tied every two feet. We waited. A few raindrops soon became a heavy downpour and, much to my surprise, we headed for shelter in a rooftop that was all that was left exposed of someone's hut. It felt strange to enter through the gable end, high in the water. It was a perfect refuge as we tied up in a stranger's attic. There was one problem, however. The boat was too long and the leper behind Loy, called Antonio, was left outside the shelter and in the rain. It was amazing since his first reaction was to laugh and soon we all shared his good sense of humor. It was time for our treat and so I dug into the bag, which my host had given to me. I gave everyone an oversized, thick-skinned orange, a fruit bursting with sticky juice and a welcomed indulgence. Loy and I ate heartily, slurping the sweetness as the juice ran down our chins. Antonio, who was behind Loy, was noticeably quiet and holding his orange, looking down at it. We finally figured out that the unfortunate fellow, whose fingers were long gone and reduced to mere stumps, was totally incapable of peeling an orange. We quickly solved that problem and we all enjoyed ourselves. Oswaldo seemed able to split his fruit and suck out the juice. I couldn't help but think if we took shelter in this lofty rooftop, what other creatures were likewise clinging in the black corners, looking at the intruders as we enjoyed our snack. The numerous snakes that lived in the Amazon also needed a refuge in the high water.

Oswaldo pulled in the lines and hauled in a dozen or so small fish, several which had huge horseshoe bites taken out of them. Piranhas have a taste for flesh. Like hunters in the jungle, our fisherman companions talked softly to one another and only when necessary. The night was warm and humid. Muskoil from Canada kept most of the flying night attackers at bay. It has been said that jaguars, snakes, alligators, stingrays and piranha all combined, sink into oblivion as enemies of man when contrasted with the insect life of this tropical rainforest.

Night sounds were ordinary at first. The usual croaking, swooping of night birds in hot pursuit of a meal, and the odd bat on the wing filled the darkness. At one point, not far off, a flock of birds suddenly awoke and sent an ear-piercing echo across the treetops, all eerie and haunting, leaving one to wonder what ever had disturbed them. The ride back was uneventful and we putted back to our quarters in the wee hours of daybreak. My backside was numb from sitting on the wooden slat and being unable to stretch. Long shadows outlined the shore, intimidating the bravest of souls. Our fishermen companions grinned a quick downcast farewell as they disappeared into the gloom. They did not want to be seen in the light of day and so another reason for our night fishing excursion. They preferred the comfort of darkness when in the presence of strangers. When I returned to Canada, I made contact with a very successful businessman in Toronto, one Mr. Bill Sorokolit. Through his generosity, an aluminum boat and outboard motor was purchased for the leper colony at Lago do Alexio, a huddle of huts on the edge of a forsaken place.

BOA VISTA AND INTO THE JUNGLE

The next day, leaving Manaus, we flew to Boa Vista, a community on a tributary of the Amazon River called the Rio Branca. The gracious gentleman who had initially met us upon our arrival in Brazil welcomed us once again. Boa Vista did not have very much to offer after the sights and sounds of Manaus. A riverbank settlement with seasonal floods, it was amazing to see the high water stained buildings, stains five and six feet off the ground. The high water also brought forth a deluge of snakes. Our plan was to hire a small aircraft and hitch a ride deep into the jungle to a clearing called Catrimani, the home of the Yanomama Indians. Arrangements to hire a small plane were confusing and it seemed impossible to pin down a definite departure time. Besides having American cash for the ride, it was necessary to have applied for the official government permits to enter this prohibited area of the Amazon. My host had thoughtfully made the necessary arrangements for us.

At 12:30 noon, July 7th, Loy and I were finally packed into a small four-seat airplane, piloted by a former Brazilian air force gentleman. We lifted off and left Boa Vista below. The idea was to avoid the torrential downpours, which made flying in this shaky aircraft a hazard, and the reason for the long delay in taking off. We peered down and saw how the forest was being slashed and raped, huge gouges missing like bad teeth. It wasn't very long before our merry chatting and finger pointing came to an abrupt halt. We flew smack into a wall of water. Our pilot left off his tour guiding conversation, which was in Portuguese, in mid sentence. He had other things on his mind. When the weather finally broke, it was amazing to peer down once again at the canopy and into what one author describes as the 'Great Silence.' One particular waterfall, far below, pitched and tumbled over an exposed outcrop and I wondered if anyone had ever walked beneath its mists that disappeared into a black hole, forbidding and perilous. Our destination was a crack in the canopy and I marveled at the expertise of our pilot to locate Catrimani.

Perhaps an excerpt from my diary will illustrate the feeling of flying over the Amazon jungle:

> *We boarded the flimsy 'Courier' at Boa Vista for Catrimani, an Amazonian outpost, and the home of Yanomama. Looking through the scratched plexiglass window of our cramped four-seater airplane, the forest canopy begins for the first time to assume a definition. Crystalline rock faces washed over by countless generations of rains, reveal a mineral wealth once deeply buried within. Silt laden rivers, sluggish and rusty in color, meander thoughtlessly beneath us, sometimes hidden under a green cloak,*

sometimes glaringly bold as the sun reflects their diamond surfaces. The jungle completely and overwhelmingly dominates our world from on high. The vastness defies comparison. Two and a half million square miles of luxuriant mantle with 1000 tributaries to feed the mighty Amazon River, which stretches across the continent for two thousand miles. This River with 1500 species of fish, (all Europe has only 150 species) have names that give a new meaning to the word exotic…pirarucu, tucunarae, tamaqui, and piranha. Jaguar and red jaguar (puma), anaconda (sucuri), alligator (jacuaru), bird eating spiders, king hawks are but a few of the denizens below. The mouth of the Amazon spills silt into the Atlantic, staining the ocean for 150 miles out to sea. This was the first clue for early explorers, which foretold of a mighty inland river. The jungle below with 8000 species of trees is a profusion of liana, gaudy parasites, air plants (epiphytes), bamboo and palms. Individual trees sometimes stand out among the bulbous green foliage more often due to color than to size. Hues of algae green drift abruptly into a patch of gold: however, it is the richness of the bleeding green that gives consistency to the mantle resulting in a solid undulating biomass Nowhere from above, can we see the haggling for position below. A soft calmness is the order of the day, which now and then is punctuated with a lone jacaranda in bloom, a drop of color in a sea of misty green. The silent struggle races on ceaselessly. One author on the Amazon jungle comments on the fact that nothing except long residence in the Great Silence, would convey any idea of the vigor of the crashing images of life and death which succeed one another with an astounding swiftness.

Sometimes a small clearing exposes itself, and immediately one searches for a lone farmhouse or a barn only to realize that this opening is only a swamp and that civilization's long finger has not yet poked anywhere near this green hell. Ridge after carpeted ridge whip by below us, only to reveal more of the same. Everything below looks so quiet, so restful, so soft and inviting.

Like the clouds above and around us, the tree crowns below touch one another producing a billowy softness to the eye. From above, the rain forest invites us gently down. There is no sign of the screaming life below us. There is no clue of the struggle for light. One is wholly unaware of the jockeying for position that is ever constant in order to seize upon the slightest environmental advantage. Sunlight is the rare commodity of the market place below. Somehow, the profusion has come to terms with the leached and infertile soil. Somehow, the struggling root systems have evolved a compromise in the sodden and often flooded floor. It is the sun, however, that powerhouse of energy from above, that drives this monstrous biomass of screaming fecundity. Parasitic plants choke and stretch upwards for the giver of life. Host plants are often consumed beneath their ever tightening, ever growing, tentacles. Like some primitive tribe, writhing in their moonlit rituals, outstretched arms stabbing towards the heavens, so too does the forests' vegetable matter grab and poke, strive and reach into every niche, always and forever upwards towards the provider of life.

Below a garish ribbon of orangey, silt laden water streaks before us. We follow this watery stain searching out a sign, a canoe, a wisp of hearth smoke. Nothing. We glide over still another wave of green. Lowering our altitude gives even further dimension to the rain forest and we can now see the riverbank hemmed in foliage with mangled roots that disappear under water. The canopy and the wall of vegetable matter bordering the riverbank give the impression that this tropical rainforest is a fertile one. Saffirio states that 92% of the humid forest is extremely infertile. When the trees are cut, the result is a desert. Only with the continuous recycling of organic matter are the elements taken from the shallow root systems to the canopy rooftop above and the giver of life, the sun. Our pilot points, there is the sign we have been straining to see, a large circus-like tent dwelling wrapped in woven fronds. It is immense, standing alone, pointed roof piercing skywards, a sentinel, and one recycled from the surrounding rain forest and skillfully fashioned. It is a Yanomama malocca.

Our first glimpse of a Yanomama Malocca

Several hundreds of yards away, glimmering roofs tell us of still another forest dweller, a much more recent arrival, a settlement built by a group of Italians. The four or five buildings look tired and out of place, weary structures. Our pilot circles, locates the 'runway,' a set of worn tracks, lines up the aircraft and noses the plane into the overgrown clearing. We bump down, the single prop chopping a path through the waist high grass and when we finally stop, we are in a sea of waving pasture, isolated and surrounded by the Amazon rainforest. We have arrived at Catrimani.

CATRIMANI

The retired Brazilian pilot broke his long silence as I grabbed for the door. My lack of Portuguese left him mid sentence with a shrug as I leapt out of the cramped cockpit and into the delicious fresh air of Catrimani. Our circling about had given our host plenty of warning along with a mob of whooping Yanomama, who came tearing out of the forest and surrounded us. Naked, except for a piece of cord tying their penises around their waist, and waving oversized bows, they came to a full stop around us and were silent. The Yanomama do not have any words for 'hello' or 'good-bye.' William, our host, broke through the crowd and welcomed us to Catrimani as the pygmy sized Indians pushed still closer for a better look at us. You immediately notice the protrusion bulging from inside their lower lip. Tobacco leaves are rolled, cigar-like and stuffed between the lower teeth and the bottom lip. Women and young children alike use tobacco this way and walk around with this odd appearance, occasionally spitting out the black juices. We must be related to William because these Indians do not conceptualize non Yanomama in their relationships and so to put us in perspective and place us into a framework they could deal with, we were reckoned as kin to William and so we fit in. William was already a classificatory brother to the Yanomama, and so he fit into their kinship scheme of things, having been given a new Yanomama name. The world outside the jungle is unknown to these people and even the concept of Brazil is foreign.

Before picking up my bags, I asked William to translate the pilot's last minute comments to me as I was leaving the cockpit. I knew he was paid and had the date for our eventual pickup and so I was curious why he seemed so intense. After a brief conversation with our pilot, William returned grinning. Apparently the pilot was telling me to be cautious as I leapt out of the plane and into the tall grass because on a previous landing, he had undergone a minor problem. He had run over large python, which then wrapped itself around the wheel carriage of the airplane and so he was telling me to be careful where I stepped.

We marched, single file, in oozing mud, making great sucking sounds as we pulled ourselves forward. No sooner were we a few paces away from the airplane, when without warning, a cloud of pium, minute black flies, engulfed us, each pest leaving a trail of blood as they fed. Loy whisked out his Muskoil and was soon glistening as the pium circled about menacing but dazzled at this new line of defence. (Days later he made the fatal mistake of going around shirtless and suffered from hundreds of bites.) I refused a dab of the oil since the building was only fifty feet away and I didn't feel like getting greasy hands and collar and sticky sunglasses. When we finally arrived at kitchen/dining room, it was about all I could stand since my hands were taken up with my baggage and the pium were enjoying a smorg. Only once before had I met insects with such dogged determination and that was canoeing in the near Arctic with a friend and landing on a burnt out island for refuge in a storm. We were met with a vast cloud of black flies, forcing us backwards to our canoe and into the water.

Once inside the nearly fly free building, it took several minutes to adjust to the cool darkness. The structure was about 35 feet long and 12 feet wide and set solidly on a concrete base. The wooden walls were constructed of crudely hewn slabs, not unlike an old pioneer stockade. These slabs were loosely fitted together, with finger-sized cracks between them. Above the walls, a 2-foot strip of wire mesh circled the room to allow any breeze to pass. The roof was peaked and supported by poles covered with iron sheets, grooved and overlapping to carry away the rains. On one wall, four rifles of a very small caliber, pointed upwards, each accompanied by a stained hat. A row of shelves, several rockers and a lawn chair, a wooden table with benches in one corner and two propane gas cylinders completed the décor. Behind a wooden partition, one could see the rear cooking area with several shelves well stocked with plantains, banana, oversized gourds split and filled with nuts, avocado, tangerines, pineapple, and heaping piles of mysterious jungle fruits varying in size and color and shape. I was relieved to see two large clay water filters sitting on the sink. Amoebic dysentery is nasty. A primitive wood burning stove with a poorly fitting oven door appeared to have seen one tapir roast too many. Several homemade cupboards, a rough chopping block, an open garbage pail overloaded with skins of the strange fruits and all covered with flies, made up the kitchen. A screen door leading to an outside woodpile, was meant to keep out some the flies and dogs. Several Yanomama could be seen huddled around the door, curious to see the trappings of the 20th century. The overflowing shelves, mixed in with the earthy smells of ashes and smoke, seemed a natural extension of the jungle itself.

Besides the kitchen-living room building, there was a small dispensary, a house for the two medical sisters, a lean-to garage of sorts, a generator shack, our sleeping quarters, and one or two small storerooms for supplies. In one of these, William had his two-way radio set up in order to contact Boa Vista. The jungle wrapped itself around the settlement like a shroud.

The Portuguese cook and her five-year-old daughter greeted us. Barefoot and bashful, she handed us a cool but weird colored drink. Two medical sisters, one from Sao Paulo, the other from Sardinia, greeted us warmly. They operated the tiny medical dispensary we had seen in the rear of the station. Franz, a former Mercedes Benz engineer from Germany, with only several teeth he could rely on, along with Sergassio, a barefooted, taciturn Negro, made up the station's personnel.

It was Sergassio who caught my immediate attention and earned my respect as a skilful dweller in the rainforest. He bristled with an inner strength that complimented his solid frame. He seemed to shout or rather bark out his comments, which were never rambling but rather abrupt and clipped. Born of slave ancestors, he was raised in the jungle as a child and as an adult, became renowned for his prowess as a hunter and survivor. It seemed the fearful jaguar was his speciality. He never appeared to blink and held your attention with penetrating black eyes. Like the smoke from the kitchen chimney, he would drift away, barefooted and silently into the greenery.

Franz, was a large German, with a few conspicuous black hairs forming a shadow around his fleshy mouth. His upper jaw housed one brown tooth with several other survivors in the lower area, resulting in a washy sort of speech. On his right foot he wore a torn, black, leather shoe, and on the other, a sporty canvas one which heaved around the toes and was in need of a lace. He never seemed to change his stained green mechanic's shirt, which depended upon several trusty pins to keep it together. His eyes were warm as they were large, and he never seemed too busy to explain the cause of a broken generator in his faltering English, liberally peppered with Portuguese and German. His temperament after a day under a diesel engine thoroughly wet and oozing mud from every pore, seemed never to change. He knew not how to complain. I found out that as a young man, Franz had wandered over to South America, met these Italians working in the jungle and volunteered his expertise as a mechanic.

The station was the proud recipient of an ancient 1941 Berne diesel truck, dark green and ponderous, donated by Switzerland, and sported wooden spoke wheels. The vehicle had been driven and then rafted over the numerous rivers between Boa Vista and Catrimani. This would be impossible today, since one major wooden bridge had recently been swept away, leaving Catrimani cut off. One reason for my journey to Catrimani was to photograph this ruptured bridge and present it as a worthwhile project to my students. Without a bridge, the Yanomama who suffered ravaging illnesses after being infected by ruthless prospectors, were helpless and dying and in dire need of professional help in far off Boa Vista.

The women in the station always seemed to be busy even late into the evening and while the cook would be washing dishes, the two medical sisters would be busy tearing up material for bandages. The cook always did the dishes in total darkness while we were bathed in the yellow light from the hissing lanterns, sprawled out on shaky chairs, sipping thick Brazilian coffee. The evenings were most enjoyable. William, Franz, Loy and I would sit around while I probed about for new stories about the jungle. Sergassio, who was rarely present, always sat just a little outside the group, and just beyond the circle of light ready to reply when called upon to settle a question about the rainforest. Sometimes, he would get caught up in the swirl of exchanges and volunteer a story about an especially harrowing experience. Of course, these stories had to be translated into English. A Yanomama mother, with her young boy, was busy in their slash and burn garden, when out of the undergrowth, leapt a snarling jaguar who carried off the youngster. Upon his return from the jungle, the boy's father hearing about the tragedy, set out to revenge his son. Covering himself with the ritual black, he left the molocca, determined to kill the jaguar or to be eaten. Narauxi is an indigenous plant and its black dye is used to paint the entire body of the males when they are angry or ready to do battle. The women use it to draw fine black lines on their faces and breasts in preparation for a feast.

Another story was told about an enormous anaconda. One afternoon, several Yanomama who had discovered the large serpent in a shallow water hole, called on our host William. With his gun shouldered, he followed the young hunters and came to the place where the snake was partially submerged. It was reckoned that it had just eaten and was gaseous and would be lying there for some weeks while it digested its recent meal. Yanomama relish snake meat and as a further indulgence, our host gave the gun to one fellow and told him he could shoot the sleeping serpent. The deed done, a rope was strung around the tail and the five of them proceeded to pull the snake to higher ground. No sooner had they begun to haul when, to their surprise, the rope slackened; they all turned to see what was happening and what they saw was the anaconda, jaws open bearing down on the hunters. Our host did the shooting the second time and the Yanomama added a quiver full of arrows for good luck. The malocca was filled with roasting snake meat that night. When I questioned the length, I was told to measure the skin myself. The crusty skin, stored above the generator shack was unrolled and after the hordes of orange cockroaches scampered off, I used rocks to keep the dried skin flat. The skin measured nearly twenty feet and I was told that it had shrunk at least a foot because it had dried out. I have a photo of this very large serpent.

William and Franz would ask me about Africa, its peoples and animals. Never once did Sergassio, with his African ancestry, show the slightest interest or comment about my tales. He was a child of the Amazon; Africa no longer coursed within him.

Catrimani, approximately 1-degree north latitude, similar to my home in Kenya, had an equal number of daylight and evening hours. At around 6 p.m., it was dusk and in the fading light the pium disappeared, only to be replaced by the hordes of mosquitoes. William insisted that Catrimani was malaria free but I was nearly certain I had slapped at anopheles malaria-bearing mosquitoes. On one particular evening, sitting around the hissing propane lamp, I asked the assembled group if there were any scorpions in Catrimani station. I described one particular species, giving minute details as to its size, color, shape and so on. In the semi darkness, everyone agreed they knew this particularly nasty creature and had encountered it numerous times. However, it was never seen in the wet season and to this, everyone heartily agreed. I was asked by William why all the concern. I pointed to the leg of my chair and informed him there was one such individual, crawling slowly towards my arm.

Our sleeping quarters, about fifty feet away from our sitting room, were of a similar construction as the main area, early Catrimani, circa 1965. We were always cautioned to walk slowly, with the aid of a flashlight and of course, using an old African trick, step heavily down with each foot, giving plenty advance warning. Venomous serpents were very common in the compound and had to be avoided at all costs. Our quarters were barrack-like, long and narrow with three bedrooms off a hallway. The hallway, a structural afterthought, was a partially covered add-on and the rusty screens no longer served any practical purpose. At the end of the hallway, was a washroom, where still more rusty screens had long since given up and a flying army of insects had free reign to visit the wash basin which housed a large resident spider, no doubt well fed with so many guests dropping in for a little moisture. A seat less toilet was located behind a wooden partition next to the showerhead. An open-ended drainage hole in the concrete floor was a source of concern for me, since I always wondered what was coming up when the water wasn't going down.

Loy and I shared the end bedroom, which had two army cots against each wall with a narrow passageway between them. At the foot of my bed was a wooden table under a window, and at the end of the other, a door led outside to a veranda and smack into the jungle. The mattresses were musty since these items never seem to keep well in the tropics, the humidity playing havoc with the fiber stuffing. The room was compact and like the entire settlement, without electricity. We were given several precious candles to light our room and were told to use one at a time and then sparingly.

With the candle placed between the two cots and snuffed out after we crawled into our army cots, we looked forward to a relaxing night's sleep with the sounds of the jungle coming alive and filling the room. I jokingly mentioned it was a jungle out there. Night birds, insect life, croaking frogs, chilly screams and the odd scrambling of a tree top predator became our bedtime lullaby, as we dozed off, recounting the events of the day. It wasn't long before we realized that we were not alone in our flaccid army cots. The room housed a myriad of visitors, which were only active once the candle was extinguished. Of immediate concern were the crawly creatures, which came out of the mattresses. You could feel the activity around your feet, legs and chest, as you scratched away in a futile attempt to gain some relief. It was impossible to ignore the abundant nightlife under the covers. Once again, the 'Black Death' spray plunger left out for us, was poised to pump a noxious stream of D.D.T. A lethal dose administered under the covers, soaked the sheets and lower body, while at the same time we tried to avoid breathing in the toxic fumes. Sleep never came easily in Catrimani. Loy captured one especially large cockroach under his sheets, which proved to be somewhat of a record in size.

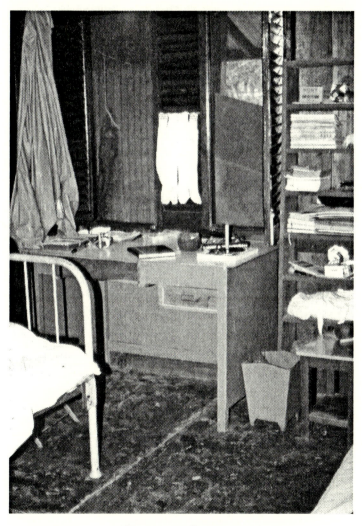

Our room in Catrimani

In the morning it was disappointing to find our precious candle had been reduced to a mere stub. I wondered if Loy had been lighting it. After examining the waxy remains it became clear that a very sharp-toothed visitor had been nibbling at our lone source of cherished light. We finally figured that late at night, when we were tossing and turning, stomping and scratching, one very hungry rat (coro coro) would snack on our candle. The rodent's entrance way was easily discovered. The backdoor to nowhere was poorly fitted with a four-inch gap across the bottom. This was duly stuffed with an army issue blanket and our remaining candles were left uneaten to burn yet another night. It was also disquieting to have so many cockroaches in the room, large orange colored creatures that were everywhere, not only in our sleeping quarters, but also all over Catrimani. If you picked up your diary off the table, orange blurs scattered all over the place and always startled me with their scurrying. Our host, William, told us it was impossible to control them and one had to learn to live with these ancient forest dwellers. It was therefore necessary, not to unpack any unneeded clothes because our travel bags were roach proof and the contents within were safe from the inhabitants in our room. The foul odor that filled our bedroom was easy enough to eliminate. Hanging outside the window to nowhere, behind the table, hung the skin of a peccary, a wild pig of the rainforest. This untreated skin was soon united with the jungle and the air was easy once again.

Catrimani was isolated by land when the rivers swelled during the torrential rainy season. Enormous trees, having been uprooted because of their shallow root systems, would ram the supports of the bridges. Unfortunately, bridges were one style only and that was to have pilings every so often, connected with beams and then covered with planks for crossing. However, when the massive tree trunks came ramming down the swollen waterways, there were no pilings or timbers strong enough to withstand the hammering forces and so the whole structure would collapse and be washed away. What was needed was a design, which had a free span beneath, so these battering ramrods could pass through unobstructed and continue their way downstream.

One of the most dangerous rivers to cross when transporting goods overland was the Ajarani. Goods had to be hauled to this river's edge from Boa Vista, unloaded, and carefully reloaded onto a raft, pushed across the river to the opposite side, unloaded again and then piled into the 1941 Berna truck and hauled away to Catrimani. William told us how he had made this trip many times, with shipments of goods from Boa Vista and upon reaching the Ajarani River, he would unload the first truck and then stack the supplies onto to the raft, jump in the water and swim alongside, holding on to the edge, pushing the whole affair to the other shore. This he had to do many times for each trip, depending upon the amount of goods he was transporting. Now the man was fearless as witnessed when one morning, as he chased after a deadly fer-de-lance (jararaca) in the tall grass near the dispensary, barefooted, stick in hand. He went on to say his most frightening experience happened not long ago when he was in the water, pushing the raft to the opposite side. It was not the alligators, or manta rays or even the piranha that bothered him. His nemesis was the deadly electric eel. This snake-like creature packs a wallop so intense, that merely being brushed by one left him semi conscious as he floated downstream, clinging on to the raft. It was the next day before he completed his crossing of the Ajarani River.

The Yanomama, like my Samburu friends of northern Kenya, were being pressed. The number of treatments at the dispensary in Catrimani between 1971-74 totaled 2,485 and between 1974-77, the number of patients soared to 12,529. The cause of this surge was attributed to the road builders who were constructing the Northern Perimeter Road – BR 210 on the outer edge of the rainforest. The epidemics they brought included measles and pneumonias, and all the familiar venereal diseases. Contacts with outsiders had been deadly for the Yanomama who were at present being administered to, from the lone dispensary at Catrimani. When the Indians left the forest as cheap labor and came in contact with the outsiders, few returned healthy. The more recent gold and diamond prospectors nearly decimated the entire tribe in the early 1980's with their contagious diseases and tried to finish off the Yanomano by hunting down whole families, sometimes shooting them in trees as they hid for cover. In the 1980's, 700 planes were ferrying 45,000 prospectors in and out of the remotest regions of the rainforest. The waters of the Catrimani River became laden and polluted with fuel, human waste and the mercury, used in the primitive recovery of gold. Game disappeared. Two out of ten Yanomama died. The Brazilian government had given these prospectors permission to explore and to exploit the area's wealth as long as there were no indigenous people present. Killing off all the Yanomama was one of their solutions. I have a copy of a diary written by one Adalberto da Silva Santos, a prospector in search of gold and diamonds in Yanomama country. He was part of a plan to exterminate the Yanomama and writes 'of one ferocious genocide' and the degradation of the human beings he encountered. He tells of murder and the raping of women, as they lay in their malocas, bound before their kin who were forced to watch. He wrote the diary hoping to appease his conscience and to make the public aware of, 'the false shine of gold.' On November 15, 1991, the Brazilian President, having been harassed by the international press, which drew attention to the genocide of the Yanomama, reacted. Stemming from advocates from Catrimani, an area of over 36,000 square miles of rain forest was created as an exclusive Yanomama reserve. The long battle had been won at a deadly cost.

There was a little Yanomama girl of about four or five years of age called Iracoma, named after an attractive flower found around Catrimani. Dimpled and coy, Iracoma was a charmer. She was a ward of the station and had the freedom of the entire compound and the hearts of everyone she met. Like all Yanomama females, she was partially covered by her skimpy waistband of wild cotton. This cotton swath, frilled at the front, comprises the total wardrobe of the Yanomano women. She had a reddish hue about her, having been rubbed with a mixture from a common plant called urucu (Portuguese) or nara wak (Yanomama) to thwart the pium and mosquitoes. This reddish brown oily seed from the urucu plant is similar to a brown chestnut with soft thorns. A medical sister I met in Boa Vista, told me she had saved this youngster three times. The first time was from female infanticide because she was born too close to an older male sibling and was deemed unwanted. The second time was when the grandmother left her to starve in the jungle by herself. The medical sister carried her for seventeen hours, often on her head through swamps and creeks in her march to reach Catrimani. The last time was when in the nearby malocca, the grandmother tried to strangle her but was unsuccessful. Iracoma was bright and knew the basics of at least three languages and showed no signs of slowing down. One morning, barefooted and smiling, she came padding down the hallway into our bedroom, stared only inches away from my face and asked for bom boms, with the only English words she knew. Notwithstanding that I didn't have any candy, she carefully undid the buckles on my camera bag in search of a prize, all the while grinning an infectious smile. She found some chewing gum an item completely unknown and foreign to these jungle people.

Iracoma with our host

It seemed my stockings and shoes have been wet forever. My feet now wrinkled and peeling ached with painful blisters. Proper attention would have to wait until my return to Boa Vista and a visit to the pharmacy. Dry shoes and socks will be a treat. Dry feet would last only a short while since we were in the rainy season, the season of overflowing paths and dripping foliage. The comfort of dryness must wait. I understood why our host William and the Yanomama went about in bare feet, probably the same reason why African nomads preferred skins to cloth. With both, it was a matter of survival since wet socks created health problems and wet clothes also kept in the dampness and were soon tattered and useless.

SPIRITS OF THE RAINFOREST

The Yanomama, like all cultures, have their own personal creation mythology. Their language is very unusual sounding and was understood by our host William, and my anthropologist friend, Dr. John Saffirio, who was called Moxiroxi or the 'bald one' in Yanomama. John remains a world authority on these people, their culture and their daily habits. John or Moxiroxi lived in Catrimani for many years and traveled the paths with the hunters. He was also threatened with his life and only survived by chasing his adversary with an axe. These Indians speak four languages understood by all Yanomama groups along with several distinct dialects. It was always necessary for me to use a translator and when asked about the creation of fire, the reply was as follows.

Children of the rainforest

'Once upon a time, only alligator possessed fire, as could be seen by the inside of his blood red mouth. The Yanomama also wanted fire, so after many long discussions they decided to hold a great feast in the jungle, and invited all the animals to attend, including alligator. The key was to make alligator laugh so heartily that they would be able to snatch fire from his mouth. All the animals were told of the plan and attempted to make alligator laugh but were unsuccessful. It seemed all was lost when suddenly, tiny hummingbird began to fly around the gathered circle of animals and proceeded to defecate on the assembly. Everyone, including alligator, broke into an uproar of laughter at the audacity of the diminutive bird. Swooping down as alligator laughed, hummingbird scooped some fire from its mouth and flew to a nearby cacao tree. Today, when the Yanomama want fire, they go to the cacao tree, cut a straight branch called the male, and between their hands, spin it into a piece of soft palm wood called the female. The resulting friction is fed with dry fibers and fire is created. It is only a simple matter of releasing the fire that resides in the hardened cacao put there by hummingbird. If you look inside the mouth of the alligator they say, it is still red and looks aflame.'

Try as I may, I have never been able to produce enough heat to start a fire with my two sticks, but I have timed the Yanomama who can have a blaze going in several minutes.

When asked what happens to a Yanomama after death, John told me the following. Upon death, the body is taken out and away from the malocca and placed in a tree to dehydrate. At one point, the bones are picked clean by an elder and then taken into the malocca and reduced to ashes in the central communal fire pit. The ashes are gathered and stored in a gourd and kept hung over the family's hammock. At one point, the timing was not made clear to me, the ashes are taken down and sprinkled into a hollowed log filled with mashed banana, which had been left to ferment. Gathered around are the deceased's family and friends. Scooping up the fermented banana and ashes in their split gourd cups, everyone has their fill until the concoction is finished. During this time, there is much wailing and sobbing because the deceased is now on his way to his final dwelling place and the farewell is filled with laments of sorrow and anguish. Having consumed the deceased in the ashes links the living with the dead in a spiritual continuum.

Where is this final place? The Yanomama understand four upper levels of existence, and one below. The frightening underworld, that nether region of darkness which fills them with terror each night, is where evil spirits dwell and will do the Yanomama great harm. These spirits of evil roam about at night and can capture the unsuspecting and so nightly outings are filled with hesitation and trepidation. The darkness is filled with these roaming 'hekuru' who will not hesitate to capture the living, especially the children. There are many rituals to thwart this malevolence, including sweeping of the front entrance with fronds.

The first upper level is the jungle and the present place of the Yanomama. It is here you must settle before going on. The next level is a halfway place whose purpose was unclear to me and seemed a waiting station of sorts. Next, was that region of long awaited glory, of total fulfillment, a place where food abounds and hunger is unknown. A place where women are plentiful and the day is filled with all the pleasures one can imagine, a nirvana of the senses, a hedonistic paradise. And how does one attain this Eden of sensuality and happiness? Well, the Yanomama say, when you enter this blissful threshold above, the Son of Thunder will question you and decide upon your admittance. He will ask if you have been a good Yanomama while on earth below. A good Yanomama is one who has shared his spoils with the whole malocco and has been a thoughtful and respectable hunter. When you answer yes, you are admitted to this Yanomama heaven. What would happen if you didn't share your meat and were a thoughtless hunter? Well, the reply was, if you were a selfish and thoughtless person, you simply had no choice except to lie, since the Son of Thunder wouldn't know the difference anyway. And the final upper level? With an incredulous shrug, the reply was that the last level was outer space of course, an empty void of nothingness.

I had done some in-depth research on the Yanomama while in Canada and although it was far removed from being among them, it was a start at understanding these interesting people. Females are seen as a liability since they were not hunters and consumed precious protein. The result was female infanticide and only an allotted number of female newborns were allowed to live. Now the practice of female infanticide, although culturally sanctioned by the Yanomama, was no less disturbing to outsiders. Of course, the long-term effect was a skewed male-female population growth. One such incident of near female infanticide happened with Iracoma, Catrimani's adopted waif. She was supposed to die but was saved by John Saffirio and the medical sister. Male babies were viewed as future hunters bringing home the meat. They were also the defenders of the village against Oka, unidentified enemies painted pitch black who attack lone hunters, usually in the evenings. Shamans are males, who cured sick people and rooted out the cause of death. Village leaders were males and gave unity to the group while patrilineal descent systems gave the male power and traced the Yanomama origins to a male ancestor. Females were in an inferior position and their status was reflected as such in Yanomama society.

Usually, Yanomama mothers suffocate unwanted newborns by stuffing leaves inside the mouth and stepping on the infant's chest. It is summarily wrapped in leaves and thrown away without any funeral rites. A Catrimani female, if asked why she destroyed a newborn, would answer with one of the following, culturally accepted answers. If the infant showed any physical defects it would be destroyed since it would have little chance of survival. Mothers traditionally nurse their children for three years and therefore a newborn is also destroyed in order to enhance the chances of survival for the nursing and dependent child. If the husband suspected the child was not his own or not sired by a 'brother,' he would not want it and she would destroy the child at birth. If the woman was lazy and felt she was unwilling to raise a newborn or was holding a grudge against her husband because he mistreated her, she would also destroy the baby. Serious illness during pregnancy, such as measles, whooping cough, or intestinal infections, was still another reason for abortion. When twins were born, it was usually the female or the smaller one, which was destroyed, since nursing two babies would be too burdensome and it was felt that eventually one of the twins would be undernourished and die. Saffirio's data shows that women destroy twice as many females as males.

Survival for females is tenuous indeed

The spiritual life of the Yanomama is enacted through shamanistic performances. The shaman uses hallucinogens to contact the spirit world and to re-enact the primeval feats of ancestors such as Oman, Yoasi, Sihirim, and so on. Included in this oral mythology is how the Yanomama received their first seeds to plant, the finding of the first woman, how the animals received their color and so forth, myths representing the collective memory of the people. Through these myths, the Yanomama interpret life around them and understanding is given to their history.

Their system of political alliances included treachery and deceit since a better offer would have them switching sides when it was to their advantage. Having a full belly was the ultimate because living in the jungle was a tenuous one at the best of times. Also, there existed a brittle coalition between the various Yanomama groups and this was due to several factors, one being the capturing and kidnapping of each other's wives, since marriageable women were scarce. When a bumper crop of banana took place, the villagers would invite a neighboring settlement to a feast. The menu could also include slightly charred or singed howler monkeys, piled high in the malocco, all black, with grotesque eyes, unblinking and cold. One such invitation came to our malocca and off we went through overgrown paths, Loy and I following a long line of naked men, brilliantly arrayed with arara feathers tied to their biceps with colorful crowns of black and white downy eagle feathers on their heads, bows and arrows trusted ahead of them, the whole group, whooping and yelling their way to an anticipated feast. Bodies were covered with severe designs, very geometric and bleeding red in color. Dust was flying as we surrounded our hosts' malocca. We welcomed the sun and the short respite from the daily drizzle. The noise made by our group had a twofold purpose. First, it was to convey their delight in anticipation of a feast and secondly, there was the intent to show their hosts they were not sneaking up for a stealthy attack.

Off to the banana party in the next clearing

As a gesture of goodwill, all the weapons were left outside the hosts' maloca before we entered. Inside, the hosts were treated to a lively dance as our friends circled the perimeter of the dwelling, all made up in their jungle finery, feathers a rainbow of blurs, as the stomping and whooping grew louder with each round of dancing. Off to one side, several hollowed logs were brimming with fermented banana, a testimony to the abundance of a rare and successful harvest. The dust swirled and the hosts smiled their approval, as gracious benefactors who also knew that such an event required a reciprocal invitation one day besides cementing a political alliance to be used against another unsuspecting village. Women stood by the banana filled receptacles, with split gourds ready to distribute the pulverized mash to their guests. Children and dogs lost in the haze watched from the edges of the crowd, eyes wide with awe at such a prestigious occasion.

The dancing and singing stopped with an abruptness, and the brimming gourds were distributed and the feasting began under the benevolent eyes of the hosts. I knew what was going to happen as I circled about unobtrusively, taking pictures in the semi darkness. I should have warned Loy, who was holding his own on the edge of the throbbing crowd. The guests were expected to gorge themselves as gourd after brimming gourd of fermented banana was swallowed, only to be immediately refilled to overflowing by the women. Soon the feasters were squatting, glassy eyed, as more of the gruel was forced down in appreciation. Tummies began to extend, haunches sank lower and lower to the ground, and gourd after dripping gourd was poured into overflowing mouths and dripping necks and bulging stomachs. It was impolite to refuse the generosity of the hosts as more of the mash was choked down. I waited the anticipated outcome and suddenly, and without warning the gushing of vomiting began, first with one merrymaker, and then another and soon the whole lot were gagging and heaving fountains of banana, spraying the earthen floor, dogs now eager participants in the feast as they lapped up the unexpected bonanza. No sooner had one coughed up his meal, than the fine hosts, only an arm's length away, were at the ready, doling out more banana mash. The feasting, finally over and after gathering up their weapons, we followed our subdued friends down the path, back to their malocca in nearby Catrimani, now a passive bunch indeed. One can imagine the stories, which were told around the fires that evening, stories, which would only be repeated when at some future time, the hosts would be showered with a banquet of food and they too would lie in comfort with stomachs full and sleep, only a hammock away.

Gorging more banana mash at the party

Perhaps it would be useful to further describe the Yanomama culture and mythology, which is fascinating because they do not 'see' the world as we do, or better still, we do not see the world they live in. We can only watch and never really understand who they are and how they became one with the place they find themselves. The Yanomama are as much a part of the Amazon as are the trees and sloths, piranha and toucan, anaconda and caiman, tapir or jaguar. These people must be seen as part of the jungle, a people who use it gently as their banquet table, never abusing, always showing a cautious respect. Gardening is the major food source. Crops consist of a variety of banana, sweet and bitter (poison) manioc, taro, sweet potatoes, tobacco, sugar and arrow cane, and a variety of gourds as well as hallucinogenic and magic plants. Forest grubs, turtles, crabs, wild fruit, honey, hunting and fishing make up the Yanomama diet. After three years when the garden is no longer productive due to the thin and infertile soil, the malocca is relocated and the tropical slash and burn garden is left to rejuvenate and to become one with the jungle again. When looking at an active Yanomama garden, it was difficult to make out where the cultivation began and where the rainforest left off. It was an inconspicuous plot, one that would readily return to a natural state if left unattended.

One Yanomama myth deals with the flood story, a tale whose contents is unique to these Indians and unrelated to our Noah and the Ark. (It seems the flood story is a common piece of oral mythology among many non technical people and bears closer examination for its near universal presence.) Apparently, a young girl left the seclusion of her hut during her first menstrual period and walked outside and into the open. This taboo was akin to opening a Pandora's box since the act brought about chaos. (It is interesting to note that once again, like Eve, women, can now be blamed for that initial indiscretion and therefore be relegated to an inferior social position.) The chaos brought about a ravaging flood and forced some Yanomama away as they rode crude logs down the swollen river and disappeared into the jungle. A few remained behind. Today, when outsiders appear, the Yanomama justify their presence as those long lost river brethren who are finally returning and can once again be reclassified into their kinship system, thus leaving their worldview intact. Loy and I would be reckoned as lost Yanomama, coming home from a distant part of the jungle.

I was given twenty odd pieces of Yanamama artwork, one depicting this flood scene. Yanomama did not have any formal artwork other than body painting prior to 1971. Saffirio, under very strict and controlled conditions, introduced paper and magic markers. The initial reason for this exercise was to test for right and left-handedness. This was an unusual experience for the Yanomama who knew neither pen nor paper and to illustrate a mental concept such as disease or chaos would baffle even the best of us. The project grew and thirty Indians, both men and women were asked to create ten different drawings each, which included geometric forms and human shapes. In 1974, they were asked to illustrate their myths and legends. These illustrations were put into a Christmas gift book and sold around the world to publicize the plight of the Yanomama who were succumbing to disease contacted from the road builders at a frightening rate while being murdered by ruthless gold miners. This publicity began the long struggle for a Yanomama reserve, one that was exclusive and unconditional. Taniki from the village of Hewenahipitheri on the

Catrimani River became the most prolific artist and produced 82 of the 104 pieces of work in a collection called, 'Spirits of the Rain Forest.'

A DAY IN THE LIFE

I have limited experience with the Yanomama people and have had to depend upon my good friend, John who lived in Catrimani for many years and traveled the paths of the warriors. He is still considered a world authority on the Catrimani River Yanomama. I met John is Brazil and we became instant friends as his enthusiasm and professionalism spilled over. Our roads have crossed many times since and we remain today, email buddies and still share a common passion for anthropology. My hands on experience with this tribe were for a limited time but my readings are extensive, having access to original material and first hand accounts. In addition, my research has been supplemented with unique and one of a kind artifacts, many of which do not exist today because of outside intruders.

It is the Yanomama who are the Amazon's largest aboriginal group, numbering about 16,000 in 1985. There were nine Yanomama villages around the Catrimani river basin and each village consisted of a name giving creek, a slash and burn garden, and a communal dwelling, all of which were connected with pathways. The communal malocca as mentioned, is a huge, round, circus tent like structure, and some 60 to 120 feet in diameter. There can be 10 to 68 people in each dwelling, with hammocks strung around the inside perimeter, leaving the central area around the huge fire pit free. This area can he used for rituals and social gatherings, which might include chest pounding, a ritual oftentimes used with serious results, and a substitute for open aggression and war.

The central communal fire pit

(I remember one afternoon, sitting with some boys outside the radio shack and being unable to communicate, we used body language and gesture. At one point, I struck my chest with astonishing results. The boys let out a yelp and disappeared into the undergrowth, terrified. Chest pounding, I realized, had very serious cultural implications, which included smashed chest bones and even death.) The Yanomama, sometimes spelled Yanomani, are a diminutive people, solid, and very closely resemble the Inuit of northern Canada.

Each family has their own fire between their hammocks, which are tied around the circumference of the malocca. These hammocks are made from crude cotton, taken from their gardens. The bottom jaws of the piranha, with razor sharp teeth left intact, are used as scissors to clip the loose cotton fibers. It is the wife who is responsible to keep the warmth-giving fire lit at all times. Because of polygyny, one man with several wives, the husband is careful to place his hammock at equal distances from each wife. Polyandry, once found among the Todas of southern India, is the practice of several men sharing one woman and it is also found amongst the Yanomama. At daybreak, the husband leaves on his hunting duties, usually eating leftovers or a banana. Brothers and other male kin often hunt together, following tracks and using their dogs where possible. As the day gets brighter, the women feed the youngsters from any leftovers, go outside to the toilet and at some point, are off to the river to fetch drinking water in their gourds, a dangerous undertaking with kidnapping a strong possibility. Because of this fear of being kidnapped, women always take their children with them and they are seldom separated. Keeping warm by their individual fires during the rains occupies the women and children, along with any of the elders or men who for some reason are not out hunting.

Mother and child

Not all of the men go out hunting each day. Some stay behind to help with the heavier chores in the gardens or work on new bows and arrows fashioned from local woods and honed with a machete and finished off using the lower mandible of the collared or white-lipped peccary. When it has been decided that fishing will be the communal chore of the day, women with watertight hand woven baskets, carrying babies on their backs, and accompanied by several adult males, make off for the river. A section of the river is blocked off and particular leaves picked for their special properties are pounded with rocks, turning the water a milky white. The fish become deprived of oxygen, float to the surface and are scooped up. Young males, practicing their skills with bows and arrows in order to be clever hunters one day, shoot larger fish to show their prowess. Older males are present to thwart any attack from neighboring villagers that would kidnap and carry off their women and children.

Mothers are reluctant to leave their children alone

Some women spend the cooler morning hours in their gardens collecting manioc roots, plantains, and bananas. Others may stay behind in the malocca, separating cotton by hand to be used for hammocks or their meager waist wraps. Once again, when the women go to the garden or to the river for water, they do so in groups of five or ten because they fear an enemy raid. I was much honored by the way the women would invite me to accompany them for water each day. I thought it a flattering invitation and a sign of acceptance, despite being painfully bitten by fire ants that swarmed near the river edge. It turned out I was being used as a decoy to foil any of their prowling enemies who might decide to attack, rape, and kidnap and confine them in some distant jungle malocca.

Being invited to fetch water with the women

The potential kidnappers would have second thoughts about attacking with a stranger present. Besides, outsiders were known to carry guns.

During the hottest time of the day, most activity comes to a halt and after food is taken, a nap is the order of the day. The hunters, who did not wander too far in the jungle in search of food, return with a bird or two. The more serious men, return in the late afternoon, having tracked game deep in the rainforest. With any luck, several large parrots, a howler monkey or even a wild pig provides many pounds of meat for the family. Its seems that everything that runs or crawls, hides or flies, swims or dies, is fair game for the Yanomama. Tarantulas to grub worms, piranha and alligator all fall within their menu. Hunger is always a real threat. Some dishes are eaten well cooked, and others slightly singed, while still others are eaten alive. Young animals are never harmed, and the malocca will have several small monkeys or parrots as pets, their parents having fallen to the hunter's arrow. Everyone notices the kill of the day as it is carried on the back of the returning hunter. Food is divided up along kinship lines. It is not long before the meat is boiling or roasting on the fire. The hunter never partakes in the food he kills, lest he gets sick. To eat your own kill is taboo. Instead, he will eat fruit picked in the nearby jungle, such as nuts and berries, or produce from the garden. He may eat meat offered by another hunter. I once had our host ask a returning hunter, how many animals he had on his back from the day's kill. He replied that he had, 'one, two' and then 'many.' There is no need for higher numerical concepts despite the fact he had four animals on his back. The Yanomama count only up to the number two and then end with many or more.

Returning with the day's hunt

As the shadows get longer, the women hack wood for the evening meal and also to keep the night fire alive. It is at this time, bathing takes place in the river and more water is carried back. As night falls, the malocca is at its height of activity. Children cry because they are hungry, younger girls are pressed into serving meat to the male members first and then to the extended family if there is enough to go around. A watery broth in a half gourd, sweet manioc, and cassava bread accompanies the food. Saffirio told me that manioc flour is weevil resistant, and a near perfect food for the nontechnical tribes of the Amazon. Gossip is exchanged at this time and women tell their husbands about their day and the activities of the children. The men will recount their day's hunting in great detail, even identifying individual trees, pathways and clearings. One may talk to a nearby neighbor or shout across the malocca. Elders tell young ones, stories and legends of the Yanomama, thus keeping their oral legacies alive. Communal activities are discussed and go beyond immediate kinship ties. A new house may be needed, or a group hunting party might be formed. Feasts and ceremony discussions take on an animated air. Some one passing wind causes uproar and everyone joins in the laughter.

The malocca has one or two roof top openings to allow smoke to escape and sunlight to pour down in piercing shafts, which move across the dirt floor much like a spotlight as the day advances. At night, the moonlight sends down eerie beams and the malocca, cathedral like, stands still in anticipation, sinks into a lull and even the bawling children are silenced and bury themselves in their mother's folds in the hammocks. A dog may bark or the 'coro coro' rat may awaken the family sending a chill over them all. The darkness is filled with evil spirits and children know they are the easiest victims. An extra piece of wood is thrown on the fire, and everyone buries even deeper into their hammocks. Another day has passed, and like a shroud, the blackness wraps the malocca in an uneasy silence.

Yanomama Malocca at dusk

One night, nearly asleep, the shaman in the nearby malocca awakened us. He chanted his mournful remedy over a dying man for the whole night and far into the early dawn when his patient finally expired. It was once thought that the Yanomama never used the plants of the jungle to heal the sick. John Saffirio, proved otherwise since various plants are used as natural remedies, their secrets known only to the shaman, a much-respected member in this society.

Hunting, exclusively a male activity can raise the social status of a young man, and as a result, many hours are spent practicing with their weapons. Bows fashioned from young palm wood are strung with a fibre called yamaasik and are waxed to prevent rotting. The lower jaw of a wild pig, with the incisor left intact is used as a plane to smooth the hard wood. Arrows are made from cultivated cane and are dried over a fire or in the sun. These seven-foot long, beautifully straight shafts, with split bush turkey feathers bound at the end with wild cotton, are prized possessions. Arrow shafts are fitted with pencil-like points of palm wood and are usually coated with poison and used when hunting monkey and sloth. The poison relaxes the grip of the animal to ensure it falls from its lofty bough, which would be otherwise very difficult to retrieve.

Poison arrow tips freshly dipped and ready for the hunt

A broader and sharpened bamboo end is inserted into the shaft for larger, land bound game such as tapir or wild pig. The quiver is made from a piece of bamboo and capped with the skin of a recently killed pig or monkey. The fresh skin shrinks around the open end and when it dries, the natural cap keeps out water and prevents the hunter from inadvertently sticking himself with a poison arrow tip.

A JUNGLE HUNT

When we were asked to go on a hunting expedition with the Yanomama, I looked forward to the day. The event turned out to be a highlight of my Amazon experience and is still the most memorable event since my time in Africa. Four Yanomama hunters and Sergassio accompanied William, Loy and me. We took off down the Catrimani River, in an aluminum boat with a tired outboard, straining under the load. The Yanomama carried their long bows and quivers filled with poison arrows and bamboo shafts, while Sergassio toted an ancient blunderbuss, surely a collector's item. The Indians were excited at the thought of being ferried a long distance downstream to an area ripe with game, an area they seldom had the chance to exploit for food. The ride in the outboard was exhilarating as we veered off the main channel and chugged headlong through the overhanging trees, not unlike driving through a tunnel of vegetation. At one point, a sudden rush of water next to us erupted and a huge, pink dolphin broke the surface and raced alongside. It was somewhat uncomfortable being so close to this rare fresh water mammal as it leered at me with one black eye, all too knowingly. The anatomy of this animal is supposed to be very similar to an adult male and so if a girl gets pregnant, the dolphin was supposed to have impregnated her during the night and therefore absolve her of any public shame. This myth is from the indigenous Brazilians who live in the distant riverside settlements on the Amazon. The Yanomama have no need for such a story.

The setting in this tributary of the Catrimani River was completely removed from any previous one I had ever experienced. The jungle hung low on either side of us, thick and uninviting. As William slowed the boat, it became clear that we were in the midst of the 'Great Silence.' Off to my left, as we kept to the middle of the narrow channel, I rubbed my eyes in disbelief and only mentioned what I saw the following evening during one our sitting room chats. There on the edge of the water, pulling itself up an overhang was the largest spider I had ever seen. It was the size of a washbasin, with brown and black stripped hairy legs and an abdomen the size of my fist. It looked prehistoric and I later found out it was not uncommon but rather the bird eating spider of the Amazon. Apparently, this creature feeds on young birds still in the nest.

An eerie wail filled the air, drowning out the sputtering of our outboard motor. Everyone became silent and waited for the long echo to end. A howler monkey calling out could be heard for miles. The howl faded on a lonesome note. Overhead, we disturbed brilliantly feathered long tailed scarlet arara, macaws with rich, crimson plumage and blue green tipped wings. Once airborne, they set the sky ablaze like a rainbow unleashed. Their coarse croaking calls are unbefitting for such beauty.

I remember in Kenya, how the Africans seemed to be without pity when a predator attacked an animal. I thought there was a definite lack of compassion, as they seemed to enjoy the death struggle of the victim. High above the tree line, as we putted through the winding river, a soaring eagle swooped down and in a crushing dive, plucked a monkey from its lofty perch and flew off with the helpless prey, its grasping arms flaying, its feet kicking in desperation. The Yanomama on board, pointed and laughed as the struggling quarry, writhed in the clutches of the airborne marauder and disappeared over the treetops. The scene was all too familiar and I again wondered at the lack of compassion. I have since come to understand that the Yanomama, like my nomadic friends in Kenya, were in fact not laughing or enjoying the kill of the hunt, but rather they, who were also counted among the hunted by predators, were uneasy. This uneasiness was because, for the time being, they had escaped the fate of the victim and being survivors, enjoyed a nervous celebration of life. Africans had an uncanny hatred for hyena and it was because this marauder always had the last meal, whether it be feasting on an aging lion, an injured wanderer, or digging up the remains of a loved one. Hyenas, nature's wraiths, became man-eaters in Ethiopia when the animals' regular diet was scarce. Likewise, the Yanomama equally despised the jaguar.

The plan that day was to drop off the Yanomama and Sergassio so they could hunt in this untouched part of the jungle and the three of us would carry on downstream, fish for piranha or whatever else was available for dinner that night, and by early evening, pick up our hunting party. As William steered into a break in the overhanging foliage, the hunters hopped into the water, weapons held high and began to wade into the blackness. I knew that this was an opportunity, not to be missed. I called to William at the front of the boat and told him I was going with the hunters. He was very hesitant and said it would be much safer to stay in the boat and enjoy the day on the river since he would be leaving the hunters alone until dusk. I assured him that I had complete confidence in the Yanomama and I asked my host to translate one request, and that was to tell them not to leave me in the jungle to find my way back alone. I had a very unfortunate experience in Africa and the bush there was low-slung acacia, a walk in the park when compared to this tropical rain forest. He called to the group to wait, as I jumped into the waist high water. They stopped to listen to William and then turned to stare at me.

On route for the day's hunt in the jungle

Now I was somewhat unprepared. I had bare feet in an old pair of running shoes, a loose T-shirt and cut off shorts. Not jungle gear to say the least but then again I never expected to travel inland with the hunters, who themselves were naked except for their penis string. William called out to me before I disappeared behind the group and under the overhang. He warned me not to sit on rotting logs since it was the favorite haunt of venomous snakes. I assured him I would follow the lead of the experienced Yanomama. The outboard sputtered away and the silence filled me with no choice but to hurry on after the group as they pulled themselves onto dry land without so much as a look backwards. They vanished in the thick growth, which enclosed the water's edge. I wondered if they resented my presence.

I had enough experience with aboriginal hunters to respect and never to second-guess their moves. And so it was, the hunters came to a fungus covered log, sat down and proceeded to take out their poison tipped arrow heads and insert them in the ends of their long, cane shafts. I sat next to them, watching closely and unable to communicate other than to show my interest in their preparations. We marched away single file; I was third in line, an old trick I had learned. If there was a dangerous snake on the path, the first hunter would spot it and sound the alarm and if he missed it, the second man would surely see the danger, I hoped. I knew this worked in Africa and as we walked I found myself wondering if maybe, to be on the safe side, I should drop back even further in line.

What happened next was truly amazing. Up until our leaving the log, the Yanomama talked in low tones, but I knew it was the language they used all the time. Now, as we marched through the jungle, they reverted to sounds of the natural world around them. Instead of their normal speech, they made calls and snorts of the animals they were tracking. They were communicating with each other and the wildness around us in a way, which was both primordial and bizarre. I felt that with each footstep, I was walking back in time, to a former moment long past, when man was one with his surroundings, a part of a whole, and inseparable. Now the Yanomama are amazing mimickers, and can repeat any sound they hear with an uncanny accuracy. So as I walked, I heard the chattering of monkeys, the grunts of the white-lipped peccary, and the calls of birds, all weird and foreign to me. I also smelled a familiar musky odor, which hung low and heavy as we trudged along.

The vegetation, struggling for sunlight under the soaring mantle, was not as heavy as I had imagined it and walking was easy as we left the fringe of the river behind. It was the numerous streams and swamps that got my attention. As I struggled to keep up with these pygmy sized hunters, bare as mentioned, except for their penis cords, the wading into the uncertain bottoms of quagmire caused me some anxiety. Unseen tentacles of struggling vines, submerged and groping caused me some nervousness as they wrapped themselves around my legs and ankles. I almost waited for the bite from some hungry bottom dweller I was disturbing. Walking in these wetlands was a struggle. At one point, I reached out to grab onto a vine as I sank into a dark hole. The hunter in front of me saw my hand, quickly pulled it away before I could take hold of the liana and turned and looked at me. Then with one finger, he carefully pointed to the vine and it was only then I noticed it was covered with minute, hooked barbs, ready to defend itself against a would be intruder. He must have wondered how I ever survived in my part of jungle, since for the Yanomama everyone lived in a similar setting, countries, cities, and streets being unheard of and without meaning. My family must go hungry often with such a hunter as myself, weaponless and clumsy, unable to distinguish a lethal vine. I since thought that grabbing onto that vine in my ignorance, would be like a Yanomama crossing a busy thoroughfare on a red light during rush hour.

Now I had counted on the hunters not to abandon me as we pushed on, deeper and deeper into the undergrowth. I really had no clue as to the direction of the river and my two friends in the faraway boat. I was completely turned around and helplessly lost. I knew up and down and little other direction. I was completely dependent upon these Yanomama. On and on we trudged, completely ignoring the leeches and sloshing shoes, my sole aim was to keep up with the hunters ahead of me. The musky odor grew more offensive and seemed to cling to the foliage. The hunters, in turn, were becoming more animated, as they forged ahead, side stepping obstacles and melting around me. I found it easier to crash headlong through the brush and leave various pieces of my body behind. At one point, the man closest to me turned and with an open palm, pressed against my chest. As I tried to walk ahead, the hunter stepped directly in front of me and without doubt, made it clear that I was to stop then and there. But I had asked William, very specifically, to inform my newly acquired companions that I was not to be left under any circumstance. Now, I was being told to stop and in a blink, the hunters disappeared and I was alone.

Being by myself was unnerving. I looked around and imagined all sorts of sounds and movements. I imagined I saw an unblinking anaconda staring from the murky swamp. Hanging lianas, mimicking the dreaded bushmaster, seemed to take on a life of their own. The sun, choked out by the surging vegetation, left long shadows and thin shafts to light the way. I knew enough to stay exactly where I was left and could only wonder why I was abandoned. At first I thought it was my clumsy trudging through the undergrowth that was scaring the game away. I never thought the hunters would permanently desert me, but the idea did float around for second or two. I waited. It seemed a long time, as I stood perfectly still and listened for a familiar clue.

There I stood, stiff legged and silent, straining to pick up the slightest sound or movement. I couldn't help but question just why I was here. My thoughts wandered back to Canada and the comfortable routine I had come to know. A walk to the local grocery store at the Glenridge plaza flashed before me and for a moment I relished the idea of filling up a shopping cart with goods.

The first sound of crashing vegetation left me stiff and straining. It was ahead and distant, but nevertheless, I did hear something. Listening with a cocked ear, the noise came again, clearly and directly in front of me where the hunters had disappeared. It wasn't long before the snapping of branches became louder and it seemed much closer. I waited, listened and realized that what ever it was causing all the commotion, something was definitely getting much closer. The first snorting and grunting had me looking for a tree to climb. Nothing offered an easy refuge and I knew I was in the path of a herd of wild pigs, probably white-lipped peccary, and the same animal famous for its ripping, slashing tusks. The animals were close now and I could make out their angry grunts when suddenly several beasts erupted through the undergrowth and came charging head on without the least intention of stopping.

The first animal, black and hairy, beady eyed and high stepping burst out of the underbrush, not fifteen feet ahead of me. I could see the stained, white tusks pumping up and down. Closer it crashed and frozen, I waited for the last moment to jump to one side, hoping my legs wouldn't let me down. I can't say how close the boar was when not more than five feet away, a Yanomama hunter, bow taunt, let loose a shaft. The animal, struck above the front shoulder, squealed and tripped over itself, rolled and kicked. The boar lay dead at my feet, the hunter, stepping next to me and smiling, looked for approval. I stared down at the pig and then at the young man and couldn't think of an appropriate gesture other than to gawk at them both and shake my head. The group appeared and showed their approval as they inspected the dead animal. One man walked over to a nearby palm, sliced off a large leaf, and proceeded to tear out the fibers in thin strips. Meanwhile, another hunter kneeled over the kill and began to butcher the animal. Within minutes, the weaver had two smartly woven baskets complete with headbands, ready to pack and carry the meat. The meat was loaded into the baskets, which hung over their backs, and strapped around their foreheads. With blood running down the small of their backs, we marched off in the opposite direction, which I would have gone in search of the river and our boat. At least that where I assumed we were headed. I had read and was told that the Yanomama were also called, 'the invisible people.' Well I could now confirm this first hand.

Their stealth and their ability to blend into the jungle was awesome since one of the hunters was at no time more than several feet away from me during my 'abandonment.'

The hunters resumed their regular language as we trudged along and it seemed we were all just a little noisier. There was a lively discussion taking place, the meaning completely foreign to me. We stopped, and the meat carriers dropped their loads, leaving trump line marks on their foreheads, and while one fellow walked off to a nearby palm, the others looked upwards at the crown of a particularly tall and prickly palm, one of the numerous species, which abounded in the jungle. This particular tree had spines, black and piercing and at least two or three inches in length, covering the whole trunk. At the very top, there were clusters of purple round fruit. I wondered how this was going to happen. The climber approached the tree with two separate pieces of newly woven twine. He looped one around the trunk, avoiding the spines and tied the ends. He then took the second piece of rope and tied the two ends together and put one foot in each end, pushed the middle of the rope against the tree, and heaved himself upwards, as he jerked up the spiny trunk using the top rope to pull himself. Up and up he went and when he reached the top, he slashed away at the fruit, which came tumbling down on us to everyone's amusement. Meanwhile, our weaver had a new basket waiting and we all piled the hard purple fruit inside as more of the nuts fell on our heads.

Off we marched, now laden with dripping meat and a hard, seemingly impenetrable purple nut of sorts. The march to the river seemed shorter and at one point, one hunter turned to me and clearly mimicked the sound of an outboard motor in need of a tune up. I strained once again and heard nothing. We continued on. When I finally heard the outboard, I could also see the edge of the water through the overhanging boughs and I knew that just beyond these limbs were William and Loy and our ride home. I shouted to William and listened. I shouted again and heard one of them yell their location, hidden well behind the overhang, twenty feet or so out in the water. We did this several times and used their calls to direct us to the boat as we waded in, first knee deep and then waist high and soon the Yanomama were up to their necks.

As we emerged from the undergrowth in the openness and sunshine, I felt a comforting relief and a rushing benevolence, as I ushered the hunters ahead of me, assisting them when I could. It was then I heard someone call out to me. Apparently, unseen by us, several large alligators were sunbathing on an outcrop, only a short distance away. We were deep in the water and struggling to get aboard, and all the while, the dripping blood of the pig, was sending out a message to both alligator and piranha. There was little we could do but to hurry. I was the last one aboard and as I set down my one foot, I felt a sickly softness and it wasn't the bottom of the boat. I let out a yell, nearly falling backwards as I looked down. My foot was just behind the jaws of a fairly substantial alligator, the mouth having opened with the pressure of my foot. William and Loy had not only caught some decent sized piranha, but this young alligator was to be added to our menu for supper. Once the laughter settled down we were on our way. I must say that the piranha filets were huge and delicious, moist and boneless, whereas the tail of the alligator was white and looked good, but tasted fishy and stagnant and all I could imagine was a summertime road kill. The purple fruit, a seasonal treat, was crushed and with filtered water, made an interesting drink.

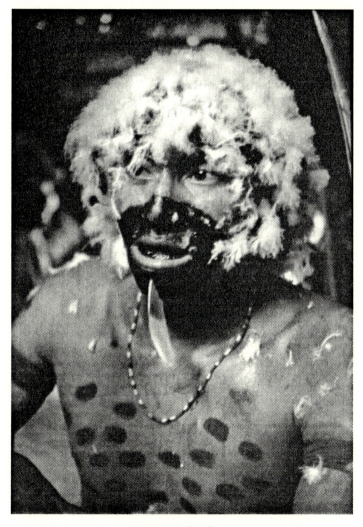

Warrior in his finery

My host was very generous and presented me with a wealth of Yanomama artifacts, which I brought back to Canada. These included a quiver made from bamboo, crudely etched with geometric designs and filled with both the thin poison shafts and the heavier type used for larger game. The raspy tongue of the pirarucu is an interesting artifact but the dried scales of this fish proved to be useful as a nail file and a great conversation piece. I also have the powder the Yanomama blow up their noses with the aid of a hollow bamboo tube, the sudden rush of this substance knocking them off their haunches and sending them into a drug induced trance. This drug called yakoana, is taken from the inner bark of the ebene tree, mixed with ashes, kneaded with saliva, dried over a fire and ground into a powder for blowing up the noses of men. The feathers given to me are spectacular and are still as bright as they were in the jungle. Some feather work, including the delicately fashioned ear and chin ones, are used to decorate the women. Some are stuck through their ear lobes, while still others are inserted into pierced holes in the chin. The men wear large arara feathers tied around their biceps and don toucan crowns for celebrating an occasion.

Warrior with Arara Feathers

Hand fashioned cotton hammocks and women's waist wraps are the only fibers used by these people and they appear diminutive and doll-like. Long bows and cane arrows were a challenge to carry home, but they are intact and are an interesting contrast to their African counterparts. Woven baskets and simple gourds and original 'paintings' complete my inventory of Yanamama artifacts, which as mentioned are a contrast to their African counterparts and so much more primitive and plain. The twenty odd foot anaconda skin would have certainly attracted the curiosity of the custom officials but was best left behind for the roaches.

YANA, YOU ARE YANOMAMA COME BACK

My friend John Saffirio, who told me the following story, had an unmarried sister living in Bra, Northern Italy. She asked to adopt a Yanomama girl who would otherwise be left out to die. As it turned out, a young female Yanomama was pregnant and John, despite the initial reluctance from the father, Machadao, finally convinced the man to let the baby live if it were a girl. He was forced to assuage the man's ego with gifts of pots and so forth. When the baby was about to be born, John had a wet nurse accompany the mother into the jungle and return the child to Catrimani, if it was a girl. The wet nurse came back with a fine baby girl and John's sister was instructed to fly from Bra, to Boa Visita in three months time, when the youngster would be old enough to travel to her future home.

The girl was named Yana and left for Europe to be raised as an Italian. She became an Italian child, student, and friend to her playmates. Over the years, when 'Uncle John' returned home to visit, he watched Yana grow into a young lady. It was most interesting to note the way she behaved in certain situations such as when she was bargaining for a favor or making her opinion known. John said she displayed a multitude of Yanomama characteristics in her social skills and thought processes. Not only did she look like a Yanomama, but also she acted out Yanomama behavioral traits, traits, which were foreign to other Italians.

Yana knew from an early age, her ethnic history and birth conditions. When she was a teenager, it was decided that she should visit the place where she was born and meet her kin. This was in part due to the many questions she had about her early beginnings. When all the tedious arrangements were finalized, John met his sister, Yana and several cousins in Boa Visita and arranged a flight to the Catrimani outpost. Yana, like many urbanites, had a dislike for creepy crawlies and all of the other insects, which we call pests. She was naturally squeamish. So upon arriving in Catrimani, the young girl was taken aback with the abundance of live things, which swarmed around the outpost. It is interesting because had she remained in the jungle, part of her daily responsibilities would have been to collect grubs and larvae for the family dinner. It was previously arranged that Yana's birth parents would make the trek to Catrimani from wherever they were in the jungle, along with their immediate extended family to meet their young girl, who had long since vanished. One can only imagine this Italian speaking young lady's expectations upon meeting her biological parents. Dressed in Italian clothes she waited in anticipation.

The Yanomama arrived and Yana was ushered outside to meet them. It must have been a shock for the parents to see this young lady who looked like a Yanomama but was fully dressed and all covered up like a stranger. The mother with only her waistband attire, and the father Machadao, donning his penis cord, would have everyone's attention. There were other family members in the group, all staring and wondering at this covered apparition who looked Yanomama.

Having left the Amazon behind, and back in Italy, Yana wrote the following letter to a friend, discussing her feelings. John has kindly provided the translation from Italian into English.

December 1, 1991

I remember nothing of my past life in Brazil, of the trip and arrival in Italy, of the moment of detaching myself from Brilliana, of my adjusting to Bra. On the other, I have heard and learned of those events so often and in such minute details that I could recount them as if I were the one who was personally remembering them. Every time some visitor comes to my house, mom tells those stories with such joy that it is a real pleasure to listen to her.

My first memory goes back to the Christmas I spent in Bra in 1975 in the Luciana Saffirio's house. Periodically my memory triggers and brings to the surface in me some flash-back from my past; my trips on the mountains, my visits to some cities, my school, my new friends. These 18 years I have spent here with my marvelous mom, with hers and my family and among friends have been splendid and I would never change anything. At the same time I have and continue to encounter a number of difficulties.

My greatest terror as a child, a fear which I continue to experience even now, is of continuously feeling that I am the object of everybody's stare; when I go for a walk, when I shop, when I go to a movie or attend a feast. It is only when I am surrounded by friends (and they are many) that I feel at peace and safe. Imagine that whenever along the road I encounter children or boys, I prefer to go in another direction or turn around and go back home. If they are adult women or girls, I lower down my head and continue. I continuously experience a great fear of people. I cannot stand being surrounded by people I do not know. The crowd terrifies me. I have already analyzed this feeling and my conclusion is that I am afraid that they may notice how different

I am from them. I feel that they may pass a negative judgment on me or that they will poke fun on me. On the contrary, I feel accepted, understood and loved by my friends and so I feel at home among them. As a child, quite often I felt the stare and heard negative comments coming from other children about my face being darker than what is usual among people. I have concluded that my terrible fear of people derives from this. I have to add that once the foreigners in (the city of Bra) were just a few, and so I was a novelty for that place. The situation has now changed. As mom says (and she has always been very close to me), perhaps, people now do not stare at me any longer, or if they do so, their evaluation of me is positive. But my fixation on that and my fears have persisted. All those embarrassments brought me to the point where I was not accepting myself. I could not stand thinking of being the daughter of an Amazonian Indian, of having to carry an unusual and difficult family name, so different from everybody else. I have cried many times and long on myself being so different. But then things gradually started to change and improve.

When I graduated from the Elementary and registered in the Intermediate School I was forced to use my real family name: Korihanateri. At that point, everyone came to know that I was not Italian but I was originally from Brazil. That was a difficult test for me. But then I gradually started to accept the reality of things. Every time people were asking me of my place of origin and I was stating that I was from Brazil, they would compliment me because they said Brazil was a marvelous country. I was proud of it yet I was still terrified at the thought that they could come to know of my real origin. I was naively hoping that they would never come to discover it. But things did not happen that way. In the meantime, I was growing, if not it height, I was maturing inside of me. I gradually started to become more and more interested in my blood family. I was studying their photos and began to accept that I was part of them. I started also to progressively love them. When I mentioned that to mom, she was very happy. She has always explaining things to me in minute details and with the greatest clarity and simplicity. For instance she never forced me to watch the projection of those film (on the Y), which she was showing to the visitors. She would always first assure herself that I was the one who wanted to see them.

Last summer I came to know a boy and I fell in love with him. I never imagined that I would have the courage to reveal to him my secret (that was the way I used to see it!) anyhow, I finally dared to tell him my story. It was absolutely the first time I was doing that with anyone. But, he, more or less, told me that he knew it. He really stunned me when he added that several other people knew of my story. That was the shock of my life. I finally saw that it was true what mom had always told me. People knew about me, but I had never realized it. Yet, to finally come to discover that did not displease me. That boy did not poke fun on me as I had anticipated. So, one day, for the very first time, I showed him their (my parent's) picture. He was not surprised and I was exhilarated. For the very first time, I had talked about my secret with someone. I came to discover that my very best girl-friend had also known about it but had never mentioned it to me, and I had never shown her their pictures.

This year, I was thrilled to have a chance to go to Brazil. Besides visiting the cities of Brazil, would finally meet up with my family. Before departing from Bra I spent several days trying to anticipate how our encounter would be, what kind of feelings I would go through. I experienced my greatest nervousness and intensity of emotions when, on that Friday, August 9 we had to take the air taxi-airplane for Catrimani. Just before departing, I wrote in my secret diary all my various contradictory feelings I was experiencing at that point. I even cried for sheer joy and nobody ever came to know about it. I did not know what it was: fear, anxiety, sympathetic emotions, sheer happiness. In those moments, I was imagining the fatidical encounter which I had anticipated for so long and now was approaching. It was going to take place in a mere couples of hours. My heart was in my throat and tears dripping while I was writing. Finally I was going to see my own family, the very person who had given me life. It was all so strange. When the airplane flew over Catrimani and I saw the children waving, I was shaking with fear, but was a new kind of fear that I had never experience before and it was not easy to define. When I saw them approaching, I was deeply moved, but I had imposed on myself that I was not going to show anyone this aspect of me. I did not want to them to see me crying for sheer happiness. As you probably did notice, both my cousins and mom started to cry while I remained normal. At that point, I almost felt guilty. But, that is because, where ever there are outsiders around me, I do not reveal my feeling. I may even seem cold. That is but a mask. The truth is that I was extremely happy and my heart was overwhelmed by emotions. While we were approaching I was trying to imagine my own very mom.

It all happened so fast. I remember that I did not have time to realize what was happening because I was conscious that all the cam-corders and cameras flashlights were on me. I had no time to make myself aware that here was the very person who, so many years ago, at 8 AM of that July 16, 1973 had delivered me. As soon as I could manage it, I distanced myself from her because my shyness would not allow me to remain close to her. I looked at her and at the other Y with a fast side-glance. I was feeling everyone's eyes

ONTO THE AMAZON

on me, yet I was not scared. My cousins were urging me to approach her. They kept repeating: 'It is your mom. Tell her something.' (This would have had to be done with a translator. Author's note.) But I just could not do it. When I met dad, it was different. I remember that he was waiting for me outside the house where we were going to reside. I felt embrace by him and received a kind of kiss. At that moment I became aware: it was daddy! My shyness made it impossible for me to show how happy I was. As soon as possible I walked away. I longed to observe them from a distance, but on that first day it was impossible to maintain a physical distance. I knew that I was continuously at the center of everyone's attention. They were endlessly snapping pictures and so, I did not have a chance to stop and consider in what kind of world I had landed. A world so different from ours. That night I dld not stop to think. I fell immediately into a deep sleep.

The following days were intensely rich and pleasant, and so were the two trips on canoe, on the truck and on foot over the beams flooded forest. I enjoyed immensely our adventure in the floodwater. Those were all experiences that I had never gone through before. My style of relating with them (my parents) was perhaps a bit too detached, but that was not all fault of mine. One has to go through all that and it is quite difficult to explain. On those moments when I was walking from the school to the office, I would observe them sitting on the cement step, or staring inside the screened windows, or calling me, and I felt a strange reaction. I had hard time to believe that I was indeed, finally, among them. I imagined that if the course of my life had been different, probably, I too would have been there doing the same things. I was observing my real mom from a distance and I was asking myself if, seeing me there, she would not, once in a while, think of me who was so different from her other children. Every time we were next to each other, we did not exchange with each other more than a fast glance, but I felt a real attraction for her. I do not think that it was real affection. It was gratefulness because she had put me in the world. For that I am grateful. I suffered, or, rather, I was displeased that she would not show me as much love as my grandmother, my dad and the other women. But in truth, who can know what she felt?

While we were waiting for the arrival of the taxi-plane and we were hoping that the rainstorm would pass, I went outside and set. No one of them (Y) was there, and I started to think while I was scrutinizing the sky, I was thinking that in a short while I was going to leave them, possibly forever (but, nobody knows that), they were not aware that I was leaving my family. Many other thought came to mind. Then suddenly I saw them coming along the pathway. They had gone to take a bath in the river. They looked so happy and were laughing. I realized that they were enjoying themselves there, *thanks to help from the medical sisters and laymen and Uncle John. When the airplane arrived and we were ready for the au revoir or goodbye, I asked if I would ever see them again. But when the airplane turned around (at the end of the landing strip and accelerated towards the outpost) and started to fly, and I saw them waving and greeting us, vivid emotions caught up with me and choked me. I did not want the people inside the plane to see me like that. I turned my face to the other side and I cried and cried. Finally, I realized that I really love them and that I intend to help them so no one will ever hurt them like it has already happened.*

I promised and imposed on myself that one day, when my studies will be completed, I will return to Catrimani to give them a helping hand. I may even remain there forever. I intend to study not only for myself but also for them. I know that it is only when I have an education that I can provide them with a valid form of help. While I was flying over that immense virgin forest, I felt that a part of my heart was remaining with them. When (much later) I bordered the last flight to depart from Brazil and return to Italy, I felt that I was leaving 'my country.' Brazil was finally that to me, and that I had no longer any feeling of shame, rather I was experiencing a degree of pride, because Brazil is indeed a beautiful country.

Since I have returned here, I have been thinking about my parents and I see them under a different light. I had been used to think that to know and see our real parents was not that important. Now I have changed my mind on that. It has been a great thrill to have experienced where they live, to see them and to know them. I have discovered that also my friends know I went to see them (my parents). To some of them I have shown some photos and also the hammock that my mom Rita gave me and I did not feel any embarrassment as sometimes ago I would have felt. Here now, l have told you a resume of my 18 years and of my feeling on the occasion of meeting my parents. I have to continuously take into account my shyness, which has now improved considerably and my fear of strangers. But now I am confident that, as I keep growing, I will be progressing through further and further steps forward.

As you have noticed, at the beginning I do not open with strangers. I remain silent. Then, when I start to know them, I am completely open. I do not like to be an intruder and I cannot stand intruders. But, within limits I like to open up. I hope this account satisfies you. If not, just let me know what further details you would like to know and I will provide them.

A big hug from Yana xxx.

ONTO THE AMAZON

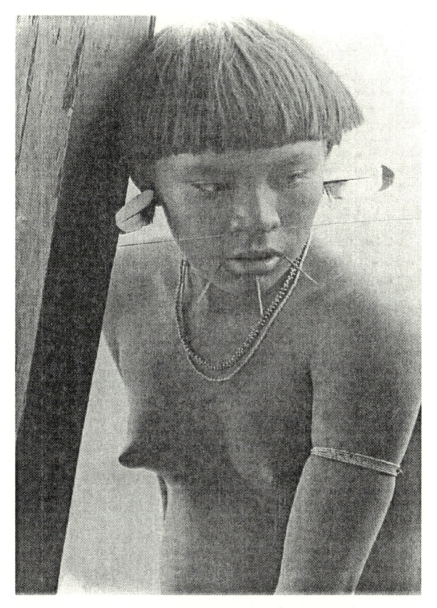

Rita Kuruanam Yanomami, Yana's mother (circa 1971)

Today, Yana lives near Turino, Italy and is married to an Italian boy. She is thirty-one years old and has recently given birth to her third male child, Lorenzo. Her Italian mother is getting nervous since it seems Yana gets pregnant every three years.

CONCLUSION

Africa and the Amazon are in the past but those times and friends are an unending source of pleasure. Some experiences remain very close for a lifetime. The lesson I have learned is that we often regret those things that we didn't do. Once lost, an adventure seldom offers one a second chance. To delight in earlier times is not a bad thing, since we are a product of our experiences with reflection being part of the human condition. To reflect and to smile and to enjoy an inward grin, is to cherish and keep alive those who have infected us with their uniqueness. In this way we can pay tribute to all of our friends, some long gone. As is often the case in reflection, we have the luxury of reliving an earlier moment like viewing the past through an inner eye. Furthermore, we may be unable to change who we are since destiny may well have chosen for us. And so like fine wine, when we inhale the aroma with deep pulls, allowing the juices to roll over the palette before swallowing, the liquid continues to linger on in its fullness for us to enjoy and savor, so too does reflection arouse the senses for us to relish and smile and relive a time long ago.

Children of the jungle

Printed in the United States
47114LVS00003B/175-204